Isaac the Infidel

*Thanks to you,
Louise!

James E. McMahney
July 21, 2016*

Isaac the Infidel

ISAAC NEWTON'S SCIENTIFIC
AND UNDISCLOSED
BIBLICAL DISCOVERIES

. . .

James E. McNabney

Copyright © 2016 James E. McNabney
All rights reserved.

ISBN: 0692572163
ISBN 13: 9780692572160

Author's Note

• • •

MUCH OF THE DIALOGUE CONTAINED in this book is fictional, but is based on conversations that did take place, and in every instance possible, incorporates actual phrases used by the persons speaking. Except for the narrator and a student named Moshe, names, dates and events are real.

About the Author

James E. McNabney is the author of BORN IN BROTHERHOOD, ISAAC THE INFIDEL, Highland, Indiana's "Bicentennial Pageant" and the Calumet College Fight Song. Some of his credits are..

BS in Business "With Distinction" from Indiana University. MS in Education. Post Graduate work in Speech, Literature and Counseling. I.U. cheerleader & founding member of Student Athletic Board. Composed and Directed ninety-voice choruses to three "I.U. Sing" winners.

President, secretary, treasurer and board member, of many organizations for many terms: Rotary Club, Model A Restorer's Club, Lakeshore Chapter of CLU's & Chartered Financial Consultants, McKinley Masonic Lodge, North Indiana Foundation of the Methodist Church, Dyer Chamber of Commerce. Grand Organist and Education Committee of the Indiana Grand Lodge of Free and Accepted Masons. Served decades as a Church organist and professional pianist.

Speech Coach at Hammond Morton High School 1962-67. One of three Directors of Indiana High School Forensic Association. Married Margaret Beckett, a teacher, in 1963.

Became a Horace Mann Insurance Agent in 1967. Twice on "Council of Six" of the nation's top six agents. Joined State Farm in 1977 -- achieved numerous awards; retired in November, 1998.

Daughter, Joy Main, lives in Bloomington, Indiana with husband, Jeff, and sons, Evan and Miles. Son, James M. McNabney, lives in Schererville, Indiana with wife, Nadia (Urzua). They have two daughters, Madeline and Jocelyn, and one son, James Sebastian.

Introduction

• • •

WITHIN A YEAR AFTER BEGINNING research on Isaac Newton, I was surprised to find the enormous influence he had on western civilization and culture. He didn't just discover truths in mathematics, space, gravity, chemistry and physics, he also discovered truths and corruptions in religion and government.

Newton was the cradle of the Enlightenment, *The Age of Reason*. He believed in using reason in all things, including government, religion and education. He used experiments to discover truth, which he called his "greater friend." And with only one exception, when he showed some bias in his "Chronology of Ancient Kingdoms," Newton's findings have been correct and indisputable. They are true.

Perhaps Newton's greatest impact on present day civilization was conveyed through his close friends who had studied and adopted Newton's beliefs, philosophies and knowledge. One of these men was John Locke, perhaps Isaac's closest friend. Newton and Locke were in total agreement philosophically, even though Locke sometimes had to treat Newton with kid gloves. For all of Newton's genius, he had an extremely touchy personality. With Locke's blessing, Newton led the campaign to oust James II from the throne of England. Locke's essays on religion and politics, which had Newton's endorsement, were the guides for many of America's founding fathers, especially Thomas Jefferson, who paraphrased Locke in the Declaration of Independence. Newton's and Locke's philosophies are a large part of America's heritage.

Another of Newton's friends who left a deep footprint in the world is John Theophilus Desaguliers (Dee-sag'-yoo-lee-ay'). Desaguliers was Isaac Newton's curator of experiments for The Royal Society, for which Newton was president for twenty-seven years. Desaguliers was a brilliant mathematician, scientist and lecturer. He was one of the rare inhabitants on earth that understood everything that Newton wrote – most of which was very complicated for people living in the 17th and 18th centuries. Although Desaguliers was an Anglican clergyman, he shared Newton's beliefs regarding monotheism. After joining one of London's Masonic Lodges, which were then "operative lodges," Desaguliers, with help from some other philosophical Freemasons, set out to unite Masonic Lodges and write their history, lectures and rituals. The rest is history. Desaguliers, a strong Newton disciple, became the Father of Modern Speculative Masonry, and the fraternity recites his rituals and lectures to the present day.

One discovery of Isaac Newton's was not well publicized for three centuries. In 1707 one of his disciples wrote about it and lost his livelihood. It is a 325 AD alteration in the "New Testament" that Newton uncovered in 1673. The discovery lay dormant until the end of the 20st century. Despite Newton's exemplary track record for revealing truth, Christian churches appear to have ignored that Biblical corruption; yet, it may be one of the reasons Christians and Muslims have fought each other for over thirteen centuries.

Table of Contents

	Author's Note · · · · · · · · · · · v
	About the Author · · · · · · · · · · · vii
	Introduction · · · · · · · · · · · ix
Prologue	A Student Meets a Professor · · · · · · · · · · · xv
Part 1	An Evolving Genius · · · · · · · · · · · 1
Chapter 1	A Christmas Child · · · · · · · · · · · 3
Chapter 2	The Formative Years · · · · · · · · · · · 11
Chapter 3	King's School · · · · · · · · · · · 16
Chapter 4	A Major Turning Point · · · · · · · · · · · 23
Chapter 5	College Bound... · · · · · · · · · · · 29
Chapter 6	Trinity · · · · · · · · · · · 33
Chapter 7	A Secluded Scholar · · · · · · · · · · · 38
Chapter 8	The Plague · · · · · · · · · · · 45
Chapter 9	Snuggery · · · · · · · · · · · 50
Chapter 10	The Lucasian Chair of Mathematics · · · · · · · · · · · 57
Chapter 11	Acquaintances · · · · · · · · · · · 62
Chapter 12	Rejection · · · · · · · · · · · 69
Chapter 13	Withdrawal · · · · · · · · · · · 78
Chapter 14	Apostasy · · · · · · · · · · · 81
Chapter 15	The Diplomat · · · · · · · · · · · 91

Chapter 16	Annoyances	99
Chapter 17	A Contemporary	105
Chapter 18	The First Disciple	110
Chapter 19	Universal Gravitation	113
Chapter 20	The Prize	116
Chapter 21	The Principia	120
Chapter 22	Resurgence of 'The Beast'	127
Chapter 23	Nearer the Gods	132
Chapter 24	The Crown Jewel of the Enlightenment	142
Part 2	From Reclusion to Involvement	147
Chapter 25	Thwarting the Beast	149
Chapter 26	A Man of the World	161
Chapter 27	Birds of a Feather	166
Chapter 28	A Flood of Followers	175
Chapter 29	Madness	182
Chapter 30	Leibniz	185
Chapter 31	Moonstruck	193
Chapter 32	A Lifelong Stint at the Mint...	202
Part 3	Fame And Its Fortunes	217
Chapter 33	Capricorns	221
Chapter 34	Catherine Barton	227
Chapter 35	Politics	231
Chapter 36	President of The Royal Society	240
Chapter 37	John Flamsteed	248
Chapter 38	1706 A.D.	262
Chapter 39	William Whiston	266
Chapter 40	Weighty Responsibilities	275
Chapter 41	The Incorrigible Royal Astronomer	280
Chapter 42	The Priority Dispute	290

Part 4	The Proliferation of Newtonianism	299
Chapter 43	The Lectures of John Theophilus Desaguliers	301
Chapter 44	Indisputable Discoveries and Decisions	310
Chapter 45	Desaguliers and Freemasonry	316
Chapter 46	Newtonianism	324
Chapter 47	Newton's "Bucket List"	331
Chapter 48	The Chronology of Ancient Kingdoms	336
Chapter 49	Final Days	346
Chapter 50	The Estate and the Manuscripts	355
Chapter 51	Newton's Legacy	360
	Epilogue	365
	Endnotes	367
	Bibliography	407

PROLOGUE

A Student Meets a Professor

• • •

YOU MAY CALL ME MOSHE. I am a graduate student at the Hebrew University in Jerusalem. A few years after the advent of the twenty-first century I was doing research at the Jewish National University Library to write a paper on the religion of Isaac Newton. Some of Newton's unrevealed writings had recently been released, and the world had discovered that more of his writings had been devoted to religion than to mathematics, optics, astronomy –or anything else. So I naturally thought I had a perfect subject for my thesis.

An older gentleman sitting next to me in the library seemed to notice the books and manuscripts I was perusing and asked, "Are you writing a paper on Isaac Newton?"

I responded, "I am."

"That is an ambitious undertaking," he said, "a most fascinating subject. Are you emphasizing anything specifically?"

"I plan to devote my thesis to Newton's religion, his theology."

"Ah yes. Isaac Newton's *religion*! An interesting topic –and one that has only recently been revealed."

"That is what I've heard, and I plan to divulge his beliefs to the world."

"A noble enterprise, indeed. Although Newton's theology is being unfolded, it is sad that it took 270 years after his death for it to be released and for us to finally see some startling truths about him. I am a professor of history, and over the past fifteen years I have found some most surprising things. I have read Newton's recently released papers in Cambridge, England; Babson College in Massachusetts, and in Geneva, Switzerland. I also have a personal interest in the Yahuda Manuscripts here in Jerusalem."

"And what startling truths have you found?"

"What's your name, son?"

"Moshe."

"And you are sincerely interested in knowing Isaac Newton's religious beliefs?"

"Most assuredly, sir."

"It will be my pleasure to tell you. He along with his friend John Locke have influenced western thought and have given us philosophies that were used by many of America's founding fathers. Moshe, I think you should also know that Newton and Einstein, two of Earth's greatest geniuses, have said that the universe was created by an intellect far superior to theirs or ours.

"Let me begin at the time of Isaac's birth, Moshe…

PART 1

An Evolving Genius

• • •

CHAPTER 1

A Christmas Child

• • •

"His life began during the time of reformation and revolution, the embryo of the Age of Reason, 'The Enlightenment.' It was a time of civil and religious war, a time of turbulence and tribulation --a time when people hungered for tolerance and truth. It was a time when Parliament rebelled against king, church assailed church and science researched and scrutinized scripture. It was the time Oliver Cromwell challenged King Charles I and his armies, and when philosophers questioned the divine right of kings. It was a time when new discoveries contradicted established beliefs and theories. It was a time of civil war in England. …

It was the year Galileo died under house arrest by the Inquisition of his church. It was one hundred-fifty years after Columbus had discovered America, and only one year after Robert Moray had been inducted into a guild of stone masons --the first nobleman ever to be admitted into an operative craft guild. It was the advent of the age of reason, an age of science and enlightenment. It was 1642 A.D. in England.

In late summer of this year a young pregnant widow from Woolsthorpe Manor in the county of Lincolnshire sobbed incessantly in front of her husband's casket in Colsterworth Church. Her mother, Margery Ayscough, vainly attempted to console her:

"Hannah, you've got to stop crying. It isn't good for you or your baby."

"You'd cry too if you were pregnant without a husband. Why did he have to die before his child was born."

"Daughter, his body and his blood are inside of you. Your baby is his legacy. Dear girl, take some consolation in that."

"Some consolation! My child will be called a bastard."

"Nonsense, your baby was conceived under wedlock."

Hannah erupted into another sobbing spasm, "The child has no father, and hardly anyone knew him anyway. Only his relatives have come to his funeral."

"Everything will be all right, Hannah Ayscough Newton. You'll see.

Early Christmas morning in this singular year, a very premature Isaac Newton, junior, arrived on the planet earth, his early arrival no doubt provoked by his mother's distress and grief. That he survived was a miracle. He was so tiny he could fit in a quart mug. On New Year's Day the rector of Colsterworth baptized Hannah's squirrel-sized son; however, his extremely delicate condition demanded constant care from his mother and grandmother. For years he would wear a neck brace to protect him from spinal trauma.

Four and one-half months later as Hannah and her mother carefully tended to Isaac, troops with pikes, spears and muskets marched through Lincolnshire, stripping much of the countryside for provisions. Hannah and her mother were on constant alert for possible excesses of a hungry and lustful soldiery. On May 13 at Grantham, seven miles from Woolsthorpe, a battle erupted between Oliver Cromwell's roundheads and the King's Royalist Cavaliers. Despite primitive weaponry and overwhelming odds, Cromwell won a decisive victory, losing only two men compared to over one hundred lost by the Royalists. Lord Cromwell, the Puritan leader, described the victory as a sign of God's benevolence and continued his war against King Charles I.

Two years later in the fall of 1645 Cromwell finally defeated the royalist army of the king, who fled north into Scotland. General Robert Moray joined King Charles after returning from the Scot Guard in France; however, Oliver Cromwell was now in absolute control of England.

At this time, when Isaac Newton was two years of age, Hannah's brother, William Ayscough, rector of Burton Coggles church, delivered a proposal of marriage to his sister from Reverend Barnabas Smith of North Witham. It appears that Reverend Smith feared rejection and sent his neighbor with the proposal. Hannah refused to read the letter and directed Smith's consort to her brother. Consequently, Reverend Ayscough, now a matchmaker by default, came calling upon his own sister. Hannah invited her brother into the parlor where he paid his respects to his mother and diminutive nephew. After he and his sister seated themselves, William handed her Reverend Smith's letter:

Dear Mrs. Newton:

I am Barnabas Smith, Rector of North Witham. You may remember me from a church function in Colsterworth. Having obtained a favorable opinion of you from discourse with mutual friends and neighbors, I wish to ask for your hand in marriage.

Although we differ in age, I can provide for you comfortably in every respect. I know you to be a widow. I have been a widower since June, and I believe a marriage will be to our mutual benefit. You will profit from my good fortune and name, and I will profit by having a wife and, hopefully, a family.

It is my understanding that you have a child. I will gladly help provide for your child; however, if you accept my proposal of marriage, I prefer not to have your child accompany you as part of your new family. It is my sincere desire that you will understand my reservations in this regard.

Your earliest reply is earnestly solicited.

Yours,
Reverend Barnabas Smith

Hannah stared at the letter in disbelief, then at her brother and her son. Isaac, of course, was now very attached to his mother and grandmother. Hannah was the idol of his life. She literally *was* his life. As she looked at her son in his neck brace she thought to herself: *How can I reveal the content of this letter to my son? Isaac is quite precocious; he would be devastated if I left him, even if I were to reside nearby. And what about the feelings he might harbor against me and Reverend Smith?*

Hannah asked her mother to take Isaac outside. She then asked her brother, "Do you know what is in this letter William?"

"Yes, it's a proposal of marriage."

"So what are your thoughts?"

"I think Barnabas would be a good husband for you. He has everything you need for a provider. He is a gentleman of high social standing. He is highly educated and quite wealthy. He would treat you well."

Hannah asked, "How old is he?"

"I believe he is sixty-three. Is that a problem?"

"You can see nothing wrong in that? I am not yet 30!"

"Age isn't so important, Hannah. Barnabas is quite healthy and wants to have a family. His previous marriage was childless. He actually looks quite good for his age."

"He may not have children, but I do! Are you aware that he doesn't want me to take Isaac with me if I marry him? I can't abandon Isaac. How could I live with myself?"

"Hannah, I don't know Reverend Smith's reasons for not wanting Isaac. Perhaps he doesn't want you to have reminders in his home of your previous marriage. There is also his position. You know how people think. They wouldn't like him marrying so soon –and to a woman with a fatherless child."

"But that isn't true. I conceived Isaac under wedlock."

"Sometimes people don't accept the truth. People in North Witham don't know you or your family, and you may not want them to. Your husband was illiterate. Perhaps it is best that he was not part of Isaac's life. You are fortunate to have caught Reverend Smith's eye. His proposal is the answer to all of your prayers."

"But what is to become of Isaac? You're a man of the cloth. How can you condone taking a mother from her child? No loving mother could do such a thing."

"Your point is well taken, sis. You have a difficult decision to make. If you do accept Barnabas's proposal, I suggest that you get some guarantees for little Isaac. He is quite sickly. You must insist on payment for his care, and for the care of Woolsthorpe manor. You also need a fund set aside for Isaac upon his majority, so that he can support himself. In truth, it may be a good idea for Isaac to remain at Woolsthorpe. If he maintains a presence here, the family of your deceased husband can lay no claim against this property. Isaac will inherit Woolsthorpe someday. Then he will be most appreciative of your decision to marry Reverend Smith because you will have preserved his inheritance. Frankly, Hannah, without Reverend Smith I doubt very much that you are in a position to hold on to this property."

Hannah reflected a moment and said, "William, I need some time to consider this. You're right. Not many widows with children receive offers of marriage."

"Think it over carefully, Hannah; you may never get an opportunity like this again. I'll tell Barnabas that you are considering his proposal. But don't wait too long."

As Hannah agonized over her response to Reverend Smith's letter, King Charles was raising an army in Scotland in order to regain his English throne. Meanwhile in England under Cromwell's Protectorate, a group of natural philosophers and theologians started an "Invisible College" dedicated to the scientific principles inculcated by Francis Bacon and Rene' Descartes. Men like Robert Boyle, Robert Fludd, John Locke, Elias Ashmole, Robert Plot, Thomas Vaughn and John Wilkins began studying nature and astronomy beyond the writings of Aristotle,

Ptolemy and even the *Bible*. Though Hannah would never have imagined it, her son would someday be a member of that college.

Soon Hannah Newton arranged to meet with Barnabas Smith. On the day of her arrival at his residence, she gazed with awe at his spacious rectory. He greeted her with a contagious smile as he kissed her hand, took her cloak and invited her into the library. He appeared quite plain, not at all handsome. As he seated her he said, "I'm glad you came."

Hannah replied, "It's my pleasure, sir."

"May I offer you some tea?"

"Yes, thank you."

As the smiling clergyman poured the tea he said, "Your brother tells me that you wish to discuss your son's future before responding to my proposal."

"Yes, sir, that is true, sir."

"Please call me Barnabas. If we're going to talk about marriage, we might at least call each other by our forenames."

"Yes, sir. I mean, Barnabas. I do have concerns for Isaac. To be quite forthright I think that a mother contemplating an offer like yours should have serious reservations. I think she would want her child to be looked after and provided for. The loss of a mother could cause permanent mental anguish for someone as young as little Isaac."

"My dear Hannah, allow me to alleviate your concerns. In my profession I have seen many children who have lost mothers. A lad of Isaac's age can adapt quite readily. If he were older and even more attached to you, I might agree with you. But be rest assured that Isaac's grandmother will gladly rear Isaac. She will be a good mother to him and provide all of his emotional and physical needs. Your own brother William has talked to her and she has agreed to raise Isaac --and with adequate compensation I might add."

"I just don't feel right. Isaac is so fragile. He needs special care. He needs me!"

"Your mother knows about these things, Hannah. She has already raised three children and is also helping to raise Isaac. Don't you think she is the best suited to care for him?"

"I ... I guess so."

"Of course you do. You will have less cause to fear Isaac's well-being than if you were raising him yourself. Nay more, let me give you further cause to accept my proposal. William mentioned that you would need some financial security for Isaac, especially since life is so uncertain. If you accept my proposal, I shall set aside my land at Sewstern for Isaac, so that when he attains majority he will have an income every year. I will also refurbish Woolsthorpe to make it more suitable for Isaac's occupancy. Isaac will have a permanent residence, and while he lives at Woolsthorpe, there will be no claims on your property. Someday Isaac will be grateful to you for giving him such a legacy."

Somewhat stunned, Hannah said, "You seem to have thought of everything."

"I want you to be my wife, Hannah. I want what will be best for both of us. I may not have as many years left as you, but I want them to be happy ones –for both of us. I want to share these years with you."

Hannah lowered her head and replied, "You make a very strong appeal, Barnabas."

"Then you accept?"

After a pause that seemed an eternity to Barnabas, Hannah uttered a faint, "Yes, ...I accept."

The wedding was set for January 27, 1646, thirty-three days after Isaac's third birthday.

Predictably, Isaac was devastated when his mother departed for North Witham. And the devastation became obsessive. Despite the opposite assurances of his stepfather, Isaac could not forget that his mother had left him --and he detested the man who had seduced her. Even at his young age, Isaac could bear a grudge and harbor vindictive thoughts. He was never able to accept his mother's and stepfather's reasoning. Even as he matured and adopted more rational thought, Isaac Newton continued to resent having been rejected by his mother and stepfather --a rejection that upon occasion could only bolster a latent vindictive nature.

The lad from Woolsthorpe was destined to be different. In fact, a superstition existed in seventeenth century England that anyone born on Christmas Day possessed superior powers –even more superior if he were born a posthumous child.

Grandmother Ayscough harbored such a superstition, and conveyed it to her grandson.

CHAPTER 2

The Formative Years

• • •

BARNABAS SMITH'S BELIEF THAT MARGERY Ayscough would be an excellent surrogate mother proved to be correct. Although in her sixties, she relished rearing little Isaac. Her son William, who had an excellent upbringing, would occasionally come by to ask how the rearing of her grandson was going. On one such day, Mrs. Ayscough anwered him:

"Raising Isaac isn't the same as when I raised you and Hannah. Your nephew is quite different. He is neither demanding nor destructive. He grasps everything he sees and hears, and he retains everything. He learned to speak and write much sooner than you or Hannah, and he always listens intently when I read the *Bible* to him. I have given him some Puritan values: a passion for work, a general distrust of human kind, a desire to excel and a strong belief in himself. Yet, I've only emphasized the most fundamental concepts of religion –to love God and your neighbor. Isaac is a very special child, and I have told him so."

William interjected, "You seem to be doing my job."

"Oh no! I certainly do not delve into religious discussion. I just read the *Bible* to Isaac. It is very hard to know what your little nephew is thinking. He reserves any show of emotion for his immediate family. At other times he appears quite stoic. He certainly is curious about the world and creation, and I'm happy he is. He loves to learn –much more than his father, I must say. I have told him that illiteracy is not a virtue. I truly believe that I am providing Isaac with more wisdom and experience than his mother could. Isaac has a talent for making mechanical contrivances and observing things others don't even notice. Although he occasionally displays a lack of patience with less gifted peers, he is compliant when I ask him to do something, provided his mind isn't preoccupied with thoughts only God knows. He is very quiet about his thoughts, yet he appears to think constantly. There is a busy mind behind his penetrating eyes.

"Although North Witham is only one mile from Woolsthorpe, Isaac has never been invited to the Smith household. On special occasions we might go to Reverend Smith's church, where Isaac can sit not too far from his mother and listen to his stepfather's sermons. On most Sundays, however, Isaac and I go to the Colsterworth church, where his father and grandfather are buried. At home in Woolsthorpe I have seen Isaac climb a haystack and look longingly at the North Witham steeple. I can only imagine what he thinks on these occasions; he never tells me. He is unlike any child I have ever known. He is not like us, William."

One day grandmother Ayscough told Isaac, "Always search for what is good and true, Isaac. You will find much truth in the *Holy Book*. Will you read from it every day?"

"Yes, grandma," said Isaac.

"Even after you grow up?"

"Yes, grandma, even when I grow up. I enjoy reading it."

At an early age Isaac thought that constant labor was the best way to improve the world. But he also felt that success could lead to vanity and pride –two deadly sins. Consequently, Isaac thwarted success by withdrawing from it, a pattern that would continue throughout his life. As with most great men, however, self-education became Isaac's greatest asset. Instead of playing or rough-housing with other boys, Isaac would be found making mechanical toys or even constructing play houses for girls. His peers saw nothing unusual or extraordinary in him; only that he was quiet, solitary and usually preoccupied.

By the end of 1648 Cromwell's parliamentary army had soundly defeated King Charles and his Scot forces. When Moray failed to persuade the king to dress as a woman and make an escape, the Scots surrendered the ill-fated Stuart sovereign to England's new "Protector." The king was branded a traitor for raising a foreign army, and despite his son's efforts to save him, he was beheaded January 30, 1649 on a scaffold in front of Whitehall Palace. The civil war and the "Thirty Year's War" in Europe were now officially over. A large entourage of royalists, including Robert Moray and Charles' wife, Queen Henrietta Maria, sailed to France for the chateau at St. Germain En-Laye. Queen Maria's Catholic faith had contributed heavily to the animus surrounding her husband, who faced decapitation with considerable courage.

Throughout England on the date Charles "the First" was executed, rumors of faintings, miscarriages and even deaths abounded. Many women of England were struck with horror, especially Charles's mistresses, who had born him many children. Scotland immediately declared Charles' son, Charles II, as King of Scotland and Jersey in absentia since he had fled for France with his mother.

When regime changes occurred in England, oaths were usually demanded of the populace. But at the conservative universities, many students and teachers balked at taking an oath to Oliver Cromwell. In fact, over 600 students and professors departed Cambridge and Oxford.[1] Nevertheless, life under Cromwell soon provided an open learning environment that had never before graced the British Isles. A true republic had been created. Religious freedom and scientific inquiry germinated, spawning an interest in the sciences that hadn't occurred since classical Greece. Unlike Galileo, Isaac Newton would be brought up in an environment in which there was less fear of inquisition. Still, Isaac maintained a solitary nature and, except for his views on Catholicism, he was careful not to expose his personal religious views.

Nevertheless, despite England's newly found freedoms under Cromwell, its universities retained their classical Elizabethan curriculum. Away from the classroom, however, students openly searched for further, even esoteric, knowledge. Under Cromwell's Commonwealth, England would produce some of the greatest scientific minds to ever emerge in such a short span of time in the history of the world. But the books and research came not only from the university curriculum of Aristotle and Plato, but from writings and findings of Copernicus, Kepler, Galileo, Bacon, Gilbert, Boyle, DesCartes' --and a man by the name of John Locke.

It was during Cromwell's Protectorate that Isaac Newton walked to and from the dame schools at Skillington and Stoke Rochford, but his observations to and from school may have taught him more than the classroom. He had a curious mind. Discovering truths in the universe would someday become his reason for living.

Reverend Barnabas Smith died before Isaac's eleventh birthday and Hannah Ayscough Newton Smith returned to Woolsthorpe with three children born from her brief union with the rector of North Witham: Mary, age six; Benjamin, age two; and Hannah, a mere ten months. When they arrived, it appeared that Isaac welcomed seeing the books from Reverend Smith's library more than his mother and his three step-siblings. In fact, in the corner of his bedroom Isaac began constructing shelves out of deal boxes to hold more than 300 books. He would retreat to this corner frequently, preferring its solace instead of playing nursemaid to Benjamin, who was ten years his junior. In a few months, to Isaac's great chagrin, Grandma Ayscough left Woolsthorpe, hoping that Isaac and his mother would be able to bond again.

One day Isaac's mother asked him, "What are those two sets of pegs doing on the south wall of our home?"

Isaac answered, "Telling the time."

"Telling time?"

"Yes, in the summer when the shadow of the top peg covers the lowest peg, it is noon."

"Why do you need two sets of pegs?"

"To tell time in the winter."

Looking somewhat confused, Hannah replied, "That is very clever of you, Isaac."

"Thank you, mother."

Isaac didn't mention that he was also working on a water clock.

Isaac's mother futilely attempted to heal the wounds caused from deserting her son. But after one year it became necessary for Isaac to attend grammar school. He was accordingly enrolled in King's School in Grantham, near the area where Roundheads had fought Royalists eleven years ago. Henry Stokes was the headmaster. Since King's School was seven miles from Woolsthorpe, Hannah called upon her friend, Mary Clark, an apothecary's wife, to provide room and board for Isaac. Mr. Clark was pleased to provide his home for the son of the twice-widowed, financially-stable friend of his wife.

Before departing Woolsthorpe for the Clark home, Isaac purchased a notebook from his mother for two and one-half pence. Although the notebook contained only 42 pages, Isaac made the most of each page, writing in his own shorthand with characters as small as one-sixteenth of an inch. He soon began recording entries in the front and back of what he called his *Wastebook*.

CHAPTER 3

King's School

• • •

THE CLARK HOME AND MR. Clark's apothecary proved to be a panacea for young Isaac. The Clarks had an easy-going nature, and Isaac felt very comfortable with them. Though William Clark was in his late forties, he became a father figure to Isaac. Mrs. Clark, his second wife, was very pleasant and not demanding. Catherine Storer, her nine year-old daughter from a previous marriage, took an immediate liking to the new boarder. Living with the Clarks was enjoyable; Isaac had much freedom. He had his own private quarters, a remodeled garret in the attic; but he also had the run of the house and the apothecary shop. All he really had to do was show up on time for dinner.

King's School was also quite palatable. The headmaster, Mr. Stokes, had earned a bachelor's degree in 1643 from Pembroke Hall in Cambridge and had served as headmaster in another school before Grantham. His residence and the school abutted a churchyard where the children played during recess. Interestingly, Joseph Clark, the brother of William Clark, was Henry Stokes' assistant.

King's School was over 120 years old. It was converted by Edward VI from a church to a classical school that taught Latin, Greek and some theology. Since Grantham was a farm community, Henry Stokes added some practical arithmetic and some exercises in polygons for the prospective farmers, who constituted the great majority of King's enrollment.[2]

Isaac did not fare well in the classroom. In fact, he was one of the worst students. Out of eighty schoolmates, Isaac ranked next to the bottom for two years. Yet Catherine Storer and the Clarks found Isaac to be highly intelligent and talented –though he was very quiet and didn't really socialize. In his first two weeks at the Clarks, he had put up two sets of pegs on the south side of the house –with his landlord's permission, of course. Throughout his stay he asked many questions about the universe, apothecary chemicals, windmills, clocks and anything else that piqued his curiosity. But he also constructed all kinds of mechanical contrivances, including windmills, clocks, watermills and sundials and at times even displayed them at dinner.

At one such time Mr. Clark asked him, "What are you working on now, Isaac?"

Isaac responded, "In truth, I have completed it. 'tis a windmill."

"Would you show it to us?"

Isaac ran upstairs and returned with an exact model of a windmill.

"Where did you find the design for such an intricate contraption?" asked Mr. Clark.

"Someone is building a windmill on Gunnerby Road. I walked over and watched them."

"Does it work?"

"Better than the one on Gunnerby Road."

"What do you mean?"

"Look inside."

William Clark opened the windmill's door and observed a vertical mill wheel with small steps instead of paddles filling its interior perimeter.

Isaac continued, "All l need to do is place corn in a little box on top of the wheel and my mouse turns the wheel as it climbs to reach the corn. Of course my windmill also works when the wind strikes its sails."

"Extraordinary!" exclaimed Mr. Clark.

Catherine chimed in, "Isaac's also making a cart that will roll without pulling it."

"Is that so?" said her mother.

"It's true, mother, and he also uses a windlass to turn the wheels."

Mr. Clark said, "You can make just about anything; can't you, Isaac?"
"No sir," said Isaac, "I can't make life, but I'm going to try some day."
The Clark family responded with a hearty laugh.

Since Isaac was smaller than others his age, he didn't engage in the trifling sports of his classmates, but he did try to engage them in other diversions. In fact, Isaac introduced kite flying at King's School as a competitive event. His classmates quickly found themselves trying to make a kite that would fly longer than anyone else's. Isaac then went a step farther; he attached candles to his kite to illuminate his way to and from school. Unfortunately, he excited some townspeople who thought they were seeing comets.[3]

When Isaac wasn't making something, he was either reading, writing or observing Mr. Clark in his apothecary shop. With his stepfather's and Mr. Clark's books he had enough information to become an authority on numerous subjects. He drew heavily from "The Mysteries of Nature and Art" by John Bate.[4] Bate's book even had instructions for making kites, lanterns, water clocks, and windmills –and had sections on recipes and medicines.

In the apothecary shop Isaac often observed William Clark mixing concoctions to cure the various illnesses of Grantham's citizenry. Perhaps because of his frail nature since birth, Isaac was concerned with his health and learned to make medicines for his own maladies. He became quite adept at mixing chemicals and grinding compounds with a mortar and pestle.

One day as Isaac and Mr. Clark were working in the apothecary shop, Mr. Clark remarked, "Isaac, you appear to remember every compound that I have shown you, and you have an ability to make almost anything you want to make. What I can't understand is why you rank next to the bottom of your class in school?"

"I care not where I rank, sir," said Isaac. "I learn more out of school than in."

"Are you not learning anything at school, Isaac?"

"I have found the first two years rather tiresome. I hear little that I don't know, and I truly do not wish to waste time copying simple lessons assigned by my schoolmaster. I prefer to spend my time and energies elsewhere."

"As you wish, Isaac. I cannot tell you what to do. That is your mother's domain."

"Mother wants only that I become a farmer and superintend Woolsthorpe Manor."

"Isn't Woolsthorpe to be your inheritance someday?"

"Yes, but I am most averse to farming."

So Isaac continued to be lethargic in his studies. Unfortunately, his diffidence in the classroom and his aloofness did little to endear him to his more bourgeois classmates.

In his third year at Grantham while on his way to school one day, Isaac was confronted by Arthur Storer, the bully of King's School. Storer, who ranked above Isaac, began taunting him about his lower standing. After a few insults the bully delivered a powerful kick to Isaac's solar plexus, driving his smaller, weaker opponent to his knees, immobilizing him.

Throughout that day's classes, Isaac's vindictive nature smoldered, and after school the normally meek Isaac Newton confronted his adversary:

"I want to meet you in the churchyard!"

Storer answered, "Happy to oblige, Mr. Newton."

An older pupil named John overheard the challenge and rushed to the churchyard with many other classmates. As the combatants squared off, John walked up to Newton and gave him a pat on the back as he winked at the stronger Storer.

Isaac, no longer a mouse, suddenly became a ferocious animal. He refused to be hurt again as he had ten years ago. He attacked Storer with an intensity no one had seen in him before. He pummeled him until the shocked bully screamed, "I will fight no more!"

John, ever the provocateur, yelled, "Grab him by the ears and drag him to the church!"

Isaac complied, and at the wall of the church pushed Storer's face against it and ordered him to apologize on his knees. Beaten and shaken, the bully humbly begged Isaac's forgiveness.

But victory alone wasn't enough. From that day on, Isaac was determined to protect his psyche. He would never again be ridiculed by anyone *for anything*. He began doing his school assignments. Not only did he pass Storer in scholastics, he passed every student at King's School. It was a turning point in Isaac's life, a metamorphosis. An episode with a bully awakened a lion. Afterward, Isaac said to himself, "Never again will anyone dominate me."

Henry Stokes, William Ayscough, the entire Clark family—especially Catherine Storer and Mary Clark's brother, Humphrey Babington of Trinity College-- all noticed a marked change in Isaac Newton. But to Isaac's mother, her son had suddenly become responsible. Surely he would soon be able to take over the management of the farm at Woolsthorpe Manor.

Naturally, a euphoric Henry Stokes envisioned a different future for Isaac. King's School had produced a true scholar. Isaac had talent surpassing any student he had ever taught, so the euphoric schoolmaster wanted him to continue his education beyond grammar school.

In the spring of 1658, Master Stokes brought Isaac into his office:

"Isaac, you are performing quite well in school."

"Thank you, sir." Isaac responded.

"Isaac, what are your plans for the future?"

"I have no future plans, sir."

"Surely you must have thoughts about your future and your worldly vocation."

"Nay, sir. I do not. If I may speak the truth, I have little choice regarding my future."

"Have you no preferences regarding your life's work?"

"I have certain interests, but I fear they are not the same interests as others in this community. I am interested in discovering phenomena and truth. I read the *Bible* daily."

"Have you thought of continuing your education? I know people who could help you."

"I know of the subjects taught in the universities. They don't interest me."

"You thought the same of subjects at King's school, but you still mastered them. You are fluent in Latin, which is the language of priests and scholars. Latin will help you in college; if you succeed during your first years in college, you can pursue and study your own interests."

"Master Stokes, the point is moot. My mother wouldn't think of me attending college. Furthermore, I would need money, which I know mother wouldn't give me. In this county almost everyone relies upon farming for a livelihood. Our land is Woolsthorpe. Mother has made it clear that my livelihood and my future lie in the land of Woolsthorpe."

In September of 1658 Oliver Cromwell died. Doctors speculated on the cause: perhaps malaria, perhaps a kidney infection or some other internal malady. Cromwell's aides blamed his death on the medical treatment he received. Parliament buried "Ironsides" in Westminster Abbey and reluctantly allowed his son, Richard, to assume his father's duties. Immediately the pervasive question in England was, "Would Cromwell's Puritan legacy live on?"

On the day of Cromwell's death, strong winds whipped across the British Isles. It seemed that the heavens were in torment. Many Anglicans and Catholics exclaimed that the wind was Satan coming after Cromwell. The Puritans thought it was an ill omen --and it was.

Ironically, on that same day the young boys at King's School were engaged in a distance jumping contest in which the thin, willowy Isaac Newton unexpectedly participated. Perhaps because of his sensitive make-up, Isaac did not enter a competition unless he thought he could win it. So when it came Isaac's turn to jump, he would wait for the wind to pick up. With his small size and weight, the wind carried him farther than the leaps of the other boys. Isaac won the contest and later called the event one of his first experiments. His victory also kindled the crush that Catherine Storer had on him –in addition to the poetry he was writing to her.

CHAPTER 4

A Major Turning Point

• • •

IN THE SPRING OF 1659 Hannah Smith withdrew her son from King's School and brought him back to Woolsthorpe. In order to prepare him for managing the farm, she began by assigning him some important responsibilities.

Whether it was rebelliousness, absent mindedness or contentiousness, Isaac was more than negligent in performing his duties. Sheep were lost under his care, corn went unplanted, livestock and crops were unattended and dinner often forgotten. Instead of fulfilling his responsibilities, Isaac made millwheels, studied dams and sluices, and conducted hydrostatic experiments. After dinner Isaac would retreat to his room and read for most of the night.

In exasperation, Hannah hired a servant to help Isaac with his responsibilities. But Isaac simply delegated his duties to the servant. When the two of them went to Grantham to sell crops, Isaac spent the day reading books at the Clarks while the unfortunate servant conducted business for Isaac. Sometimes Isaac jumped out of the wagon immediately after it left Woolsthorpe and told the servant to pick him up on the return trip. But after the servant related these transgressions to Isaac's mother, many heated exchanges erupted when she confronted her oldest child about his responsibilities.

As Hannah bemoaned Isaac's conduct, Royalists in England were moving to retake control of the throne. Therefore, when Parliament could not find a competent leader in the Cromwell family, and despite the enmity between Royalists and Cromwellians, it offered Charles II, King of Scotland and Jersey, the English throne. Charles II arrived safely from France on May 29, 1660, his 30th birthday. Other exiles, including Robert Moray, soon followed.

Charles II promptly ousted Cromwell's appointees, including Dr. John Wilkins, Master of Trinity. The new king appointed former general Robert Moray as director of the Royal Laboratory in the palace at Whitehall. And on January 30, 1661, the twelfth anniversary of Charles I's execution, Charles II ingloriously exhumed Cromwell's body and decapitated it. He impaled its head on a pike, placed the torso in chains and paraded it throughout the kingdom. He ordered the body to be thrown in an unmarked pit, and never returned to Westminster Abbey. All records of Cromwell's Protectorate were destroyed, and Charles II declared his restoration date as January 30, 1649, the date of his father's beheading.

Robert Moray and the king engaged in many conversations. However, one that is known to have occurred shortly after November 28, 1660 is of particular interest in the history of western civilization, and is believed to have gone as follows when Moray addressed the king:

"Your highness, on November 28, I invited twelve of England's best minds to Gresham College to hear a speech by Christopher Wren."

Charles interrupted, "Christopher Wren!? You invited gentlemen to listen to a supporter of Cromwell? I dismissed him as the Royal Architect months ago."

"Yes, I know. You have replaced some other Cromwellians whom I also invited to hear Wren."

"Just what are you up to, Moray?"

"Quite frankly, I am starting a society of some of England's best minds in order to rebuild our navy, which Cromwell all but decimated. Truthfully, if we hadn't had Dr. William Petty's greyhound, the Dutch fleet might have overtaken you in the Channel and captured you after you left France. I need you to give support to this society."

"The idea of a society to rebuild our navy appeals to me, but I want to know who else you invited to hear Christopher Wren."

"Well, I also invited six royalists besides myself: William Brouncker, Alexander Bruce, Sir Paul Neile, Dr. Robert Boyle, Mr. William Ball and Elias Ashmole."

"Excellent men all. But why did you invite followers of Cromwell?"

"We need their expertise, Your Highness. Besides, like you and me, all of them except for Wren are in a Masonic lodge."

"Hmm. So you think that will make them loyal to me?"

"Yes I do. They have all taken vows to be true to the government under which they live. They simply want to understand nature, God, and Biblical truths. We all consider ourselves as equals. We elect officers to preside over us."

"So which of my former enemies did you invite besides Wren?"

"John Wilkins…."

The king loudly exclaimed, "What? I say, **John Wilkins**! He is married to Cromwell's sister! What are you doing, Moray?"

"I assure you that he is a loyal subject and will conform to our rules."

"I would certainly hope so. Please continue."

"John Goddard…"

"My God, Moray! He was Cromwell's personal physician!"

"Dr. William Petty."

"Cromwell's statistician!"

"Laurence Rooke…"

"Didn't I dismiss him as Professor of Geometry? Isn't he also a Cromwellian?"

"Yes, your Highness, but we need his knowledge. I also invited a twenty-six-year-old businessman by the name of Abraham Hill, who has no preferences politically, but he has volunteered to help pay dues for some indigent members. I hope you will forgive me, my Liege, but many whom you have dismissed because of their politics are now almost destitute."

"General Moray, you have assembled men who have been on both sides of England's brutal civil war, and now you are placing them in the same society. You must be quite persuasive. Are you seeking my approval for this society?"

There is something else, Your Highness. I would like you to grant this society a royal charter under the name, *The Royal Society of London?* We need this society to provide our people with truth, not superstitious beliefs."

"Hmm... perhaps you have latched onto something, Moray. If your society can provide indisputable truths, I'm fairly confident they would be accepted even if they differed from established church, governmental or academic superstitions."

"Then you will give us a royal charter?"

"Heaven help me, Moray, I am persuaded. You shall have your royal charter."

"Thank you, my Liege."

The Royal Society opened up freedom of conscience and the development of ideas in England.[5] Its goal was "To scrutinize the whole of Nature and to investigate its activities and powers by means of observations and experiments, and in time, to hammer out a more solid philosophy with the widespread approval of civilization."[6]

Meanwhile, Henry Stokes began visiting Isaac's mother at Woolsthorpe, hoping to convince her that Isaac belonged in a university. But Hannah would have none of it. Even William Ayscough, upon hearing of Isaac's discontent at Woolsthorpe, told his sister that Isaac should go to college, but Hannah also rejected his advice despite Isaac's irascible behavior.

The last straw occurred when Isaac *lost a horse*. One day when he was riding home from Grantham, he dismounted and held the horse's reins while he walked up Spittlegate Hill with the horse behind him. As was his usual custom, he became preoccupied with thoughts other than leading a horse up a hill. Consequently, at the top of the hill when he turned to remount his filly, he discovered that he was holding an empty bridle. The horse was gone.

After the horse incident, the Clarks did their best to convince Hannah to let her son attend the university. Mary Clark's brother, Humphrey Babington, who had returned to Trinity after the Protectorate, said he would gladly recommend Isaac to his alma mater. Doctor Babington and Isaac had actually become close friends despite their age difference.

Henry Stokes, upon hearing of Isaac's latest misdeeds, made another attempt to change Hannah's mind. Hannah reluctantly welcomed the schoolmaster, offered him a cup of tea and commented with tongue in cheek, "Pray tell, Master Stokes, what is the purpose of your visit?" "I confess, Widow Smith, my purpose is unchanged. I still feel strongly that your son belongs in a university. I came to entreat you to let Isaac take entrance examinations for Trinity. I will gladly help him to prepare for them."

"Master Stokes, I have told you before and I tell you now, Isaac will someday inherit Woolsthorpe. This manor will be his sustenance. We must work for a living and this manor has many mouths to feed. I have no title, no office; nothing except Woolsthorpe and a modest inheritance. Land is what matters to me, and land is all that matters in this world."

"Widow Smith, your son has a very good mind, but it needs cultivation. Knowledge can be a great asset, perhaps even greater than land. Didn't your late husband rely on knowledge for his livelihood? Your son has an opportunity greater than other lads of Lincolnshire."

"I grant you that Isaac is different from other lads, but are you quite sure about his mind? He has not shown much use of it to me."

"Milady, it would be a great loss to the world to bury a genius in rustic employment that is undoubtedly unsuited to his temperament. The way to improve Isaac's fortune is to prepare him for the university."

"I'm not so sure about that."

"Indulge me to offer you a proposition. Were you to change your mind, I think Isaac can be accepted at Trinity University, where your brother and Mary Clark's brother attended. They will gladly recommend Isaac, and I will prepare him for the entrance examination. I will even pay the forty-shilling annual fee for non-residents."

"I…. I cannot accept your offer, Master Stokes. I have high hopes for Isaac to become a squire at Woolsthorpe Manor. However, I shall speak to my brother about your proposition."

On Isaac's eighteenth birthday William Ayscough, fully aware of Hannah's plans regarding Isaac's future, told his sister that he endorsed Henry Stokes' proposition –as he had endorsed a proposal of marriage to his sister years ago. With everyone seemingly against her agrarian plans for Isaac, Hannah tearfully took Isaac aside and spoke to him:

"Isaac, I know that you are not happy. In spite of my efforts to provide you with a secure future, you are obviously not inclined to be a farmer. Master Stokes thinks you are qualified to go to the university and wish to do so. Is it so?"

"Yes, mother."

"Then so be it. I will no longer stand between you and your desires. I will make arrangements for you to return to the Clarks, where you can prepare for some testing that Master Stokes says you must take. …..Isaac, I want you to know that I only want what is best for you, and that I hope you are doing the right thing."

Mother and son engaged in an embrace, and Isaac said, "Thank you, mother."

Hannah turned to her brother and said, "William, I more than anyone know one thing is as certain as mortality. My son, Isaac Newton, is his own master –*no one will ever own him*. He has a mind of his own that most of us simply can't understand."

CHAPTER 5

College Bound...

• • •

WHILE ISAAC STUDIED FOR HIS entrance examination with Master Stokes at the Clark home, Mary Clark's brother, Humphrey Babington, called on Isaac and inquired:

"Isaac, would you be interested in some information about Trinity? I've spent a few years of my life at that institution, and if you'd like to know anything, I'd be glad to tell you."

"I would be interested, Dr. Babington."

"Just call me Humphrey, all right? Trinity is one of the oldest universities in England and has some ancient traditions."

"I have heard talk to that effect."

"Before I tell you more, if you are accepted into Trinity, will you be able to pay your room and board and your tuition?"

"I think so. My step-father's inheritance now pays me fifty pounds per year, and Master Stokes will apply for me to be a sub-sizar."

"You are willing to be a sub-sizar?"

"Yes, I can perform odd jobs for upper classmen for which I will be compensated."

"Isn't your mother giving you an allowance?"

"No. She feels that I will appreciate my education more if I work to earn it."

"So you will be content in doing menial chores?"

"I will do them. They won't be time-consuming; mainly errands and such."

"Well if you are accepted into Trinity, your first two years may be somewhat tedious for you –perhaps even boring. Trinity has a very classical curriculum –especially for the first two years. Student codes are still governed by the Elizabethan Statutes, not that many students abide by them. The bawdiness of the students caused Trinity to prohibit female housekeepers under age 50."

"Then why are the first years so boring? Is it the subject matter?"

"For you? Precisely. Your first year is filled with rhetoric, poetry, classical history, geography, scripture and classical languages, in which you are already proficient –except for Hebrew. You will be introduced to Aristotle and Plato, whom you already know; so I fear these subjects may not be particularly stimulating to you."

"I believe I can then find something interesting beyond the established curriculum, Doctor Babington."

"I'm sure you will, Isaac, when you aren't running errands or listening to tutors. You will be assigned tutors, you know; mainly upperclassmen who may know less about the subject matter than you.

"In the second and third years you will find more freedom to choose your own areas of interest. In these years you will be studying dialectics, which is simply logic from which you must derive conclusions from matters of your own choosing. And should you survive to the fourth year, you will select from a menu consisting of metaphysics, physics, arithmetic, geometry, astronomy and optics. Regrettably, your texts will be Tonstall's arithmetic, Euclid's geometry, and Ptolomy's astronomy. The university has not as yet endorsed the recent findings by Bacon, Oughtred, Kepler, Descartes, or Galileo."

"But I can study them, can't I?"

"Of course; however, you must study on your own --without tutelage."

"I would prefer to do that anyway."

"I rather thought you would, Isaac. But first you must pass your entrance examination. Are you aware that Trinity is the only university whose master is appointed by the king? It is the only university to bear the king's standard. England is quite fortunate to have kept her institutions of higher learning at Cambridge and Oxford."

"Fortunate?"

"Most fortunate. Henry the Eighth dissolved all other universities and confiscated their assets, as he did the Catholic Church's."

With a quizzical expression, Isaac responded, "But he spared Trinity. Why did he spare Trinity?"

"Catherine Parr."

"Catherine Parr?"

"Yes, Henry's sixth and last wife. After Henry abolished the Catholic Church, Catherine convinced him to keep Trinity in order to prepare clergymen for the Anglican Church as the new state religion. Henry was close to death at this time; therefore, he undoubtedly sought favor with the new church. He spared the university and named it 'The Holy and Undivided Trinity'."

"So if I enter Trinity, must I be a clergyman?"

"Everyone who attends Trinity obtains a degree in theology, but you are allowed to get degrees in other subjects also."

"I don't mind theology; I read the *Bible* daily. But I'm not inclined to be a clergyman. I have found that I have some problems with some church doctrine."

It came as no surprise to anyone who knew Isaac Newton that he easily passed his entrance examination, and as he prepared to board his coach for Cambridge on June 2 in 1661, his family and friends gathered for his send-off. Uncle Ayscough approached him,

"I've bought you the book, Logick, Isaac. Logic will be the first lesson that you will receive from your tutor."

"Thank you, Uncle," Isaac responded.

Isaac's mother sobbed as she gave her son a big hug, "I wish you well, Isaac. Please take care of yourself."

"I will, mother."

The Clarks and Henry Stokes also gave Isaac their best wishes. Then Catherine Storer came up to Isaac, gave him a big hug and said,

"Will you write to me, Isaac?"

"Yes, Catherine," he replied.

Isaac boarded his carriage and was soon traveling south for Cambridge, sixty miles away. Perhaps to view the property deeded to him by his stepfather, Isaac spent his first night at Sewstern. After spending the second night in Stilton, Isaac arrived at Cambridge on June 4. His driver dropped him off at the White Lion Inn and headed back to Lincolnshire. Isaac, who had never travelled farther than Grantham, was most impressed with the sights and size of Cambridge.

The next day, Isaac hired a coach to take him to Trinity. His first observations of the university were as overwhelming as his views of the city of Cambridge. He first saw the massive Great Gate and the huge statue of Henry VIII standing guard in front of it. After passing the towering gate, Isaac looked upon a sweeping court surrounded by Tudor Gothic facades that extended to the Chapel, Master's Lodge and a magnificent dining hall with a hammer and beam ceiling, a minstrel's gallery and a portrait of Henry VIII looming over the oaken tables.[7]

Isaac reported to the proper officials and was admitted to the university as a sub-sizar. He was assigned a room, a roommate and a tutor. He carried his bags to his room and began settling in, which involved purchasing school supplies, a chamber pot, fruit and *candles*. Isaac bought a lot of candles; he was accustomed to working at night while others slept. From his constant reading he had learned that food poisoning was the cause of many deaths, and since fruit resisted spoilage, Isaac preferred to have an apple or pear in place of any food left uneaten.[8]

CHAPTER 6

Trinity

• • •

EVEN THOUGH MOST STUDENTS AT Trinity gained their knowledge from tutelage, Isaac began attending classes at Trinity a day after his arrival. Other than storming out from his roommate's raucous party and going into town on a rare occasion, Isaac's first two years at Trinity were uneventful. He spoke very little, rarely socialized, and stayed primarily to himself; in fact, most students didn't recall seeing him. The Puritan conscience instilled in him by his grandmother during Cromwell's Protectorate conflicted with the rather loose moral values of the students at Trinity, so Isaac preferred to isolate himself.

Nevertheless, it was primarily due to Cromwell that the Puritans stood at the cutting edge of educational reform. In fact, it was the Puritans who believed that the last obstacles to knowledge had been overthrown and the spirit of man would soon stand forth exalted in the unblemished light of divine wisdom. Even after the purges that followed the Restoration, the Puritan mindset had established a new pedagogy that could not be stamped out. It was a mindset that wanted every member of society to prepare for a vocational life of public service; it was one's religious obligation. It was a mindset that wanted everyone to be educated, not only with established knowledge, but also with new discoveries that hadn't yet penetrated the ivy clad towers of the traditional universities. Without a doubt, freedom of expression and of discovery had arrived.

As early as the late 16th century, Francis Bacon had adopted an experimental method for natural philosophy [science]. After Bacon came Galileo and Descartes, all hoping against hope that, despite occasional church and monarchical opposition, the truths they had discovered would somehow, someday, be accepted in the world. Having faced arrest, exile and even death, they already knew how difficult it would be to disclose newly discovered truths in the face of established beliefs that, despite blatant flaws, had been ingrained into humanity by the most powerful governments and institutions in the world. These early "natural philosophers" could only hope that somewhere a country might be created to tolerate the ideas and discoveries of great men who were attempting to bring "light" into a dark and rather unbrotherly world.

At Trinity University, Isaac obediently read his *Bible* and studied the classics. His Puritan ethic and his solitary nature, however, made him appear aloof. It didn't take long before the candles in Isaac's room began burning late into the night –sometimes until dawn. Many times he would forget his supper, which caused his cooking housekeeper to think her meals were unsuitable. Isaac ignored not only his food but his sleep. His mind seemed always to be preoccupied. But what Isaac studied all night was a mystery to the Cambridge students, even his roommates. Trinity appeared to be the perfect refuge for an intellectual and emotional monastic like Isaac. The servants at Woolsthorpe had said that Isaac was only "fit for the 'versity',"[9] and they were probably right --though in Isaac's first two years the subjects at Trinity were not what Isaac desired most.

Later in Isaac Newton's life, biographers and relatives managed to extract information about Isaac regarding his first years at Cambridge. Over fifty years after Isaac's freshman year, John Conduitt, the husband of Isaac's step-niece, wrote:

"When Isaac came to hear his tutour's lectures upon logic, he found he knew more of it than his tutour, and after the lecture proceeded to convey that fact. Hearing that Isaac was so knowledgeable, the tutour then said that he would soon be reading Kepler's *Opticks* to some commoners outside of the university and that Isaac might wish to hear that lecture. Later, when the tutour gave notice of the lecture, Isaac responded, 'I have already read the book through.'"

When Isaac was reading a book of ludicial astrology, he came to a formula that required some knowledge of trigonometry. Isaac then bought an English book on Euclid's geometry and used its index to find titles relating to the two or three problems that vexed him. However, he found the content of the book so 'self-evident' that he thought it foolish to read anything but the titles. He laid Euclid aside as a 'trifling book' and was soon convinced of the vanity and emptiness of the pretended science of ludicial astrology.[10]

In Isaac's second year at Trinity, he read Oughtred's "Clavis Mathematica," but not in its entirety; he took exception with many of the author's cubic equations. Nevertheless, Isaac wrote one sentence about the book that was not discovered until long after Newton's death:

"Mr. Oughtred's *Clavis* --being one of the best as well as one of the first essays for reviving the art of geometrical resolution and composition– I agree with the Oxford professors who say that a correct edition thereof to make it more useful and bring it into more hands will be both for the honour of our nation and advantage of mathematicks."[11]

Newton's daily *Bible* reading and strict Puritan upbringing manifested itself during his first and second years at Trinity. He made lists of his own sins, placing sinful thought on a similar level with sinful deeds. He listed many violations of the Sabbath: "making a mousetrap on Thy day, squirting water on Thy day [etc., etc.]." Since puberty he had handled more than his share of feelings of guilt, and of craving independence from his mother and stepfather. He wrote about "unclean thoughts and dreamese, peevishness with my mother, threatening my father and mother Smith to burn them and the house over them, not loving Thee for Thyself, not desiring Thy ordinances."[12] Feelings of guilt arose continuously during Isaac's first two years at Trinity.

As Isaac began his third year he purchased a new 140 page leather-bound notebook in which he began recording notes in Greek about Aristotle and his discoveries. But one day he suddenly stopped writing about Aristotle. He left a few pages blank and began a new section entitled "Quaestiones Quaedom Philosophical" with a subtitle indicating a complete break from Aristotle to a new order of knowledge –of "truth." Newton wrote the subtitle in Latin, but it translated, "I am a friend of Plato, I am a friend of Aristotle, but truth is my greater friend."[13]

On the day that Newton selected truth to be his "greater friend," he began a lifelong quest to find the nature of primal matter. He had learned much from the *Bible* and books of contemporary thinkers, and he wrote in his new notebook –his *Wastebook*-- the topics he would attack: "Aer [air], Earth, Matter, Time, Eternity, Soule, Sleepe" and many others. He had experienced an epiphany and decided to be a natural philosopher. He began by first investigating matter. Following the example of the natural philosopher, Walter Charleton, he recorded the possibilities of matter's composition, but dismissed most of them except for atoms.[14]

In order to understand nature and study the topics listed in his *Wastebook*, Newton digressed considerably from the curriculum of Trinity. Nevertheless, he had benefitted much from mastering syllogistic logic, Latin and Greek. But now he began reading books that were not used at Trinity nor recommended by his tutor, Benjamin Pulleyn, nor anyone else at the college. **Euclidis Elementorum**, the book on geometry that was part of Trinity's curriculum, had been scanned by Isaac. Though it was the text used by Dr. Isaac Barrow, who held the Lucasion Chair of Mathematics at Trinity, Isaac labeled it a "trifling book."

Isaac did look at Dr. Barrow's text again to help understand "a figure of the heavens," a subject which had appeared in a book on astrology; however, Isaac then needed more knowledge of trigonometry. Therefore, he purchased a book on that subject which, in turn, demanded more knowledge of geometry. So Isaac again pulled out Euclid's **Elementorum** and gave it a little more attention, though not too much more. He then consulted Oughtred's **Clavis Mathematica**, but had some difficulty with quadratic and cubic equations.[15]

Isaac then took up Descartes' **Geometry**, which was purported to be very difficult. Isaac read the first ten pages, stopped and reread them farther than before; then he stopped, again went back to the beginning and read farther than before until he had mastered the geometry of Descartes' without aid from tutor, professor or anyone else. In his *Wastebook* Isaac wrote at length about vertices, axes and diameters of curves. He definitely preferred Descartes' analytical geometry instead of the more pristine geometry of Euclid.[16]

Isaac then read Dr. Wallis's **Arithmetica Infinitorium** in order to interpolate a quadrature of a circle. Through Wallis's book Isaac found the theorem for raising a binomial to any given power, and later, upon being given a coordinate system and some defining equation, to draw the crooked line which that equation represented and to evaluate its properties.[17]

Though the world didn't know it yet, Isaac was probably the rarest human to have inhabited the planet Earth. And rare indeed was a man with such a gifted mind and a determined work ethic, a man capable of solving the phenomena and mysteries of the universe by teaching himself the most complex mathematics available –and expanding on them. Isaac Newton was well on his quest to learn the meaning and substance of the universe.

CHAPTER 7

A Secluded Scholar

• • •

"IN HIS THIRD AND FOURTH years at Trinity, Isaac worked day and night to research the topics in his *Wastebook* and to correct some fallacies and errors he had discovered in the writings of earlier scientists, mathematicians and theologians. Unfortunately, the curriculum offered at Trinity did not contribute significantly to his new found mission, and as a result, his grades suffered, though not quite as much as in his first two years at King's School. ...

But Newton was happy. He was in his element; his mind was truly being challenged and he loved it. He wanted to know everything about every *thing* and what made everything tick, and he was now in pursuit of doing just that. He had his own method of scientific investigation: the logical outlook of Rene' Descartes along with the experimental process of Galileo and Francis Bacon. He was fusing the rational and the empirical, the scientific and the religious, but unlike Descartes, Isaac saw that behind the clockwork precision of the universe there was purposeful direction.

He wrote in his *Wastebook* under "Of God:"

> *If men and beasts were made by fortuitous jumblings of atoms, there would be many useless parts; many beasts would have one eye and some more than two.*[18]

At the end of Isaac's third year at Trinity, his tutor, Benjamin Pulleyn, recognized the vastly superior intelligence of his pupil, and believing Isaac might need financial help someday, struck up a personal conversation with his reclusive pupil:

"Isaac, may I ask ye a personal question?"

"If you wish."

"Are ye planning to continue on at Trinity after thy Bachelor's Degree?"

"I am, God willing."

"Aren't ye still a sizar and don't ye still lend money?"

"Aye, 'tis so."

"Ye wouldn't have to do such things if ye had a scholarship. Have ye thought of applying for one?"

"Yes, but my academic record would disqualify me."

"Maybe not, Isaac. Would ye allow me to make an appointment for ye to see Dr. Barrow? He is on the scholarship committee. Once he knows your mathematical expertise, I'm sure he would recommend ye for a scholarship."

"Dr. Barrow knows little about me."

"Once he examines ye, he'll know enough."

"Enough? What do ye mean *enough*?"

"He'll find out that you're a very intelligent student, Isaac!"

"Balderdash! What sort of man is this Professor Barrow? I've only heard him twice when he gave Lucasian lectures. "

"He's a man of many talents with friends in high places. He's been quite fortunate."

"Fortunate?"

"Aye. He refused to take the Cromwellian oath and sailed for France in 1655. He held to his own beliefs among the Jesuits in Paris, and he charmed the elite of Smyrna and Constantinople; he even bested a Turk in hand-to-hand combat. On his return to England in 1659 he fought Maltese pirates who attacked his ship. He was greeted in London like a conquering hero. After the political winds had changed upon Charles II's restoration, Barrow was appointed Regius Professor of Greek at Gresham College in 1662 and became one of the original Fellows of the

Royal Society of London. This year Charles II appointed him Lucasian Professor of Mathematics at Trinity. He is considered a friend of the king. Henry Lucas endowed the Lucasian chair just last year."

"Didn't Barrow catch the *Popery disease* in Europe?"

"Nay, not even a trifle."

Isaac hesitated, then said, "I suppose I could talk with him."

Pulleyn arranged the meeting, but during the interview with Dr. Barrow, Isaac was quizzed at length on Euclidian geometry, a subject which Isaac had only glossed over. Regrettably, Dr. Barrow posed no questions on Descartes' geometry, and Isaac apparently thought it best not to mention his prowess in it. In Barrow's defense, he probably thought that no one could understand Descartes' before mastering Euclid.[19] After Newton botched the oral exam, the Lucasian Professor drew only an indifferent opinion of Benjamin Pulleyn's prize pupil.

Isaac was embarrassed with his performance with the professor; furthermore, he had embarrassed his tutor. And judging from Isaac's past, he did not like being negatively thought of. Therefore he reacted as he had reacted at King's School after being harrassed by a bully; he attacked Euclidian geometry with a vengeance. It wouldn't be long before Dr. Barrow was very impressed with the student from Woolsthorpe, especially after **Euclidis Elementorum** became the most thumb-worn annotated book in Isaac Newton's library.[20] The two Isaacs soon became very close friends.

Before his senior year, Isaac had ventured beyond the science and mathematics of Bacon, Euclid, Galileo, Oughtred and Descartes; and like those geniuses before him, he ventured alone in his own private world and studied in solitude. In a few years Isaac would ask Charles Darwin how he made his discoveries, and Darwin would answer, "Truth is the offspring of silence and unbroken meditation."

In addition to Isaac's penchant for solitude, his personality did not endear him to the other students --the fact that he was a money lender didn't help either. Newton really didn't like his classmates at Trinity –except perhaps for John Wickins. Isaac and Wickins shared similar Puritan beliefs and both of them were viewed as pariahs by other students. Though Puritanism still reigned in most of England, it wasn't the way of life at Trinity, where drinking, gambling and whoring had become commonplace since the Restoration –despite the religious heritage of the university. Nevertheless, Wickins and Newton didn't talk much to each other.

Isaac had met Wickins entirely by accident. Having bolted from his room because of his boisterous roommates, Isaac retreated to a bench on one of Trinity's walkways. As he sat, Wickins walked by and, noticing the disconsolate look on Isaac's face, inquired as to the reason for his dejection; then, after hearing it, told Isaac that he was out walking for the same reason. They immediately decided to room together and abandon their current roommates.[21] They roomed together until Wickins left Trinity; their friendship, though not close, lasted many years.

From reading Wallis's "Opera Mathematica" in his senior year, Isaac gained his first insight into the naïve calculus of invisibles. He also learned how to compound and interpolate integrals better than Wallis himself. Later, these developments led to Isaac's series expansion of the general binomial. However, Schooten's "Exercitationes Mathematica," based on Descartes' "Geometrie," was the stepping stone that led Isaac toward unprecedented mathematical creations. He was now surging headlong from "pure" geometry to the "analytical geometrical construction of equations."

In the Spring of 1664 Trinity's fledgling mathematician had not yet deeply studied the complexity of Kepler's elliptical orbits, but he had studied Galileo's principle of uniformly accelerated rectilinear and circular motion, which became the foundation for his future laws of more complicated motion.[22] In late 1664 Isaac recorded his first two axioms of inertia:

1. A quantity in motion will never rest unless hindered by some external cause.
2. A quantity will always move in a straight line unless some external cause diverts it.[23]

Using his principles of inertia, Isaac experimented with a ball moving in a straight line within a circle, striking the interior wall of the circle many times until it eventually moved in a circular path with the circle, all because of the pressure exerted by the circle's interior surface against the ball. Newton concluded that all bodies that are moved in a circular motion have some "endeavor" (centrifugal force) from the center, or axis, about which they moved. [24]

Newton then formulated a mathematical formula regarding the total number of times the ball would strike the interior of the circle, or the sum of the sides of a polygon the ball had made; the number of sides was divided by the force of the ball, or the radius of the circle. This formula became Isaac's version of the law of centrifugal force, a concept developed by Christiaan Huygens five years previously, but not published. Soon, instead of having the ball constrained by a spherical surface, Isaac allowed it to proceed on a plane. Using his own independent research, Newton's investigation of the property of curves by transforming their Cartesian equations into new axes preceded his research on Wallis's binomial expansion.

Years later, geometry would be called the first and noblest of sciences. Newton's first research into mathematics stemmed directly from Descartes' "Geometrie" and its appendixes. Slowly, by mastering the intricacies of the geometrical and analytical theory of conics, he became fascinated by the mathematical descriptions of curves, understanding ovals and drawing the "crooked line" from multiple coordinates and some defining equation. By using his newly acquired knowledge of mathematics, Newton attempted to reduce "the defining equation" by a mathematical transformation to a curve –a technical implementation that was difficult to say the least. The theory of such a transformation –from one oblique pair to another—had never been solved.

Yet, Newton solved it in three months, from October to December of 1664. And for an easier, more practical application of this transformation, he constructed lengthy, complicated tables of coefficients. In the spring of 1665 Isaac probed even further into his concept regarding the extremes of curvature and formulated a general rule of tangents from reading Gregory and Slusius.[25]

And nobody really knew the extent of Isaac's studies. No one in the vicinity of Trinity knew that Isaac was establishing new frontiers, nor were they capable of understanding some of his discoveries and their implications. But many knew that Isaac was one of the "brisk part of the university" –meaning those students who were venturing into Cartesian ideas.[26]

While Isaac experimented in mathematics, he was also delving into optics, dynamics and space. He had started tracking comets in December of 1664, having seen his first comet on December 8 and then again on December 15. He made regular observations of that comet until it disappeared a month later. He scanned the skies all winter until he saw another comet the next April.

Unfortunately, in studying the heavens he put his eyesight in jeopardy by looking repeatedly at the sun through a looking glass. Then he would look into a dark corner and see circles of colors. He repeated this process until the imprint of the sun was always present wherever he looked. He had to stay in the dark over three days to regain the use of his eyes. At one time he even inserted a bodkin into his eye socket and pressed it against his eyeball until those dark circles appeared again. Isaac was gifted with remarkable visual and auditory acuity. He could count rings of colors from a prism, a feat unmatched by any of his peers. When he was nine years of age he could see the steeple at Grantham from a haystack in Skillington six miles away.

In 1665, Isaac began reading **Philosophical Transactions**, a publication of the Royal Society about recent scientific discoveries. In one publication Isaac read an article "Micrographia," written that same year by Robert Hooke, who with Anton van Leeuwenhoek, became known as the fathers of microscopy. However, Isaac disagreed with Hooke's hypotheses that light consists of "vibrating motions" and that colors result from a "confused" mixture of impressions. Robert Hooke, the curator of experiments for the Royal Society, endorsed Descartes' color scale from red, the strongest; to blue, the weakest. However Isaac Newton, from his work with prisms found that the two thousand year-old theory regarding this "scale of colors" was flawed. The disagreement with Hooke's findings may have been the spark that ignited a lifelong feud between these two natural philosophers. Isaac also may have felt that Hooke was not high enough on the intelligence scale.

In 1665 Catherine Storer gave up hopes of marrying her childhood sweetheart and married a Grantham attorney named –homophonically-- Francis Bakon. Her uncle, Humphrey Babington, Isaac's friend, performed the ceremony. Interestingly, Catherine carried a torch for Isaac the rest of her life. In her 70's she would read poetry Isaac had written to her on the walls of her stepfather's home.

In the spring of 1665 at the age of twenty-two, Isaac Newton stood for his Bachelor of Arts degree. Unfortunately, he was placed in "second posing," the lower part of his class. To coin a derogatory term used by students at Trinity, Isaac "lost his groats." But Isaac had spent his time in "solid learning," not in "trifling logic or rhetoric." Isaac's exact ranking was never discovered because the "Ordo Senioritatis" for the year 1665 mysteriously disappeared from Trinity's Grace Book.[27] When Isaac eventually became famous, some historians thought that Benjamin Pulleyn and Humphrey Babington may have helped Isaac in his final disputations --not to mention the mysterious disappearance of the Grace Book.

CHAPTER 8

The Plague

• • •

"IN 1665 THE WORLD WAS unscientific. Most people turned to scripture in order to explain disasters, wars, famines and plagues. The Black Plague had struck Europe in 1347, and the Bubonic Plague had decimated London in 1625. Since that scourge of forty years ago, and despite high infant mortality, London had multiplied geometrically to a population of over 500,000. Unfortunately in April of 1665 another plague struck outside the city walls, where most of the poor people lived. By the end of June the sickness had spread so rapidly, people began putting their affairs in order. Even Samuel Pepys, Secretary of the Admiralty, had boarded up his home and written his last will and testament. ...

Mortality at this time was approximately 90% of those infected by the plague. Within one year over 100,000 people met an agonizing death. Quarantining the infected was the only means of containing the disease.[28] Pets were prohibited from homes; therefore, cats were not available to kill the rats which carried the dreaded affliction. Everyone seemed to possess a remedy. The majority recommended prayer; some, astrology. But the only effective way to deal with the pandemic was an exodus: *cito, lange, tarde* --fly quickly, go far, return slowly. At the end of June Isaac escaped to Woolsthorpe. The king, parliament and the university students began fleeing to the countryside. On August 6, 1665 Trinity officially closed its doors.

The "plague period" became Isaac Newton's epoch of discovery, the greatest creative and mental productivity in the life of any scientist, before or since. But Isaac thought he was just making discoveries as a result of his personal work ethic and his desire for truth –for more light. It was during this time he became the most advanced mathematical thinker history has ever known. Before Isaac had departed Trinity he wrote a paper on the summation of the infinitesimal arcs of curves. In November, 1665 at Woolsthorpe, he wrote his second paper on fluxions (calculus) and their applications to tangents and the curvature of curves.

During the summer Isaac spent some of his time in Boothby Pagnell at Humphrey Babington's home, where he successfully calculated the area of a hyperbola. He was so pleased with this accomplishment that he carried out his answer to fifty-two places. Throughout the summer and into early autumn this recent graduate of Trinity reworked the theoretical basis of his recently accomplished formulae for calculus, moving from the small discreet increment of a variable to the product of its fluxion and the unit increment of the variable of time.[29]

For the first time Isaac attached simple fluxional equations without much success; however, it is remarkable that he would attempt to resolve these equations at his current stage of development.[30] It was in late autumn that Newton returned to tangents and attempted to define a curve in an arbitrary coordinate system by compounding the limit-motions at a given point. He wrote a correct construction of tangents to mechanical curves on November 8, 1665.[31] As far as calculus is concerned, his greatest period of creative discovery occurred from the middle of 1664 through all of 1665 when Isaac accomplished the following:

1. Introduced finite difference techniques in the study of factoring polynomials.
2. Extensively researched the theory of equations to find their complex roots.
3. Made findings in the general theory of angle sections and was the only person in his day to address circular motion.[32]

However, Newton kept these accomplishments and discoveries to himself. Why should he have to prove them to anyone? He knew what he had accomplished and that fact alone was his remuneration. He was ecstatic to make new discoveries and to find new light --to uncover the truth. Isaac had found facts about God's universe, and wasn't that enough? Besides, wasn't vanity sinful?

In March of 1666, Trinity sent word for its students to return. The plague had subsided. Isaac returned to the university and resumed his experiments on colors. Unable to grind lenses of ellipses and hyperbolas to make a perfect focus, he bought another prism and started recording his findings in a Wastebook section entitled "Of Colours." Never had anyone used prisms so well. Descartes, Hooke and Robert Boyle refracted light from two to four feet away from their prisms to produce circular images. In contrast, Isaac Newton projected a sun's beam through two prisms producing an oblong image onto a wall twenty-two feet away. He found that white light was heterogeneous, and that the different rays which produced colors are refracted at different angles.

But Isaac went further; he introduced mathematics into his study of light. He found that each color had its own proportion of sines, so he calculated sines for each color, something Descartes was only able to do for a refracted beam of white light. Soon Isaac discovered that by using three prisms, he could combine individual rays of colored light to form a white color. Thus, Isaac single-handedly reversed the relationship of colored and white light and proved his findings mathematically.

Later on, when Isaac released his findings, he found himself doing verbal battle with Robert Hooke, who would strenuously defend his own findings. Unfortunately, Isaac Newton's first revelations of his new discoveries prompted many objections, many by persons who were no match for Isaac's superior intellect. And Isaac took much time trying to answer all of them.

When June arrived, the plague returned. Even the learned men of Cambridge had not yet discovered that plagues become dormant in winter due to rat hibernation. So Isaac returned to Woolsthorpe, where he soon made an observation that not only changed the world, it opened the windows to understanding the planets and the universe. One day while Isaac was looking out a window, he saw an apple fall from a tree, and the thought struck him:

If an apple is drawn to the earth, why not the moon or any planet? Isaac then mathematically attempted to estimate the force with which a globe revolving around a sphere is drawn to that sphere. Using Keplers' 3rd law that the squares of the time period of the revolutions of the planets are to one another as the cubes of their average distances from the sun, Newton made a new discovery. He calculated that the force of a planet's gravity is in inverse proportion to the distance from the center of the planet around which it is orbiting. He theorized that the attraction of planets to the sun decreases inversely as the squares of the distance separating them from it. At twice the distance, the force is one-fourth as great; at three times the distance, one-ninth as great. Newton wrote his inverse square formula on the back of one of his mother's old leases and named the force of a planet's rotation *centripetal force.*

Isaac's fascination with gravity and the moon's orbit seemed to mesmerize him his entire life. Unfortunately, in mathematically testing his theory of lunar attraction and planetary motion, he arrived at an incorrect figure for the earth's radius. Galileo and other scientists had theorized that one degree of latitude equals 60 miles, however Newton could not prove that theory using Italian or English miles. He temporarily abandoned his moon research, but it still remained his most captivating subject. Unknown to him at the time, his inverse square law was 100% accurate. Isaac's error was in not using nautical miles. A few years later Jean Picard wrote that a degree of latitude was equal to one nautical mile, or 6077.28 feet. Newton then knew that his inverse square law was perfectly correct. He modestly described it "as one of my guesses."[33] Yet it became one of the world's most important scientific discoveries.

During 1666 Isaac codified plane and spherical trigonometry and investigated musical octaves. He also fine-tuned his papers on calculus and entered them in his Wastebook in a small tract on fluxions and series methods.[34] He also experimented in optics and dynamics during his miraculous years of mathematical discoveries --his *Annus Mirabilis*.

CHAPTER 9

Snuggery

• • •

"On Monday, September 2, 1666 an ember from a bakery on Pudding Street ignited a fire that destroyed the London that was home to Chaucer, Elizabeth I, Christopher Marlowe and Shakespeare. The fire lasted four days and nights and burned down every wooden structure in the walled city; 436 acres of buildings were destroyed --over 75% of the town. Royal Society member, Christopher Wren, was commissioned to rebuild the city --this time with stone. ...

Fortunately, Isaac Newton was in Woolsthorpe when the Great Fire struck. It was the fourth life-threatening catastrophe Isaac had survived; the other three: premature birth, the Civil War and the Plague. Of course, Isaac had his own internal fires which had been burning in his mind for years. Instead of rebuilding London, he was restructuring the universe. Though Isaac was just a novice in natural philosophy, he was putting the world together for the first time since Pythagoras.

Isaac also continued to experiment with colors, optics and mathematics. In his volume "Of Colours" he drafted steps that he would later submit to Henry Oldenburg, the Royal Society secretary. He eventually sent Book I of his "Opticks" to Oldenburg, and within the next six years would tell him that mathematics could be used in the science of light: "There is much certainty in it as in any other part of "Opticks."[35] Isaac's experiments in light continued to refute the arguments made by Robert Hooke and Descartes' –primarily because he had employed three prisms and combined individual rays of colored light into white light.

On March 25, 1667 Isaac returned to Trinity to complete his Master of Arts degree, but he needed to obtain a fellowship to survive financially. Fortunately three vacancies occurred during the summer of 1667: two fellows had fallen down a staircase in a drunken stupor and injured themselves, and one more also fell victim to the bottle -- he passed out in a field, caught a fever and died. Ironically, the three vacancies were caused by a vice especially spurned by Isaac Newton.

In September, at the urging of Babington, Isaac applied for a fellowship. He undertook three days of oral examinations and one day of writing themes. On October 1, 1667 fellowships were announced and Isaac Newton was formally declared a Minor Fellow the next day. He may have been helped by Humphrey Babington, who was involved in the selection process. Upon completion of his M.A. degree Isaac would be elevated to Major Fellow, and be required to accept the "true religion of Christ." Then in seven more years he would be required to take Holy Orders of the Anglican Church in order to retain his fellowship and remain at the university.

But Isaac was now snugly entrenched at Trinity, and he wanted to remain there. He had a stipend, a livery allowance, room and board. Although he and roommate Wickins were assigned a ground floor apartment, they rented it out and moved to the second floor north of the Great Gate, a place later to be known as the "heart of the scientific revolution."[36] Since he was now a minor fellow, Isaac celebrated for only the second time in his life. He went on a shopping spree, visited some local taverns and entertained in his room, all because it was customary for students to celebrate accomplishments. Nevertheless, Isaac was never "one of the boys."[37] His closest friends, if one could describe them as such, were older, successful, intelligent men like Humphrey Babington and Isaac Barrow.

On March 10, 1668, Isaac officially became a Major Fellow, and on July 7 he received his Master of Arts. He was now receiving some additional income from his properties at Sewstern and Woolsthorpe. With his extra money, Isaac purchased a lathe and table, drills, gravers, hone and hammer, a mandrill, a magnet, compasses, glass bubbles and three prisms. He bought eighteen yards of tammy to tailor his bachelor's gown into a resplendent gown of a Major Fellow. He also bought many books including Bacon's "Michelangelo," Thomas Sprat's "Ye Hystory of ye Royall Society," and a subscription to "Philosophical Transactions," the Royal Society's official publication; however, he decided to wait until next year to acquire two furnaces and some supplies for alchemic experiments.

During 1668 another natural philosopher, Nicholas Mercator, published the treatise "Logarithmotechnia," in which he constructed a square equal in area to a hyperbola by using infinite series, a procedure already employed by Isaac Newton. But Newton had extended infinite series to all types of curves (not just hyperbolas) by using cubic equations and mathematically extended curves in three dimensions –a calculation more complex than the two-dimensional mathematics of Mercator. In fact, Isaac approached analytical geometry the same way that he had approached calculus –algebraically and kinetically, using points of curves moving through space.[38]

In 1669, John Collins, a member of the Royal Society, sent a copy of *Logarithmotechnia* to Isaac Barrow, who, knowing Newton to be competent in mathematics, showed the manuscript to him. Isaac recognized the treatise and said:

"Dr. Barrow, I saw this document during the plague before its publication. I had already calculated logarithms from infinite series; however Mercator uses infinite series in only two dimensions. I have carried logarithms into cubic equations, a computation that is far more advanced than the mathematics in *Logarithmotechnia*."

"Would you be so kind as to show me a sample of these calculations, Isaac?"

Isaac produced a scratch sheet of paper, started to draw and said, "These are examples of curves moving through space. By placing points on these curves, I can develop cubic equations algebraically and kinetically."

The younger Isaac began writing equations, and soon his perplexed professor asked, "Have you written anything on this subject?"

"Certainly, Dr. Barrow. I have written the paper *Analysis by Infinite Series*; however, it is in Latin."

"May I see it?"

"I suppose."

A few days later, after studying Newton's *De Analysi per Aequationes Infinitas*, Professor Barrow wrote to John Collins:

A friend of mine here, that hath a very excellent genius to these things, brought me some paper shewing methods of calculating dimensions of magnitudes like that of Mr. Mercator concerning the hyperbola, but very general.[39]

Barrow soon spoke to Newton about his paper:

"Isaac, may I send your paper on infinite series to Mr. Collins of the Royal Society?"

"I would prefer not, sir."

"Think on it for a time, Isaac, then give me your answer."

Isaac remained recalcitrant, but Dr. Barrow continued to prod him. On July 31, Dr. Barrow again took his prize student aside. "Isaac, I'm not asking you to publish *De Analysi*, but I am requesting that you show your treatise to a member of the Royal Society in order that you might establish precedence to your remarkable work."

After a long pause, accompanied by an equally long stare, Isaac responded: "You may send it, Dr. Barrow, but it must be returned at Mr. Collins' earliest convenience. And you must not mention my name."

"Thank you, Isaac. You may edit my letter to Mr. Collins if you wish."

Isaac watched as Dr. Barrow wrote:

"I send you the papers of my friend, a Fellow at Trinity. Please return them after perusing them, per his desire. Please give me notice of your receiving them with your earliest convenience.[40]

Barrow then turned to Isaac, "Is the letter to your satisfaction, Isaac?"

"Aye, sir, 'tis most acceptable."

Within a week Collins responded quite enthusiastically, "The papers of your friend are most extraordinary. Please tell me his name?"

Dr. Barrow's third letter to Collins finally revealed Isaac Newton's name to the scholastic world of the Royal Society, describing him as a fellow of our college and very young, but of an extraordinary genius and proficiency in these things. Barrow also wrote "Master Newton has given his permission to impart the papers, if you so desire, to my Ld. [Lord] Brounker, President of the Royal Society."

Upon receipt of permission to show Newton's papers to Lord Brounker, Collins carried *De Analysi* to other scholarly virtuosi en route. The unpublished papers were communicated widely,[41] proving without a doubt that Newton had invented and perfected the logarithmic method over two years before Mercator had published anything.

By this time, Dr. Barrow and Isaac Newton were close friends. The Professor had even enlisted Newton to edit his optical lectures before he published them, and Isaac displayed remarkable tact by not telling Barrow of his own revolutionary discoveries in optics and colors. Newton's discoveries would certainly have discredited much of Barrow's work, which had been drawn primarily from the writings of Kepler, Descartes and others. Barrow also helped Newton financially by assigning Isaac the tutelage of a wealthy student, St. Leger Scroope,[42] part of whose tuition would be paid to Isaac.

Dr. Barrow's "Optical Lectures" went to press in the summer of 1669 with a preface praising Isaac Newton as "a man of great Learning and Sagacity who revised my copy." No other student at Trinity had ever received such praise, and Isaac Newton had no better friend than the Lucasian professor. Friendships have rewards, one of which is being privy to a friend's wishes and desires. And Isaac knew that the professor was not happy holding the Lucasian Chair. Barrow was a theologian, not a mathematician. He aspired to be Master of Trinity College, but as Lucasian Chair he was ineligible for college office. In fact, Isaac may even have known that Dr. Barrow, who was close to King Charles, was aspiring to be the king's chaplain. Patronage was king in England, and the king did the patronage.[43]

Patronage was not only rife in court, but also in the universities; in fact, under Charles II it was pervasive. Appointments were political, not elected nor earned, and almost everyone sought favors. Fellowships were sought as a basic means of support, especially with stipends and perquisites amounting to 60 pounds per year --a considerable amount considering skilled workmen working six days a week for 52 weeks earned less than 30 pounds a year. Students desiring a life of ease and indolence sought fellowships, and those who attained them usually succumbed to a snug life, too often relieved by the solace of the table and the tavern.[44]

Until late in the 17th century, Trinity had been the leading academic institution in England, producing great scholars like John Pearson and Isaac Barrow. The Puritan revolution had stopped politically appointed positions, but the restoration brought them back. A small oligarchy of college masters appointed by the king began to dominate the universities. Before 1670 university officers were elected by regent masters from their ranks. After 1670, university officers were imposed from outside or selected by rotation from the senior fellows, who were primarily appointed through patronage. The patronage mushroomed to such an extent that most of the teaching masters did not even teach.[45]

Of the 41 students who became fellows from 1664 through 1668, including Newton and his roommate Wickins, only Isaac became known as an intellectual. One became prominent as an educator and a horticulturalist. Nine others did a little writing or educating, but none, other than Newton, became known by any standard, nor were they impressive as tutors. Four became pupil mongers, and of the other 37, ten tutored a total of 16 students –Newton and Wickins accounting for five of them. All of these fellows stayed at Trinity an average of seventeen and one-half years. Four men stayed over 40 years *and tutored no one*. None of the four ever published a word, yet they stayed to reap Trinity's ripest monetary rewards. [46]

On his quest to understand the universe, Isaac Newton was surrounded by fellows in search of a comfortable place to spend their lives. None was by any stretch of the imagination a true scholar. Most Trinity fellows only wanted snuggery.

This was the setting in which Isaac Newton would spend the greater part of his creative life –provided, of course, that he take Holy Orders before March 15, 1675-- and taking them was quickly becoming a problem. Isaac had religiously abided by his grandmother's wishes and daily studied the *Bible*. However, he also began examining original texts, especially those regarding the "Trinity." Ironically, as a result of his intense study, he began to privately question the authenticity of certain scriptures that had been the basis of the Christian church since the first quarter of the fourth century.

CHAPTER 10

The Lucasian Chair of Mathematics

• • •

"AFTER CROMWELL'S DEATH, ISAAC BARROW returned to England from the continent and received three professorships and the Lucasian Chair of Mathematics at Trinity. Being an original fellow in the Royal Society of London undoubtedly helped him gain this last appointment. Nevertheless, since 1664 Barrow coveted a higher position. ...

The Lucasian Chair was indeed a plum; it was the first endowment at Trinity since Henry VIII established the five Regius professorships in 1549. Wealthy benefactor Henry Lucas wanted a scientific lectureship to match the Savilian Chairs established at Oxford in 1619. Included with Barrow's chair was a salary of 100 pounds of tax-free income every year and a light teaching load of one lecture a week during three of the four terms. Unfortunately, Barrow found attendance very poor at these lectures, and he found himself lecturing only during one term –at times to no one. He once said "I have sat on my chair incessantly alone."[47]

It did not take a genius to recognize that Isaac Barrow was dissatisfied with the Lucas chair; after five years he had taught only a handful of students. Furthermore, he was prohibited from holding an administrative position in the university due to Trinity's statutes. Therefore becoming Master of Trinity was out of the question; yet, Dr. Barrow wanted it. He began submitting articles to Trinity's "Valedictory Volumes," not on mathematics, but on matters designed to attract the king's attention, such as a very flattering essay about the death of the king's daughter. The fact is, Isaac Barrow had two very good reasons to resign. First of all, King Charles II had suggested Barrow to be his personal chaplain, and secondly, Dr. Barrow had found *an excellent replacement for his Lucasion Chair.*

In autumn of 1669, not long after Newton had released *De Analysi* to John Collins, Collins showed the treatise to Dr. Barrow, who promptly summoned Isaac Newton to his office. Isaac soon knocked at his professor's door. Dr. Barrow admitted his prize student and directed him to sit in a chair across from his desk. Barrow spoke first:

"Isaac, over the last few months I've been observing some of your work and I'm not at all hesitant to tell you that I believe you have the best mathematical mind I have ever known or heard of. "

The professor halted for a moment, possibly expecting a response; but when none came, Barrow continued:

"I am truthfully envious of your abilities and your knowledge, knowing full well that I, myself, in the highest position of mathematics awarded in England, am not capable of creating your complex formulae and equations. Other members of England's intellectual community have also written to me about the knowledge you have disclosed to my friend, John Collins of the Royal Society. Your *De Analysi* has reached the best mathematicians in Scotland, France, the Netherlands, Italy and England. You are no longer anonymous, Isaac."

"I did not desire such dissemination of my work, sir."

"I know, but it is all for the best, Isaac. I brought you here for another reason. As you know, I am primarily a theologian. I prefer theology and administration over mathematics."

The younger Isaac interrupted, "But sir, you are still a good mathematician."

"Not as good as you, Isaac. You are the best mathematician I have ever known. So I have a proposition for you. Were I to resign and recommend you to succeed me in the Lucasian Chair, would you accept the position?"

"Dr. Barrow, I am but twenty-six. Surely, an older candidate would be more suitable."

"There is no one to whom I would relinquish this chair except for you, Isaac. There is no one more qualified. Again, were I to resign, would you accept the position if it were offered? The position has a great many benefits in remuneration, but it would offer you the opportunity to give lectures on subjects that only you have mastered in the field of mathematics. Although I can't guarantee your appointment, my recommendations are generally accepted by the executors and survivors of the Lucas estate. What say you?

"I suppose that if I were selected, I would accept sir, and I thank you for your consideration and your kindness."

"I will speak to executors Raworth and Buck. After all, I dedicated my book to them and I doubt sincerely that they would not submit your name to the university."

Dr. Barrow soon resigned his chairmanship and the Lucas executors accepted his recommendation that Isaac Newton, a fellow of the university, succeed him. Consequently, on October 29, 1669, Trinity University appointed Isaac Newton as the Lucasian Professor of Mathematics. It was a mercurial rise in a short span of time. Starting with John Collins' sending Mercator's *Logarithmotechnia*, which led to the dissemination of Newton's *De Analysi* and then to his appointment as Lucasian Chair, the whole process took less than six months.

Interestingly, Isaac Newton's first lectures were not on mathematics, but "opticks," and attendance was as poor as it had been for his predecessor. Although Isaac had worked on analytic geometry --specifically "The Enumeration of Cubics"-- and on fluxions prior to his appointment, he had worked more intensely on his study of colors and optics. Drawing from his earlier study, this time he did a thorough investigation of colors to formulate his final theories, including: 1) Blue rays are refracted more than red. 2) The color white was simply the sensation caused by a heterogeneous mixture of rays.[48]

While experimenting with colors and optics, Isaac used not only his prisms, but also lenses which he had ground himself –and which required much time and effort to perfect. The degree of perfection that he demanded of himself would astonish any human being. Isaac expected accuracy within one one-hundredth of an inch, precision unheard of in the 17th Century. No one ever demanded even half this accuracy.[49]

Throughout his life Newton was consumed by the desire to know; he had an unrelenting passion for knowledge. His new position at Trinity did much to help this passion --he was now isolated as well as alienated. No one ever saw him take any recreation –no riding, walking, bowling or even stepping out for fresh air. He rarely left his chamber or went to the dining hall –except for some special event-- and then, if he weren't reminded, he would go very carelessly and unkempt with his hair scarcely combed. He rarely went to morning or evening chapel, but did on occasion attend services on Sunday at St. Mary's.[50]

Within a month of his appointment, Isaac made his second trip to London. Dr. Barrow had informed John Collins of this excursion, and Collins eagerly called on his mathematical idol late on a Saturday night at the inn where Isaac was staying. After obtaining the location of Isaac's room from the innkeeper, Collins proceeded to knock on Newton's door.

"Who knocks?" came from within.

"'Tis I, John Collins. Would this be the room of Professor Isaac Newton?"

"Aye" said Newton as he opened the door. "Greetings, Mr. Collins. Please come in."

Neither gentleman had ever seen the other before. Collins was aware of Newton's young age and was somewhat startled to observe the premature graying of his hair. The caller thrust out his hand and said:

"I am so pleased to meet you, sir. I truly am honored."

"I deserve no honors for only labors and the labors of those before me."

"Ah, but you have expanded far beyond the scope of any of them, sir."

"Exceeding the abilities of others is not my concern, John. I simply search for knowledge and further light, and I fear I am addicted in so doing."

"And thank the Lord you are, sir; thank the Lord. Mr. Newton, may I inquire as to the nature of your visit to London?"

"Of course, but first I wish to thank you for sending me Wallis's *Mechanics*."

"Why, you are most welcome, sir."

"I am in London primarily to purchase supplies for some chemical experiments and for constructing a reflecting telescope. I also plan to visit The Royal Society."

"A reflecting telescope?"

"Yes, it reflects images within the scope, and I believe will magnify them up to 150 times their size. I make, grind and polish all of its parts. I use mirrors instead of lenses."

"I don't believe I have ever seen such a scope. It must be much larger than the current refractors."

"On the contrary, Mr. Collins, it is no longer than six inches. Now may I ask what might be the nature of your visit?"

"In truth, I am again seeking more information from you. I need help in mathematically formulating a musical progression. This is what I have accomplished thus far."

Collins showed his mathematical musical progressions to Isaac, who said, "Let me send you something by post on this, John."

"Mr. Newton, I thank you so much for even considering my request. May I invite you to have dinner with me at the Rummer and Grapes tomorrow eve –say at the hour of six?"

"I will be glad to. I shall see you tomorrow then."

Newton escorted Collins to the door and returned to his shopping list. *Let's see.. two furnaces, three lenses, pitch, putty ...*

CHAPTER 11

Acquaintances

• • •

"With Dr. Barrow's prodding, Isaac Newton allowed a chink in his armor of privacy. He had now revealed some of his own calculations and discoveries to John Collins, who prior to November of 1669 had been a perfect stranger. And this 'perfect stranger' had now revealed a mite of Newton's mind to a few other mathematical virtuosi. Furthermore, Dr. Barrow had convinced his prize protége' to edit and annotate the Algebra text of Gerard Kinckhuysen, which Collins had translated from Dutch to English. ...

In January of 1670 Newton responded to Collins' request for a mathematical solution to musical progressions by sending various methods to sum up some definite terms in a harmonic series,[51] methods which Collins struggled to understand. Consequently, Collins responded with some of his own harmonic thoughts and another question: "Would you be so kind as to provide me a formula for computing the rate of interest **N** on an annuity of **B** pounds for thirty-one years purchased for **A** pounds?"[52]

On February 6 Newton sent an annuity formula to Collins along with some notations on Kinckhuysen's *Algebra*. On February 18 Collins sent a question from Michael Dary. Newton obliged by sending Dary a formula for calculating the zone of a circle. However, in his February 18 letter Collins also asked permission from Isaac to publish his formula for annuities in the Royal Society's "Philosophical Transactions." Newton responded quickly: *Soe it be wth out my name to it. For I see not what there is desirable in publick esteeme, were I able to acquire & maintain it. It would perhaps increase my acquaintance, ye thing wch I chiefly study to decline*. Isaac went on to say that he had a method to compute harmonic series with logarithms, but he did not send it. He only mentioned that the calculations were "troublesome."[53]

Collins persisted with his apparent friendly relationship with Isaac by sending Moses Pitts, a bookseller, to meet Isaac regarding the publication of Kinckhuysen's Algebra, but Isaac avoided meeting him. Nevertheless, before summer's end, Newton provided Collins with annotations on Algebra that simplified many of Kinckhuysen's cumbersome procedures and revealed Isaac's mastery of the subject. In the same letter Isaac said, "I hope I have done what you have requested. I send them [annotations on Kinckhuysen] not so much with a design they should be printed as that your desires should bee satisfied to have me revise ye book. And so soon as you have read ye papers I have my end of writing them."[54] Newton added that he didn't want his name to appear ---even though it was obvious from his revisions that every mathematician would benefit from them.

John Collins was so pleased, he responded immediately and enclosed three books, from which Isaac was to pick the best one for discussing surds. By this time Isaac had become rather unsettled with Collins' interruptions. He sent back Collins' books and asked him to return the manuscript on Algebra. Collins was simply not close enough to Newton's intellectual plane.

Collins promptly sent back the manuscript, but with even more questions and the faux pas of his life; he wanted to use Isaac's name as the source of the notes on Kinckhuysen's *Algebra*, a request that must have caused Newton much anxiety. Collins had written:

"Your paines herein will be acceptable to some very eminent Grandees of the Royal Societie, who must be made acquainted therewith." It was a stupid remark, especially since Newton had already told Collins that he studied mainly to *diminish making acquaintances.*[55]

Two months elapsed without any response from Isaac Newton. He finally answered Collins on September 27:

"I am considering a completely new introduction to Algebra, and since there are already several introductions published, I have chosen to let it passe wth out much altering what I sent you before."[56]

Collins heard nothing more from Isaac Newton for ten months –nor did he get the *Algebra* notations back. But he learned something: Isaac was more than just a mathematical genius; he guarded his discoveries and his privacy. Two or three times Isaac had told Collins how to do something but had not imparted the "general method." Newton had communicated some of his individual series and given out a formula for annuities –but hadn't divulged the "general method" perhaps to test a recipient's mental capabilities. Having recognized a definite reticence on the part of the mathematical genius, Collins decided to leave Newton alone.

Isaac, of course, had been working day and night on other projects, one of which would have raised the ire of the outside world, had it be known. But, as usual, Isaac kept controversial subjects to himself and to his private papers. In July of 1671 Collins finally broke his silence and sent Newton a verbose letter about mathematics, especially the mathematics in Kinckhuysen' *Algebra*. Collins also said that the book would have sold much better with Newton's name on it. Accompanying Collins' letter was a new book by Borelli. Newton responded that he hadn't been able to visit Collins that summer due to illness, and tersely suggested that Collins not send him any more books.

Newton also mentioned something else –something he had been doing during the past year. It was a discourse, *De Methodis Serierum et Fluxionum* (A Treatise of the Methods of Series and Fluxions), the most ambitious undertaking of fluxional calculus Isaac had ever undertaken.[57] In almost every respect, Newton expanded upon his work in October of 1666 and also upon his De Analysi of 1669; he also made his calculations more systematic. He especially concentrated on two important problems in the analysis of curves:

1. Given the length of space continuously to find the speed of motion at any time.
2. Given the speed of motion continuously, to find the length of the space at any time.[58]

Later he added a third problem: To calculate areas under curves. He applied his method of fluxions to questions concerning the maxima and minima of quantities, the drawing of tangents to curves, nascent ratios, and determining the curvature of curves. Regrettably, Newton never really completed his *De Methodis*; nevertheless, had Collins ever received it, he would have done everything possible to put it into print. If it had been printed, it would have prevented a great controversy that arose in the future.

Of course, Newton would move heaven and earth to prevent the publication of his treatises. Yet if he had allowed *De Methodis* to be put into print, it would have revolutionized mathematics thirty years sooner. Quite the opposite, Newton killed every attempt to publish his work. He never did resend his annotations on Kinckhuysen to Collins; instead, he bought out the interest of the publisher for four pounds. [59] Although he might initially succumb to modest praise, he would nevertheless withdraw from any recognition, whether due to anxiety, fear of criticism --or the loss of his treasured privacy. No one knew why he rejected recognition.

From 1669 to 1671 much of Newton's mathematical work came from the urging of others. First it was Barrow who recognized Newton's superiority to Mercator; later on, it was Collins who wanted notes on Kinckhuysen. But what Isaac was doing in his cloistered quarters was more than just mathematics. He was researching religion, making telescopes and experimenting with optics and "chimicall studies." Collins and Barrow had leaked his genius in mathematics to a few members of the Royal Society, however, and by 1670 Newton did not possess the absolute anonymity he religiously cherished. Yet within his cloistered chambers he had amassed a voluminous body of scientific and mathematical information which he had accumulated since 1665 --and kept all of it hidden from the world.

One might also assume that Newton might gain some acclaim due to praise by one or more of Trinity's students. In his resplendent scarlet robe, he conscientiously appeared once a week to lecture for any student who came to listen. However, Isaac lectured in Latin and, with rare exception, students didn't understand him or his subject matter. With few lecture attendees, Newton had few student acquaintances; consequently, his genius remained obscure. To students he was probably just an eccentric, reclusive, absent-minded professor.

The truth is that Newton didn't enjoy teaching. His first loves were experimenting, discovering and creating; however, his strongest trait was his tenacity of purpose, the power of will. Nothing short of illness or death would stop him once a project occupied his mind. Even during entire nights, he never rested during his productive time. In fact, time was his enemy. If he did not devour it, it would devour him. There was no end of the day. There was only work until exhaustion. When sleep would try to overtake him, he wouldn't succumb. He could meditate without parallel in intensity and duration. It is humanly impossible to put this kind of genius into words. Newton had no peers in solving complex problems, in contemplating end results, and in working until achieving them.[60]

Unfortunately, one of the reasons behind Isaac Newton's gargantuan work ethic was a distaste for contact, let alone intimacy, with the outside world. Although he probably had the best brain on the planet, he lacked many social skills. Having been psychologically wounded in Woolsthorpe, Grantham, and Cambridge, he was now known as an odd mathematics professor with scarcely a student. With such a wounded psyche, Isaac's pleasure came from the isolation he guarded so tenaciously. He did not interact well with other people.

But Newton's sanctuary of anonymity would be short-lived. In fact, his name would soon be known to the scientific world, not because of his mathematical genius, but because of a telescope, a product of his hands and mechanical skills. It appears that Isaac was quite proud of his reflecting telescope. He had made every part of it from its copper plates to the putty, pitch and polish he employed to put it together. He had even boasted about it to Collins in December of 1669 and had shown a second one to some Trinity faculty by December of 1671. One faculty member, a Mr. Gale, wrote about the wonders of it to John Collins, who then relayed the information to some of his scientist friends in the Royal Society. John Flamsteed, a young astronomer, heard about the telescope both from a relative and from the Royal Society.

Though Collins hadn't yet conveyed Newton's mathematical skills to the Royal Society, his account of Isaac's reflecting telescope prompted the society to ask to see it. In the latter half of December Dr. Barrow again called on Newton and convinced him to show his creation to the Royal Society. Before the end of the year Barrow demonstrated the instrument to the Grandees of the Royal Society. Although only six inches in length, the telescope magnified items to 150 times. It caused such a sensation that Henry Oldenburg, the society's secretary, promptly sent a letter to Isaac Newton containing the following extract:

> ....*You have been so generous, as to impart to the Philosophers here, your invention of contracting telescopes. It having been examined here by some of the most eminent in optical science & practice & applauded by them....*[61]

Oldenburg also said that the members of the society wanted to secure Newton's name as the inventor by describing all of the telescope's features and sending them to the society's most eminent scientist, Christiaan Huygens in Paris. Isaac was told he could "adde & alter" as he saw fit.[62] Furthermore, Oldenburg said that Seth Ward had proposed Isaac for membership in the Royal Society. Before receiving a complete description of Isaac's telescope, Huygens was sent a general description dated January 1, 1672. He immediately praised the "marvelous telescope of Mr. Newton,"[63] and on January 11, the Royal Society unanimously elected Isaac Newton into its ranks.

Newton was so grateful that the Royal Society had secured his name as the inventor of the reflecting telescope, he allowed his name to appear on its description in the *Philosophical Transactions*. Before being admitted to the society he also sent a letter to Henry Oldenburg thanking Seth

Ward for his nomination and expressing a desire to be a member. And then, perhaps to his later regret, he said:
...I shall endeavor to testify my gratitude by communicating what my poore & solitary endeavors can effect towards ye promoting your Philosophicall designes.[64]

In a second letter dated January 18, Newton followed through on his promise by telling Oldenburg that he would be sending for the society's consideration and examination:

"...an accompt of a Philosophical discovery wch I doubt not but will prove much more grateful [gratitude] then the communication of that instrument [telescope], [such new discovery] being in my Judgment the oddest if not the most considerable detection wch hath hitherto beene made in the operation of Nature."[65]

As evidenced by such a bombastic statement from a quiet unspoken recluse, Isaac was extremely proud of his "Theory of Light and Colours." Many years of experiments had proved his discoveries to be perfect --without a shadow of a doubt.

So Isaac came out of his shell. However, preparing, editing and copying his theory –even with Wickins' help— took over two weeks, after which he sent it to London. The overwhelming acceptance of his telescope and his unanimous election to the Royal Society had allayed his fear of being criticized by such an intelligent fraternity whose purpose was his purpose: to discover truth –or *light* as some called it. And what could be more fitting than a theory about "light" itself. He was now associated with acquaintances of similar minds and consciences to whom he could present findings without fear of ignorant or prejudiced criticism. In his fondest dreams he had never envisioned such acquaintances ......or so he thought.

CHAPTER 12

Rejection

• • •

"Isaac stepped into the arena of great natural philosophers and offered them his findings, not simply as a discoverer or inventor, but as a creator of scientific law.[66] He believed the Royal Society contained great minds with which he could share his findings. He did not conceive of it as a killing ground. Furthermore, Isaac thought of himself as a phoenix bringing light from darkness. He left no stone unturned in his experiments. His findings were proved beyond question. ...

He displayed how exacting he was in his February 6, 1672 letter to Henry Oldenburg. That letter by itself would assure Isaac's immortality in modern science. It started with his optical research with prisms and then masterfully presented his experiments and propositions in the following order:

1. Explaining refractions of light
2. Deriving colours from degrees of refrangibility
3. Species of colours and degree of refrangibility not muted by refraction
4. Transmutation of colours
5. Two basic types of colours: primary and other
6. Mixing of colours
7. Whiteness; a proportionate mixture of primary colours –the color of light
8. The disbursement of colours into oblong forms from prisms
9. Explanation of the refraction of the colours of the rainbow[67]

Perhaps because of his current high opinion of the Royal Society – and of the confidence he placed in the accuracy of his discoveries in light and colors-- Newton wrote a final statement in his letter:

"If anything seem to be defective, or [seems] to thwart this relation [relating], I may have an opportunity of giving further direction about it, or of acknowledging my errors, if I have committed any."[68]

Newton's paper on light and colors was enthusiastically received by the Royal Society with uncommon applause. Secretary Oldenburg immediately asked Isaac to publish it in "Philosophical Transactions." A changed Isaac Newton responded:

> .... *Believe me Sr I doe not onely esteem it a duty to concure with them [the society] in the promotion of reall knowledge, but a great privilege that instead of exposing discourses to a prejudic't & censorious multitude (by wch means many truths have been bafled & lost) I may wth freedom apply my self to so judicious & impartiall an Assembly.* [69]

But he also mentioned that his paper was only a synthesis of a larger, more complex work, and could be subject to the "criticism of superficiality."[70] By now Oldenburg understood Newton's tantalizing style of not revealing everything even though Isaac had proof for every "mystery" he hinted at. He seemed always to be holding a carrot just out of reach.[71]

"Theory about Light and Colors" appeared in "Philosophical Transactions" on February 19, 1672 with Isaac Newton as author. A description of his telescope showed up in the next issue. Isaac Newton had burst on the stage of natural philosophers like a whirlwind. He would never again be unknown to the outside world.

Original reactions to Newton's discourse drew high praise –even Christiaan Huygens called it "ingenious." Isaac was pleased. After all, articles in "Philosophical Transactions" had never been disputed –not even mediocre ones. Nevertheless, the former theory on colors had been accepted for 2000 years. Robert Hooke, the Curator of Experiments for the Royal Society since its inception, supported the old theory. Consequently, the new discourse on colors instigated an immediate response from him.

Robert Hooke, the co-author of "Micrographia," was seven years older than Newton and was considered to be one of two men who were the foremost experts on light and colors. He was an unattractive figure; he walked with a limp, had a humped back, a pale face, one popping gray eye, a large head and a small body. He also had a temperament of sudden peaks and horrible valleys, which started at age 13 when his father hanged himself. Although Hooke was a creative person, he lacked the analytical ability to take his visions to concrete principles. He claimed more than he could prove, and at times watched while others reaped a harvest from seeds he may have planted in their heads.[72]

Like Newton, Hooke's love was his work. But unlike Newton, who lived a monastic life, he had many mistresses. Newton worked alone, but Hooke employed a number of people in doing experiments. Hooke engaged in social functions; Newton rarely left his chambers. Perhaps due to his sensitive nature and his aversion to criticism, Newton only revealed the results of his experiments after they had been proven without a doubt.[73] Hooke, however, published at every possible opportunity.

Newton's personality has been previously discussed; however, six years of searching and testing a theory to arrive at an indisputable truth only reinforced the wall that protected his psyche. Six years spent in a state of rapture, passing up sleep and regular meals to discover truths in places unknown to the human mind, can take a toll, not to mention the exasperation that could result if ignorant criticisms were to come from a source where ignorance was supposedly absent.

Within two weeks of Newton's first letter, Robert Hooke sent an extensive rebuttal to Secretary Oldenburg. Hooke, the English expert on light and color, implied in a condescending manner that he had conducted Newton's experiments with different conclusions. In essence, Hooke reasserted what he had published in "Micrographia," that light is nothing but a pulse or motion traveling "through a homogeneous, uniform and transparent medium; and that Colour is nothing but the Disturbance of ye light ... by the refraction thereof." He then added salt to the wound by protesting Newton's use of prisms instead of refracting telescopes and labeling Newton's theory as a "hypothesis" throughout his refutation. [74] Oldenburg forwarded the letter to Newton, who responded:

> *I received your Feb 19th. And having considered Mr. Hooks observations on my Discourse, am glad that so acute an objecter hath said nothing that can enervate any part of it. For I am still of the same judgment & doubt not but that upon severer examinations it will bee found as certain a truth as I have asserted it. You shall very suddenly have my answer.*[75]

Though Isaac did not say it, he was offended by Hooke's criticism, and no answer came for three months. Newton spent those months agonizing over his response. Hooke had unknowingly aroused a dormant lion. Not only had he impugned Isaac's veracity, his affrontery and lifestyle were an abomination to Isaac's puritanical foundations --not to mention the fact that Isaac did not like being refuted. Newton had found Hooke's conclusions in "Micrographia" galling. In Isaac's copy of that book he wrote"Descartes and Hooke are mistaken. Light does not turn corners. ... I shall not mingle conjectures with certainties."[76]

In the meantime, Oldenburg received a few more comments and critiques, one of them coming from Sir Robert Moray, the first "speculative" member of a Masonic lodge and the first president of the Royal Society. Moray, without really examining or understanding the theory, proposed four experiments to test it. Another objection, however, came from a French Jesuit priest, Ignace Gaston Pardies, a professor and a member of the Parisian scientific community.

Though not having yet replied to Hooke, Newton responded to the other comments amicably at first; but when the priest obviously assumed Newton to be a rank amateur and that his theory was an hypothesis,[77]

Newton responded, "If I did not know it to be true, I should prefer to reject it as vain and empty speculation, then [than] acknowledge them as my hypotheses."[78]

So Pardies sent a second letter through Oldenburg apologizing for the use of the word "hypothesis," stating simply that it was the first word that came to mind. But then the priest relented a bit and offered his opinion that instead of a hypothesis, Newton's diffusion of light might be an "alternate explanation" of this disputed phenomenon. Newton responded to this second letter by stating that his doctrine concerns the properties of light, not hypotheses nor alternate solutions. "The first and safest method of philosophizing is to inquire diligently into the properties of things and establishing those properties by experiments. …If the possibility of hypothesis is to be the test of the truth and reality of things, I see not how certainty can be obtained in any science."[79] Pardies responded that he was satisfied with Newton's new answer… "I now clearly perceive …what I did not before understand. I have nothing further to desire."[80]

Secretary Oldenburg had previously written Newton that critiques of his theory would appear anonymously in the Royal Society's "Philosophical Transactions," and that Newton was not to use names in his responses. At first Isaac acquiesced; however, he soon told Oldenburg that Hooke's comments would be easily recognized; consequently, he would name the curator in responding to him. In fact, Isaac had used Pardies' name earlier and received some raised eyebrows from some society members. If one dared criticize Isaac, he had better be right.

Unfortunately, after Hooke's rebuke and Oldenburg's letter, Isaac did not submit his complete research on "Opticks" to the Royal Society. In fact, no one would know the depths of his discoveries for thirty years. Before responding to Hooke, Isaac answered ten other letters with eleven responses and became convinced that he didn't need the stress of dealing with lesser minds. Isaac decided not to publish anymore. One thing was certain: his creative work had been interrupted by defending his theories. Even though he had made many mathematical and scientific breakthroughs, he went into an emotional abyss instead of disclosing them.

But Isaac Newton still had some unfinished business. On June 11, 1672 he finally replied to Robert Hooke. The months taken before his response were truly a time of turmoil. Isaac had a fragile ego. He made many drafts of responses, all of which were blunt and harsh, but filled with both brilliance and rage. Furthermore, though all of his letters were directed through the society's secretary, Henry Oldenburg, he made **thirty** direct references to Hooke --one for each year Isaac would postpone publishing "Opticks." Newton not only challenged Hooke, but by using Hooke's name seemed to be challenging the society to censure him –as Oldenburg had mentioned as a possibility. By now Isaac didn't care what the society did. If he were censured he would have his privacy back; if he were not, Hooke would be the one suffering embarrassment. In either case, the science of optics would remain inaccurate for thirty years.

Newton started his letter in a condescending tone: "I was troubled to find a person so concerned for hypothesis. I expected an indifferent examination of what I propounded." [81]

Then came the venom:

> *...Mr. Hook thinks himself concerned to reprehend me for laying aside the thoughts of improving Optiques by Refractions. But he knows well it is not for one man to prescribe rules to the studies of another, especially [if] not understanding the grounds on which he proceeds. Had he obliged me by private letter on this occasion, I would have acquainted him with my successes in the tryalls that I have made of that kind, which I shall now say have been less [than] I sometimes expected, & perhaps less then he at present hopes for.*[82]

Isaac went on to say that had he not given up using the refracting telescope, he "might not have examined what could be done by a complication of divers successive mediums."[83]

He then attacked Hooke's criticism of his theory of light as "ascribing an Hypothesis to me which is not mine, ...and by denying some things, the truth of which would have appeared by an experimental examination."[84] Newton said that it didn't matter which mechanical hypothesis one might subscribe to, whether corpuscles, waves or some other, the doctrine of colors remained unaffected. He further stated that Hooke took no notice that when the color at the lens is intercepted, the whiteness changes to other colors. Therefore, "if there be yet any doubting, 'tis better to put the event on further Circumstances of the Experiment then to acquiesce in the possibility of any Hypothetical Explication."[85]

Newton's replies were brilliantly struck blows from a genius whose reasoning was affected by a distrust of mankind in general due to a Puritan upbringing; Newton may have even believed Calvinistically that he was one of the "Chosen Few" --one who was always correct. Only after Robert Hooke's death did Newton place anything but the lowest interpretations of Hooke's opinions, believing that he was motivated by the basest or most selfish of motives.[86]

Though Isaac had allowed a few prejudiced opinions to torment him, he unknowingly had garnered some admiration and respect from some members of the society, especially Henry Oldenburg. At the June 12 meeting of the Royal Society in Gresham College with Robert Hooke in attendance, Oldenburg read Newton's response to the curator's criticisms. Hooke was devastated –especially upon hearing his name thirty times. As the secretary read Newton's blistering rebuttals, society members began shifting uneasily in their seats or staring wide-eyed at the ceiling. By the time Oldenburg finished, a deadly silence had gripped the room. The proverbial "dropped pin" would have caught everyone's attention.

To make matters worse, proceedings at society meetings were public information. In order to arrive at truth, freedom of speech and open debate were exercised. Furthermore, Oldenburg published all proceedings in "Philosophical Transactions" and sent copies to absent members. In deference to Hooke regarding Newton's letter at the June 12 meeting,

Oldenburg substituted the word "considerer" in place of Hooke's name, but anonymity was fruitless. The publishing of Newton's letter infuriated Hooke, especially since Oldenburg did not read Hooke's critiques nor publish them. On June 19 the maligned curator even sent a rebuttal to Newton's June 11 letter, but was advised by Oldenburg to "make more experiments."[87] Hooke even sent a letter to the President of the Royal Society, Lord Brounker, to no avail.

The rebuttals by the society's curator were neither read at a meeting nor published. Hooke had been slighted in favor of a young, unknown, rarely known Cambridge professor who had never set foot in Gresham's halls. Nevertheless, Hooke's criticisms alone were enough to wreak havoc on Newton's sensitive nature. Perhaps to escape from the disquietude, Isaac left Cambridge for a month during the summer of 1672. He visited his mother at Woolsthorpe, checked out some university property at Bedfordshire, and then spent two weeks at Stoke Park, Northhamptonshire with some "friends" whose names are unknown. However, it is known that an alchemist or two resided in that area.

In the fall of 1672 Christiaan Huygens, the scientist who had called Newton's Experimentum Crucis "ingenious," joined Hooke in supporting existing scholastic knowledge instead of Newton's discoveries. Later Huygens wrote to Oldenburg that Newton "might content himself with accepting his doctrine as likely hypothesis."[88] As was Oldenburg's practice, he sent the letter to Newton.

Hooke and Huygens, by criticizing Newton and defending traditional belief in place of scientific proof, were probably responsible for Newton's concealing most of his research on optics for decades. Unknown to the world, however, Isaac Newton was now also delving into areas that could be considered heretical by the established churches. Fortunately, Isaac lived in a different time and place than Galileo and probably would have been ostracized and not arrested like his scientific predecessor. He undoubtedly would have jeopardized his livelihood. At least civilization had become a shade more tolerant over the past forty years.

On the other hand, even with proven facts about light and optics, Isaac had been criticized severely. He had released truth beyond a shadow of a doubt. Yet some members of the scientific world, whose theories were being refuted, could not accept it. Not getting acceptance was a burden Newton could not carry. He was again psychologically wounded. He was deeply sensitive to criticism, and throughout his life he felt that most criticism of him was incorrect.

Isaac again resorted to his most reliable defense mechanism and, like a woodchuck startled by its shadow, he retreated to his sanctuary at Trinity to become obscure again.

CHAPTER 13

Withdrawal

• • •

"Huygen's letter to Henry Oldenburg may have been the last straw. With negative reaction from two supposed giants, Isaac Newton felt that the Royal Society had not accepted his findings. In January of 1673 Isaac read an article in 'Philosophical Transactions' by Huygens on light and colors in which he had said in a correspondence to Secretary Oldenburg: 'Yellow and blue colors were sufficient as primary colors.'[89] Isaac was taken aback by this reversal by Huygens and wrote to Oldenburg in March of 1673 regarding the article:

'They are but the abstract of a private letter sent to you and concern me not to take notice of them... Sir, I desire that you will procure that I may be put out from being any longer [a] fellow of ye Royal Society. For though I honour that body, yet since I see I shall neither profit them nor partake of the advantage of their assemblies, I wish to withdraw.'[90]...

By now Oldenburg had begun to understand Isaac Newton and knew that "distance" was not the problem. In April the Royal Society Secretary began remitting Isaac's dues without terminating Isaac from membership. Oldenburg had correctly judged Isaac's letter as a plea for emotional support, so he told John Collins about Newton's threat to resign. Collins soon wrote to Newton, and Isaac responded:

"I suppose there hath been done me no unkindness, for I met with nothing of yt kind besides my expectations. But I could wish I had met with no rudeness in some other things. And therefore I hope you will not think it strange if to prevent accidents of that nature... I decline that conversation wch hath occasioned what is past."[91]

Collins wasted no time showing Newton's letter to Oldenburg, who entreated Newton to let the "incongruities" committed against him pass by: "Every assembly had members who lacked discretion. The Body in general esteems and loves you which I can assure you of fide viri boni."[92]

Unfortunately, before Isaac received Oldenburg's gracious and supportive letter, he had already sent another comment to the secretary about Huygen's January article:

"Mr. Huygens takes an improper way of examining the nature of colours. Whilst he proceeds upon compounding those that are already compounded."[93]

Newton then went on to describe the tedious and difficult process of correctly conducting experiments. He concluded by stating:

I could not be satisfied till I had gone through it [the experimental process]. However, I only propound it, and leave every man to his own method. No one questions the indefinite variety of waves of the sea or sands of the shore. Why should the properties and movement of light be any less varied?[94]

Of course, Huygens also had an ego and did not appreciate being lectured. He retorted through Oldenburg that Newton had expressed too much concern, and he refused to argue any more about it.

On June 23 Newton answered Oldenburg's latest –and most kind-- letter. He first thanked the secretary and then said:

The incongruities you speak of, I pass by. But I must, as formerly, signify to you yt I intend to be no further solicitous about matters of philosophy. And therefore I hope you will not take it ill if you find me ever refusing doing more in that kind.

Isaac then reiterated his determination that the Royal Society secretary prevent *as far as you can ... any objections or other philosophical letters that may concern me.*[95]

Other than a short comment to Collins about a book sent to him on gunnery and cannon ball trajectory, Newton never wrote to Collins again --and even in that letter, Isaac asked that his name not be mentioned regarding his comments."[96] This short letter of Newton's is the extent of his communication from the summer of 1673 until the end of 1674. Except for a visit to London to see Lord Monmouth installed as Chancellor of Trinity and to attend the funeral of Robert Moray, Past President of the Royal Society who died on July 4, 1673, Newton became secluded.

In fact, it took over 200 years before historians finally knew what Newton was doing during this period of silence.

CHAPTER 14

Apostasy

• • •

"In the last months of 1673, the upstart Lucasian Professor of Trinity University shunned every opportunity for social intercourse – even with the Royal Society, which was currently paying his dues. He now relished returning to his lifelong ambition of understanding the universe and discovering everything in it. He could eagerly devote every minute to research, because every minute lost in searching for the meaning and reason of life was a minute lost forever. To Isaac Newton, time not spent in researching the universe was wasted time. There were numberless stars, worlds and truths to discover in this vast machine that undoubtedly was framed by a divine artist and conducted by the unerring law of nature. ...

In pursuit of such ambitious goals, Isaac Newton undertook some unorthodox study, including *Chemistry*, even though chemistry was not a science and was rarely practiced in the 17th century. From reading works by Robert Boyle, Newton had written some notes and a glossary on chemistry in 1666.[97] Unlike his contemporaries in this area, Isaac first studied *chemistry*, not *alchemy*; however, he soon surrendered to the more profound alchemy. Typically, as with his other studies, Isaac Newton demanded perfection and went into great detail with each topic in his notebook. One mark of his genius was his ability to organize and retrieve data on any subject long after he recorded it. So would it be with alchemy.

Late in November of 1669 on his second visit to London, Isaac Newton dropped in to see John Collins, but alchemy, not mathematics, was the primary purpose of his trip to London.[98] Isaac bought two furnaces at that time and brought them back to Cambridge, where he immediately began using them in alchemic experiments.

Alchemists in the late 17th century were often referred to as rogues attempting to find a way to make gold. At that time alchemists believed that gold was the only metal. Other metals were simply "growing" until they emerged as gold, the most precious of metals. Other metals were "purified" by using sulfur and other chemicals to extract mercury. Many alchemists believed that mercury was the "philosopher's stone," the basic substance of all matter in the universe. Newton did so much alchemical research during his life that some said he died from mercurial poisoning. Of course, no one was able to manufacture gold, and by the latter part of the 17th century, skepticism of alchemy abounded.[99]

In 1669 Isaac immersed himself into alchemical literature and research. He would experiment in alchemy throughout his life. At his death over ten-percent of his library consisted of books and pamphlets on alchemy, and he wrote over 1,100,000 words on the subject – one-sixth of them before 1675.[100] His first alchemical experiments, however, were primarily to extract mercury from metals, the primary practice of alchemists. Isaac believed that alchemists were a chosen few, and he was one of the chosen.

As Isaac plied his alchemical skills, probably no one except his roommate observed what he was doing. Newton, like Boyle and John Locke, was driven by a love of truth;[101] however, his alchemic papers were never revealed for almost three centuries. Regrettably, no evidence was written or spoken by Wickins about Newton's activities. Had all of his papers been released, the opinion that Isaac was a cold, rational scientist would have changed. In fact, he may have been the spark that started a new world order built on a new intellectual foundation similar to the Babylonians and the Sumerians 10,000 years ago.

From his research and his experiments Newton realized that by applying pure unbiased thought to certain evidence, he could find clues which God had planted to direct him in the path of an esoteric brotherhood. These clues were found from evidence in the heavens [space], from the composition and constitution of elements, and in papers and traditions handed down by "the brethren" in an unbroken chain dating from the cryptic revelations in Babylonia almost 3,700 years ago.

The world already knew the outward objective of alchemy: to find a pure matter, the Philosopher's Stone, a substance so powerful it could transform base metal into silver or gold. But this "outward alchemy" spawned interest in an inner "mystical alchemy," which may have a power greater than any outward physical transformations. The very same Philosopher's Stone might even be the elixir of life, which could bestow immortality on its discoverer –provided he had disposed of himself in a manner "pleasing in the sight of God." Therefore, if the "esoteric" alchemist would conduct himself correctly, he might be transformed from a sinful person to one worthy of divine grace.

In practice there were three types of alchemy: 1. Materialistic 2. Transcendental and 3. A mixture of both.[102]

Isaac was definitely #3. Eventually the world would discover how deeply he studied and wrote about both materialistic and transcendental alchemy. His study of alchemy was intended to expand his understanding of creation and his Creator. In addition to studying material from Robert Boyle and the books of William Clark, the father figure in his youth, Isaac garnered knowledge from Henry More of Trinity University, who was also an alchemist. Isaac read More's book, **Immortality of the Soul** in 1659 and wrote about it in his notebook:

"The excellent Dr. More in his book hath proved beyond all controversie that matter cannot be divisible in infinitum."[103]

Dr. More tried to reconcile natural philosophy [science] with a "rational theology." He devoted his entire life and his energy refuting what he believed was "insipient atheism." He even had used the term "stupid atheists." Isaac Newton agreed with Dr. More that the mechanical universe must not be separated from its creator. Newton also believed that the study of alchemy was to extend man's understanding of the Creator and His universe. He was seeking a key to the universe and to *universal matter* in order to explain the very structure of the world. He had to delve into nature's most concealed recesses in order to find these answers –and his pursuits occupied every minute of almost every day.

Later in his life Isaac Newton had other secrets that were revealed only to a few of his disciples, who kept the secrets in their faithful breasts even after Isaac's death. For example in late 1673 Isaac had immersed himself deeply into *Theology*. Since childhood he had already read volumes on religion; however, since he was soon to be ordained into the Anglican Church, Isaac intensified his study of the subject. He became so obsessed with theology that by the time he died he had written more words and read more books on that subject than on any other. Unpredictably, however, when he began his more intensive study of religion, Isaac had no idea that his findings would alienate him from established church orthodoxy.

As usual, when Isaac started any serious research, he would enter headings in his notebook and record findings under each heading from the most authoritative sources. He would then enter his own insights. He went from total objectivity to mastery of the subject, and then to final conclusions. Headings such as "Incarnatio," "Christi Miraculi," and "Christi Vita." were entered for his research. One heading that overflowed the pages allotted to it was "Deus Filius," which defined the relationship of the Son of God to God, the Father. From <u>Hebrews</u> I Isaac recorded:

> *God set Christ on his right hand and told him that because he had loved righteousness, therefore God, even <u>thy God</u> [underlining by Isaac Newton], hath anointed thee with the art of gladness above thy fellows.*

Isaac then wrote in the margin:

Therefore the father is God of the Son even when the Son is considered as God.[104]

Later, Isaac clarified the implication he had drawn:
"Concerning the subordination of Christ, see <u>Acts II, 33-36; Phillipians 2, 9-10; 1 Peter I. 21; John: 12.44; Romans I.8 and 16.27.</u>" Isaac listed over a dozen more Scriptures with the same emphasis.

Isaac then wrote in his notebook:
"There is one God and One Mediator between God and Man, Ye Man Christ Jesus. <u>I Timothy, 2:5.</u>"

"The head of Christ is God. <u>I Corinthians.</u>"

"From <u>Luke I.32:</u> He shall be great and shall be called ye **Son** of ye most <u>high</u>."[105]

Interestingly, Newton had underlined "<u>most high</u>."[106] It was now obvious that the intense study Isaac had undertaken in preparation for ordination had changed his mind about the status of Christ and the doctrine of the Trinity. Now his new beliefs could threaten his upcoming ordination by a university that bore the very name of a concept he abhorred. Isaac had read about a "War of the Trinity" that occurred in the fourth century between two church leaders, Athanasius and Arius. Arius opposed changing the doctrine of the Trinity and Athanasius accused him of heresy. To prove that Jesus was God, Athanasius had drawn upon the theory of "homoousios" [the Son is equal to the Father] from the writings of Dionysius of Alexandria. But Newton, in his exacting research discovered that Athanasius had deliberately misquoted Dionysius. **Dionysius actually had said that "homoousios"was heretical**.[107]

Isaac then found that Athanasius had altered words of other church fathers. He had "foisted" the epistles of Ignatius and the proclamation at the Council of Serdica.[108] True scripture had been deliberately changed to convict Arius of heresy --not to present the truth. Accepting Athanasius's distortions had become more important than charity, or love, the basis of Christianity. Isaac now believed Jesus was *not* "God" and shouldn't be thought of as such.

His longest notebook entry, "De Trinitate," was filled with facts about men who contrived the concept of Trinitarianism. Newton obsessed over its most stalwart advocate, Athanasius, whom Newton now detested for perpetrating a massive fraud against the legacy of the early Church.[109] It wasn't long before Isaac extended his antagonism to the Roman Pope who had supported Athanasius. To Isaac, the "Horned Beast" in the Revelation of Saint John was the Roman Catholic Church, and from **Revelation** Isaac knew the consequences of being seduced by power and authority; even orthodox Anglicans' souls were endangered. *Scriptures had been corrupted in order to support Trinitarianism.*[110] Isaac began listing these Scriptures starting with I John 5:7 and I Timothy 3:16, and by the end of 1673, had summarized his lifelong views of the nature of Christ:

1. The Father alone is supreme.
2. The son is a separate being, both in substance and in nature. He is human.
3. Christ transmitted the Word and Wisdom of God in the flesh. Divine, yes; but only with the divinity communicated through him by the Father.

In the First Chapter of John he read: *For there are three that bear record in heaven, the Father, the Son and the Holy Ghost; and these are three in one.* Then Isaac wrote in his notes: "It is not read thus in the Syrian Bible, not by Ignatius, Justin, Irenaeus and others. Perhaps Jerome is the first who reads it such."[111] The original text reads *Father, the Word and the Holy Spirit.*

In First Timothy Isaac read: "And without controversy great is the mystery of godliness: *God was manifest in the flesh.*" However, Isaac found the earlier versions read: "Great is the mystery of <u>**godliness** which was manifested in the flesh</u>." **The word "God" did not appear in early scripture**; it had been changed in the fourth century. Isaac then wrote that worshipping Christ as God was idolatrous, "a breach of the first and greatest commandment; …it is forsaking the true God to commit whoredom with other lovers. It makes the entire church guilty of apostasy --a synagogue of Satan."[112]

To underline his disdain for current orthodoxy, Isaac developed a great appreciation for Arius, the original scriptures, and the fundamentals of Christianity: to love God and one another –Isaac preferred simple moral truths, not complex theology. As he continued his research Isaac found that at the Council of Nicaea in 325 A.D., the leaders of the Christian Church voted to make Jesus Christ equal to God. The vote was not unanimous, but those who opposed it (Arians) were considered heretics to be punished by death. To Isaac, such a penalty was tantamount to murder, a violation of the sixth commandment.

Newton wrote his findings in his notebook, but spoke of them to no one, not even his roommate. After his death, his notebook revealed that Trinitarianism, the Papacy, the invocation of saints and the veneration of the Virgin Mary were insults to original Christianity. Isaac only drew conclusions after long research; he knew that his findings were true.

As Isaac continued his study of religion –his most prolific study— he eventually arrived at the Renaissance and the early Protestant writings about Mochus, who lived prior to the Trojan War. The writings indicated that Pythagoras had met followers of Mochus at Sidon and that Mochus was indeed Moses, the great monotheist. Moses, like Newton, tried to fit everything in heaven and earth into a rational framework –a universal truth. Moses, who possessed the knowledge of ancient Egyptians, had dissolved the Golden Calf that was worshipped as a God.

The search for universal truth naturally led to Solomon, king of the ancient Hebrews, and the son of David, "ye greatest philosopher in ye world --the first to build a temple that served as a model of the universe …in the name of Yaweh: God."[113] According to Newton, that temple was "the first institution of true religion, [a] true temple of the great God they worshipped."[114] Consequently, to help understand the Deity, Newton undertook to draft a floor plan of Solomon's Temple from the writings of Ezekiel after the Babylon Captivity when the Temple had been destroyed. This became an arduous task and demonstrated the extent to which Newton labored to discover answers to life's greatest mysteries. Though he did not regularly attend church, he had a demanding regimen of worship and knew more theology than the "milk for babes" dispensed by Trinity's theologians. Isaac needed stronger nourishment.

By the end of 1674 Newton firmly concluded: *Christ is not truly God, but the word and wisdom made flesh —divine only so far as the divinity communicated from God to the greatest messenger on earth since Moses, David and King Solomon.* Isaac began concentrating on the Book of Daniel and the Revelation of Saint John the Divine, and then to merging the philosophies of science and religion. He predicted the fall of "the Beast" about 1867 AD. To Saint John's question, "Who is worthy to open the book and loose the seals thereof?" Newton confidently answered "I am!" And his 1,400,000 words on theology appear to support him.

During this silent contemplative time, Isaac wrote his most radical theological thesis, "Theological gentilus origines philosophicae" (*The Philosophical Origins of Gentile Theology*). It formed the basis of his heterodoxy, yet the world was not privy to it for almost three centuries.

Origines traces religion to Noah, a monotheist, and then to Egypt, where Noah's religion was corrupted by adding additional gods. Other nations adopted these gods, which were essentially named after planets. Therefore, gentile theology had origins in natural philosophy, astronomy and the science of the universe— but it had abandoned the true religion of Noah.

Then along came Moses (Mochus), who reinstated monotheism. In the center of a tabernacle or temple he placed a perpetual flame representing the sun or center of the world. God, the creator of the universe, was to be worshipped for what he has done and not for the aspect of his being; for his wisdom, power, goodness and justice -- not his omnipotence and omniscience. Newton wrote that humankind should also not be celebrated for their essence, but for their actions and accomplishments – and this includes Jesus Christ. Newton claimed that Christ was a prophet like Moses who returned mankind to the original and true religion --to the worship of one God *and no others*. Trinitarianism, which worships Christ as God, is a throwback to superstition and idolatry for which Newton blamed Athanasius.[115] "Origines" also suggests that the kingdom of heaven could someday be found on earth.

Unfortunately, Isaac's research placed him in a serious quandary. He had researched Christian dogma and found flaws in it; yet, he would soon be required to pledge his support for a "corrupted orthodoxy." If he refused to take Holy Orders, he would lose his fellowship and the Lucasian Chair. To other fellows the decision might be easy: "Take the vows and keep your livelihood." But to Isaac it was the greatest moral issue in his life, and he agonized over it:

> *How can I take an oath I do not believe in? I have found that scripture concerning the very foundation of the church has been corrupted. If I am to stand for truth, I cannot take Holy Orders. Yet, I need to stay at Trinity to have an income and continue my research. If only Martin Luther had protested the Doctrine of the Trinity in 1519, I wouldn't be in this situation.*

Isaac indeed had a problem. If Trinity's administrators knew of his Arian beliefs, he would be undone. His only hope was to obtain a dispensation from the king without revealing his reasons—a daunting task indeed.

As Isaac obsessed over his problem, a Jesuit professor from Liege, Francis Holly, better known as "Linus," wrote to Henry Oldenburg about Newton's experiments with prisms on light and colors. Linus had duplicated Newton's experiments and could not obtain an elongated spectrum on clear days. Oldenburg forwarded Linus's letter to Newton in October of 1674. Isaac replied to Oldenburg: "Ye experiment as it is represented *was tried in clear days.*"[116]

In the January issue of "Philosophical Transactions" Oldenburg anonymously published Newton's answer. Newton now considered the matter closed. He undoubtedly thought: *I have more important concerns than the problems of amateur experimenters. I need an exemption from the king from taking Holy Orders. I cannot swear to something I do not believe.*

CHAPTER 15

The Diplomat

• • •

"IN LESS THAN ONE MONTH after Isaac's response to Linus was published in "Philosophical Transactions," he was in a coach heading to London with a petition for King Charles II. In brief, it requested that the *Lucasian Chair* be exempt from ministerial duties in the Anglican Church. Newton's timing couldn't have been worse. Only one month previously, Francis Aston, who also held a chair at Trinity, submitted a similar request that was denied. In fact, Newton's mentor, Isaac Barrow, who had been recently appointed Master of Trinity University, sent a letter opposing Aston's petition with the words: *It would destroy succession and subvert the principal end of the college, which was the breeding of clerics.*[117] ...

Though he supported college tradition regarding Holy Orders, Dr. Barrow had been an advocate of Isaac's and knew that Newton was of a different breed –and held a different chair than Aston's. Therefore, before Newton left for London he asked for a meeting with his Lucasian Chair predecessor and current Master of Trinity University. Dr. Barrow granted his request and greeted his former student with an embrace when he arrived.

"Have a seat, Isaac. What is on your mind today?"

Both men sat as Newton responded,

"Well, sir, I have found myself in a quandary."

"That's indeed hard to believe, Isaac. You have always been resolute and decisive. Your dedication to work has seemed to solve any perplexity in the past. What could possibly present you with a quandary?"

"In a word, sir, 'ordination'."

"Ordination? What is wrong with being ordained? Every fellow takes Holy Orders; just take them and be done with it."

"Well, Dr. Barrow, of all the people who know me, you are the only one who is aware of the time I devote to natural philosophy. I devote almost every minute of my life to research and experiments. ...What I am trying to say is that any interruption to this research would be devastating to me. My mind seems to find answers after long and dedicated effort; however, any interruption to these efforts could hinder finding solutions to some of the great truths of nature and our universe. I feel that dividing my efforts between my research and the ministry may do great harm toward uncovering fundamental laws of nature. When my mind is on the verge of discovering a great truth, that truth may be lost forever by an interruption that obliges me to perform ministerial duties."

"Isaac, you are asking me to help exempt you from taking the vows of the ministry at a time when I have just persuaded the king to keep this Trinity tradition alive."

"Yes, I am, Dr. Barrow, but not for me personally, but for the Lucasian Chair. It is a relatively new chair and it must not be a position that is compromised by dilution."

"So you are asking me to change from a position that I took just one month ago."

"No, Dr. Barrow. I'm not asking that you reverse yourself from a time-honored tradition; I am asking that you establish a new precedent for the progress of science. I ask that you support the mathematical and experimental sciences as a separate profession, not as an adjunct to the profession of theology."

"Hmm... You make a salient point, Isaac. If it weren't you, I wouldn't even consider making such a change. But I know you wouldn't have requested such an exemption unless you were convinced that it could harm the progress of your research. ...All right. I will support your petition to the king, but only as an *elected* exemption of the Lucasion Chair of Mathematics –not for any other position."

"That is all I ask, Dr. Barrow."

Dr. Barrow replied, "So be it."

After speaking with Dr. Barrow, Newton talked with Humphrey Babington, who had always been a faithful friend. Once Isaac had obtained the backing of both of these men, he prepared to present his petition to the King of England.

As Newton rode to Cambridge in his coach he thought to himself:

What I must do at all cost is avoid a cross-examination concerning my reasons against ordination. If anyone discovers my true persuasions, I will lose my fellowship and my chairmanship. I could quite possibly be evicted from Trinity College. But Isaac Barrow and Humphrey Babington have the ear of the king and the senior fellows respectively, and if both men argue for me, I may not have to undergo examination. Nevertheless, despite their support, King Charles might still reject my petition. What will I do then?

Isaac remained in London for five weeks awaiting the king's reply. During his extended stay, he decided to attend a meeting or two of the Royal Society. He first visited this venerable body on February 8, 1675; after all, currying favor with this organization couldn't hurt his petition. Wasn't the Royal Society established by the king and didn't it have a regal name? Not only did Newton attend the meetings, he went so far as to strike up conversations with its members –including Robert Hooke— whom Isaac thoroughly disliked.

Newton attended every weekly meeting of the Royal Society during the five weeks he remained in London. He appeared to enjoy associating faces with the names he had read in "Philosophical Transactions."

As he socialized he thought: *Enlisting friends will profit me. I do not need enemies at this time.*

As fate would have it, while Newton was in London, a second letter arrived from Professor Linus insisting that Isaac's results with prisms "are never scene on a clear day."[118] Upon receipt of Linus's letter, and while Isaac Newton was attending meetings, Secretary Oldenburg instructed Robert Hooke to conduct an experiment on light and colors at the March 18 meeting. Many society members, including Isaac Newton, arrived to see the experiment only to find the weather uncooperative. But Newton had cause to rejoice on that date; Dr. Barrow had given a message to Henry Oldenburg that the king had approved Newton's petition. Early the next morning a relieved Newton was on his way back to Cambridge.

Newton's trip to London had been a resounding success in more ways than one. Everyone in the Royal Society had received him with warmth and affection. His reputation had indeed preceded him. Most importantly, however, on April 27, 1675 King Charles II officially excused the Lucasian Chair of Mathematics *in perpetuity* from taking vows of ordination if the chair elected to do so. The King gave no names, just the "Lucasian Chair of Mathematics." A century' old tradition had been uprooted –or at least revised. The only problem coincidental to Newton's trip was an oversight: neither he nor Henry Oldenburg had replied to Jesuit Professor Linus's second letter.

Linus had now waited seven months for a reply. By this time he and his Jesuit colleagues felt they had been slighted and Linus took umbrage. On September 11, 1675, Linus wrote to Oldenburg and asked why his second letter had not appeared in *Philosophical Transactions?*:

"It is to my disadvantage & prejudice of the truth, being apt to make the reader conceive yt Mr. Newton's theory of light is still good ...and that I sayd more against the same [than] I could mayntayne."[119]

Oldenburg promptly forwarded Linus's letter to Newton, who quickly responded to the 80 year-old professor via Oldenburg in November. Newton wrote that Linus had used 30 year-old methods in experimenting. He then drafted detailed instructions on how to conduct a correct experiment and said that he would be happy to perform one at a meeting of the Royal Society on his next visit. But Newton also said, "If Mr. Line [Linus] persists in his denyal of it, I could wish it might be tried sooner." Included with the letter was a note for Oldenburg and an ear trumpet for "an ancient gentleman [in the society] whose name I cannot recollect."[120]

On December 7 Isaac sent a very thick packet to Oldenburg. It seems that on Isaac's visits to The Royal Society, he had started a rebirth of discussion regarding his previous paper on light and optics. Although Isaac was not in the habit of mixing hypotheses and scientific fact, that first paper left an opening for Hooke and a few others to label Newton's theory as "an hypothesis." Now, since the society had elicited much warmth and friendship on his latest visit, Isaac decided to entrust them with most of the research on light and optics that he had compiled since reading Hooke's "Micrographia" in 1669. The packet contained "An Hypothesis Explaining the Properties of Light" and a "Discourse of Observations," which was actually Parts I, II, and III of Book II of "Opticks," which Newton continued to refrain from publishing for three more decades. "An Hypothesis..." was actually a justification of the circumstances leading to an hypothesis. With the packet Isaac also included a note stating that he didn't want "to be obliged to answer objections to this script; for I desire to decline being involved in such troublesome and insignificant disputes."[121]

Isaac Newton's "Hypothesis..." monopolized the Royal Society throughout January, and his "Observations" through February. He discussed subjects such as "universal aether," gravity, cohesion, electricity, animal sensation, reflection, refraction, planetary orbits and revolutions. The packet was filled with detailed accounts of his experiments. In fact, Robert Hooke attempted to duplicate Isaac's experiment on electricity, but needed two more letters from Isaac to complete it.

"Hypothesis of Light" showed a quality in Newton that he had in common with the philosophers preceding him –a scientific imagination. Newton simply could not abide an accidental, unplanned world of nature. He was constantly driven to seek a system, an order, and a connection between them. Underneath the ambiguity in some of his writings was a divine wish, a testament that the universe is a vast coherent and rationally ordered machine. He searched to find a pattern and symmetry in nature – to connect the microcosm to the macrocosm.[122]

As The Royal Society observed Newton's meticulous measurements and quantitative analyses, it couldn't help but notice the disparity between Newton and Hooke, who relied on observations alone. For example, Hooke accused Newton of plagiarizing the thickness of light. Newton countered that he had taken pains to measure the thickness, which Hooke never even learned how to do. Hooke considered Newton a fearsome rival, while Newton thought Hooke an intolerable nuisance, "a fly to be swatted on occasion." [123]

Hooke felt he had been a whipping boy far too frequently and began to suspect that Oldenburg was taking Newton's side against him –and it appeared that he was. Henry Oldenburg had printed Hooke's heated remarks, but not Newton's. Oldenburg had also read criticisms of Hooke to the Royal Society, but did not read any criticisms of Newton. He even read Hooke's pathetic explanation of two unsuccessful electrical experiments, which Newton had performed with ease. Therefore, in an attempt to avoid contention and feuding for all to see in print, Hooke wrote a letter directly to Newton without sending it through Oldenburg. Newton recognized the curator's handwriting immediately and opened the letter:

To my much esteemed friend, Mr. Isaack Newton,

Please forgive me for this direct communication, however I feel that I have become the victim of a sinister practice to arouse your suspicions concerning my intentions. I want you to know that I do not approve of contention or feuding and proving in print. I desire to embrace truth by whomever discovered.

I truly admire your excellent disquisitions. Though I may have initiated some of the same studies, you have gone farther and completed what I did not, mainly because of other troublesome employments. I am sufficiently sensible, however, that my meager accomplishments are obtained with abilities much inferior to yours.

By this letter I entreat you, kind sir, to consider that we correspond privately to each other to prevent reasonable differences of opinion from erupting into open hostility. This way of contending I believe to be the more philosophicall of the two, for though I confess the collision of two hard-to-yield contenders may produce **light** *yet if they be put together by the ears of other's hands and incentives, it will produce rather ill concomitant heat which serves for no other use but to kindle cole."* [124]

R. Hooke

Newton's response on February 5 was even more conciliatory:

Honored Friend,

I am I receipt of your letter of January 20. You are a true Philosophical spirit. There is nothing wch I desire to avoyde in matters of Philosophy more then contention, nor any contention more then one in print. I loathe intellectual warfare and accept your offer of a private correspondence.

You are to be commended for your contributions to Opticks. What Descartes did was a good step. You have added much several ways. If I have seen further it is by standing on ye shoulders of Giants. [125]

I. Newton

Though the letters of Hooke and Newton expressed some lofty sentiments, neither man endeavored to institute a "philosophic correspondence" that both professed to desire. Their antagonism toward each other continued until Robert Hooke died. The two letters displayed some diplomacy and praise toward each other, but lacked any expression of true friendship.

CHAPTER 16

Annoyances

• • •

"IF THERE WERE ONE THING that Isaac Newton couldn't abide while engrossed in research, it was being disturbed. At this point in his life, he had found his mission, his destiny. His search for truth in the universe had found its way into theology as well as natural philosophy, and in each of these areas Newton hoped to undo the myths and corruptions that lesser men had professed. Newton's mission now extended beyond surveying nature and her proportions. It extended to the Scriptures and prophecies. It expanded the study of mathematics, natural philosophy, alchemy and theology to a higher plane, their ultimate substance and purpose –the meaning of life and the purpose of creation. ...

Starting in the mid 1670's as Isaac mixed and melted concoctions and heated them in his furnaces, he devoted most of his waking hours toward theology. It bears repeating that Isaac, who one day would become the symbol of the Enlightenment, wrote and read more on theology than any other subject.

Nevertheless, as isolated as he was in his academic sanctuary, criticism of his work still reached and distracted him. Although Linus, the spurned Jesuit, had died in November of 1675, one of his pupils, John Gascoines, sent Newton a letter, again by way of Oldenburg. Newton received the letter in December; it supported Linus' findings and criticized Newton's. Unfortunately, the letter also implied that Newton had "impugned Linus's honor."

This time Isaac wasted no time in responding. He first gave Gascoines instructions for correctly conducting prism experiments, and then gave a strong rebuttal to Gascoines' implication that Isaac had impugned Linus's honor.[126] Unfortunately, Secretary Oldenburg had published Isaac's heated rebuttal in "Philosophical Transactions" alongside Linus's second letter that stated Newton had snubbed him. When Isaac witnessed these two letters in January's "Philosophical Transactions, " he recalled the chain of events behind them and again became incensed. Undoubtedly, Newton must have thought:

Why must Gascoines impugn my honor? Oldenburg and I made every attempt to conduct an experiment on a clear day --as Linus had requested. Perhaps we made an oversight in not responding to Linus's letter --but it was only an oversight! We scheduled an experiment solely because of that letter. Now I bear insults from another Jesuit, who claims we had deliberately ignored his predecessor. Again I must suffer inconvenience because of mediocre mathematicians and philosophers.

Isaac immediately wrote to Secretary Oldenburg and asked that the Royal Society conduct his experiment on Light and Colors in order to settle the dispute with the English Jesuits in Liege. The experiment was performed in front of numerous members of the Royal society on April 27, 1676. The results were as Newton had promised and were published.

Upon reading the results, Gascoines had difficulty understanding them and turned Linus's cause over to Anthony Lucas. In June, Newton received a letter from Lucas, who conceded the major point of contention: that a prism projects a spectrum perpendicular to its axis. But Lucas went on to claim that after performing nine experiments, the length of the spectrum came to only three and one-half times its breadth, not **five** times, as Newton had stated.

Although Lucas probably deserved a decent response, despite the fact that his experiments could not have been carefully executed, Newton had become irrational and truly believed that "the papist" Jesuits were conspiring to engage him in continuous disputes. He replied to Lucas but refused to discuss the Jesuit's experiments. In fact, he insisted that Lucas limit his correspondence to Isaac's experiments, especially the *experimentum crucis*. Lucas obliged but, due to his lack of expertise, told Newton that the *experimentum crucis* also wasn't conclusive and didn't work as Newton had described.[127]

Newton bristled upon reading Lucas's correspondence. And when Lucas said that Isaac's entire theory of colors was flawed, Isaac responded with a blistering letter:

> *That it was only three and one-half times its breadth as Mr. Lucas has represented it -- To this I desire a direct answer to take off all suspicion of my misrepresenting matters of fact. Tis ye truth of my experiments which is ye business in hand. On this my Theory depends, & which is of more consequence, [whether I have been] wary, accurate and faithfull in ye 'reports I have made.*[128]

Isaac said to Oldenburg, " I have made myself a slave to philosophy, but if I get free of Mr. Linus's business I will resolutely bid [adieu] to it eternally, excepting what I do for my privat[e] satisfaction or leave to come out after me. For I see a man must either resolve to put out nothing new or to become a slave to defend it."[129] Slavery to Newton at this time was sending fourteen printed pages to Liege in one year. Eventualy, Lucas mentioned that he had performed his experiments between six and seven in the morning, a time during which it is almost impossible to find a room capable of projecting a spectrum on a screen perpendicular to the spectrum's trajectory. Unfortunately, Newton's dogmatic attitude preempted Lucas's sloppiness and caused the Jesuit to do battle instead of accepting scientific truth.

In February of 1677, Newton received a *third* letter from Lucas. By this time Isaac had decided to publish a volume of all of his papers on optics in order to confirm his theory and settle all annoying disputes. Even

David Loggan of Trinity College "had drawn Newton's picture for an engraving to be included in a book on light and colors." [130] Regrettably, Henry Oldenburg died during work on the book, but evidence exists that Newton gave Robert Hooke, the new secretary of the Royal Society, the first pages for such a volume.

Although Isaac Newton had survived many life-threatening catastrophes before 1677, he did not get the highest marks in disseminating and gaining worldly acceptance of his discoveries. So would it be with optics, because early in 1677, while on the verge of publishing his book on light and colors, a fire erupted in his chamber destroying the book and many other valuable papers. Thousands of experiments which had been conducted over twenty years at a cost of hundreds of pounds and uncounted hours were lost forever.

Years later a student in Johns named Abraham de la Pryme was told the story of Newton's chamber fire and recorded it in his diary:

> *Febr: [1692] What I heard today I must relate. There is one Mr. Newton ....fellow of Trinity College, that is mighty famous for his learning, being a most excellent mathematician, philosopher, divine etc. ...but of all the books that he ever writ there was one of colours and light ..which he valued so much, and which was so much talked of, [that] had the ill luck to perish and be utterly lost just when the learned author was almost at putting a conclusion [to it].... In a winter morning, leaving it amongst his other papers on his study table, whilst he went to chapel, the candle which he had unfortunately left burning there ... cached hold by some means or other of some other papers, and they fired the aforesaid book, and utterly consumed it and several other valuable writings. ...when Mr. Newton came from chapel and had seen what was done, every one thought he would have run mad[.] [He] was so troubled therat that he was not himself for a month after.*[131]

It was obvious from Newton's tone in some of his letters in the first months of 1677 that he had lost partial control of himself. The tone in his letters to Lucas seemed to show a loss of control compatible with a breakdown. Newton was in a state of acute intellectual tension throughout the 1670's, not only from having to answer objections to his optics, but from newer studies that were occupying his very soul.[132] To add to Isaac's misery, Henry Oldenburg, Isaac's faithful supporter, and Dr. Barrow, his closest ally, both died in 1677. For almost a year Newton retreated again into his shell.

Finally on March 5, 1678, he sent two letters to Lucas on the same day. One was in reply to Lucas's first two letters; the other was in reply to Lucas's third letter of February, 1677. Lucas undoubtedly did not expect the candid, brutal last words that Newton would ever write to him:

> *Do men [desire] to press one another into Disputes? Or am I bound to satisfy you? It seems you thought it not enough to propound Objections unless you might insult over me for my inability to answer them all, or durst not trust your own judgment in choosing ye best. But how know you yt I did not think them too weak to require an anwere & only to gratify your importunity complied to answer one or two of ye best? How know you but yt other prudential reasons might make me averse from contending wth you? But I forbeare to explain these things further for I do not think this a fit Subject to dispute about, & therefore have given these hints only in a private Letter, of wch kind you are also to esteem my former answer to your second. I hope you will consider how little I desire to explain your proceedings in public & make this use of it to deal candidly wth me for ye future.[133]*

Lucas sent two more letters in May of 1678. Newton declined to answer the first and refused delivery of the second. This brought all correspondence about colors to an end, and Newton again secluded himself. Throughout the rest of 1678 and 1679, he may have written two letters. Only one, to Robert Boyle, has survived. Newton later said that he deliberately withdrew and that it marked an epoch in his life. In Isaac's last years of life he wrote to Otto Mencke about this time of his life and said that he had declined "correspondences by Letters about Mathematical & Philosophical matters," and that they tended toward "disputes and controversies..."[134]

Although dealing with novices was irritating to Isaac, it was not as troublesome as the problems that would arise primarily because of the puritanical beliefs instilled by his grandmother —especially that he was chosen by God with a superior mind. Perhaps because of this belief Isaac thought that no one else was capable of achieving the complex mathematical results that he had reached. Isaac Newton appeared content to let the world wait until after his demise for people to see the depth of his genius.

CHAPTER 17

A Contemporary

• • •

"AT THE TIME WHEN ISAAC Newton was using his pen to swat at the pests who interrupted his labors, other natural philosophers were experimenting in areas Isaac had all ready explored. By this time Isaac had crossed horns with Linus, Lucas, Gascoines, Hooke, Huygens and others. Even Guillaume Cassegrain and James Gregory tried to claim priority over Isaac's reflective telescope. However, a deformed mathematician from Germany by the name of Gottlieb Wilhelm Leibniz would become Isaac's most serious challenge. In fact, Leibniz became known as Newton's 'greatest adversary. ...

Leibniz was three and one-half years younger than Newton and by the age of 15 had entered law school at the University of Leipzig. When Leipzig refused to grant him a doctorate in law because of his age, Leibniz went to Nuremburg and received his doctorate from the University of Altdorf. He then entered the University of Jena and mastered Euclidian geometry by the age of 17. By this time he had already met Francis Bacon, Johannes Kepler and Rene' Descartes.[135]

At age 26, Gottlieb Leibniz sailed to England where he met Robert Hooke and Robert Boyle and was admitted to membership in The Royal Society. Before he returned to the continent, Henry Oldenburg and John Collins gave him many mathematical papers, four of them with Newton's name on them including: the squaring of curves and the use of infinite series to solve complicated geometrical problems.[136]

By the end of 1675 at age 28, Leibniz invented differential calculus on his own, one decade after Newton had developed his fluxional method; however, both methods yielded the same results. Newton immediately suspected plagiarism and was not pleased that Collins had given many of his mathematics papers to Leibniz. In 1676, to avoid a priority dispute, Collins asked Newton to publish a paper on fluxions, but Newton refused. However he did consent to write eleven pages on fluxions to Leibniz in order to demonstrate his priority on the matter. Fortunately, Isaac was a meticulous recordkeeper and –even during his "Annus Mirabilis"—had sent letters on almost everything he had discovered *except for calculus*. Isaac hinted to Leibniz: "I have no time to explain nor to report on some other things I have devised."[137]

By the time Newton's June letter reached Leibniz, it was August 26. The German responded the next day: "[your] discoveries are worthy of [your] genius." He also mentioned Isaac's optical experiments, reflecting telescope, method of obtaining roots of equations and infinite series, which he said was "quite different from mine."[138]

In October of 1676, Leibniz again visited London and viewed more of Newton's papers on file with The Royal Society. In fact, John Collins gave Leibniz access to Newton's "De Analysi." When Leibniz returned to Hanover, Germany in November, Newton sent a second letter elaborating on the expansion of infinite series, but still held back details of his fluxional method; Newton instead sent an anagram:[139] "6accdae13eff713ign404qrr4s8t12vx,"[140] which Leibniz deciphered even though Isaac thought he had carefully hidden his formulae.

Leibniz responded to Newton's nineteen pages with ten pages of diagrams and calculations –including the gist of his differential calculus. And on July 12 he sent a letter to Oldenburg asking for any important developments that might have escaped publication in "Philosophical Transactions." By now Newton had ceased corresponding with Gottlieb Leibnitz; consequently, the two men never had an open dialog on calculus. Their two egos would collide later over who had originated calculus, and an acrimonious relationship resulted.

That Newton had a strong ego is indisputable. Since he believed he had been chosen with superior intelligence, no one else would be able to arrive at his discoveries. It seemed as if someone had ingrained in his mind a superiority complex, a type of complex renowned throughout history that a belief, even a religion, justified a form of egotism. Since time immemorial people of earth have been victimized by egotistical thinking to the point of being deliberately kept in ignorance or otherwise infringed upon –even exterminated.

This same type of egocentric thinking that Newton abhorred in the organized churches of his day perhaps existed in his own character: a superiority complex over others, the need to be right for the sake of being right. It is a mindset that has caused some of the world's greatest injustices – and in Isaac's case was depriving those in darkness from receiving the light of truth.

Needless to say, Newton's penchant for concealment had already sneaked up to bite him. Others had now printed information on subjects Isaac had discovered years ago. Nevertheless, Isaac still believed he had been given his gifts from God. He had a "highly privileged relationship with his Creator." Just one year earlier he had said, "...no one, including Leibniz, could ever rival my mathematical achievements, no matter how long I kept my findings from the rest of the world."[141] Isaac was content to let posterity decide.

Nevertheless, by 1677 Newton realized that calculus was not his alone, and he eventually rationalized by alluding to Leibniz as a thief. Later on, others also began to make great advancements in mathematics, and Isaac would be forced to act with haste to head them off --and perhaps even to get some revenge on Leibniz.

In the spring of 1679 Isaac's mother died after nursing her son Benjamin back to health from a malignant disease, which she unfortunately contracted. Isaac rushed to her side, but despite his deft hands, constant care, unique potions and dressings, was unable to save her. Though he had rarely visited his mother in the past, Isaac was named heir and executor of Hannah's estate and guardian of the children born of her union with Barnabas Smith.

For the remainder of 1679 Isaac stayed in Woolsthorpe, primarily because of problems with two of Hannah's tenants, who were deeply in arrears with rent payments. However, both tenants learned that when Isaac Newton fixed his sights on a problem, he never swerved from solving it. Isaac wasted no time and minced no words in letting the wayward lessees know that he intended to collect the money they owed. Finally, in 1681 Isaac brought three actions in Chancery against the two tenants and another individual who had attempted to illegally claim land that was a part of Woolsthorpe. Needless to say, Isaac obtained judgments against the three defendants and received all monies and lands owed him. Interestingly, one of the tenants was Edward Storer, the step-son of the apothecary, William Clark, with whom Isaac lodged while attending King's School in Grantham. Assuredly, Isaac had a strong will –and when he thought he was right, heaven help his adversary, regardless who it might be.

In 1680 and 1681, Isaac developed another friendship at Trinity. Charles Montague, cousin of Trinity's Master John Montague, had heard of Newton's extraordinary skills and attended some of Newton's lectures. Montague, who had a taste for literature, seemed to have an effeminate nature but was never characterized as a homosexual. He received a Master of Arts in 1682 and a Fellowship in 1683. In addition to his attendance at Newton's lectures, his kinship with Trinity's Master undoubtedly appealed to Isaac.

In 1683, after many extended absences from Trinity University, Isaac returned to his quarters in Cambridge to find that his roommate of 20 years, John Wickins, had resigned his fellowship to become the rector of Stoke Edith. Under a Thomas Foley patronage, a Wickins had served the rectorship of Stoke Edith for more than a century. John Wickins undoubtedly wished to continue that legacy; furthermore, he had also decided to get married. Either status would make him ineligible to continue his fellowship at Trinity. Although Wickins had served as Newton's amanuensis (scrivener) for twenty years, nothing could be found by historians to describe his personal relationship with Isaac. It appears that the two men lived together but rarely spoke, and that something finally caused a breach between them.

On March 28, 1683, Wickins and Newton both left Trinity; Wickins for good; Isaac until May 3, though he left again on May 21. No record exists as to Newton's whereabouts for six weeks during 1683.[142] The only correspondence between the ex-roommates occurred 30 years later concerning a contribution of *Bibles* from Isaac to the poor at Stoke Edith. Apparently Wickins first wrote to Isaac, but Isaac's response was brusk, perhaps curt: "I am glad to hear of your good health, & wish it may long continue, I remain."[143]

By the end of the year 1683 Newton had arranged for a young employee of King's School in Grantham to be his new roommate and amanuensis. Though Humphrey Newton would never officially enroll as a student of Trinity, he copied the valuable papers of his roommate during the remainder of Isaac Newton's life at Trinity.

In the meantime, Gottfried Leibniz was sending letters about his discoveries, one of which Isaac believed had been purloined. To Isaac, Leibniz had become a bad penny that would continue to show up even after the German's death.

CHAPTER 18

The First Disciple

• • •

"In the decade of the 1670's, Newton bantered with critics, contemporaries, and even delinquent tenants. During those ten years, an enthusiastic teen-ager at Queens College in Oxford became noticed for his prowess in astronomy. Rather than compete with famous astronomers like Flamsteed and Cassini, Edmund Halley, the son of a wealthy soapmaker, decided to leave Oxford in 1676 at age nineteen to sail to St. Helena in order to chart the constellations of the southern hemisphere. He returned to England two years later with a catalog of stars entitled *Catalogum Stellarum Australium*. At age 21 the youthful astronomer was promptly accepted into the Royal Society and given a Master of Arts degree by order of King Charles II. ...

Edmund Halley, like Isaac Newton, buried himself in study and scientific experiments. He was especially concerned with calculating longitude at sea –almost as consumed as Isaac was with calculating the moon's orbit. Regrettably, Halley never found a reliable method to calculate longitude. Nevertheless, for sixty years he actively involved himself with the Royal Society, contributing over 84 papers --most of them on astronomy— to "Philosophical Transactions." One day he would also achieve his dream of becoming the King's Royal Astronomer.

On December 12, 1680, while caught in a storm crossing the English Channel, Halley caught sight of a comet, and twelve days later wrote to Robert Boyle about it. Ironically, Isaac Newton had seen the same comet and scrupulously recorded 21 detailed sightings for the next 42 days, not only from Cambridge, but from observers in Venice, Paris, East India and the colony of Maryland in the Americas. Royal Astronomer Flamsteed verified that some astronomers had observed the same comet in November.[144]

In 1682 Halley saw another comet, which was eventually named "Halley's comet." He observed that this comet didn't move in a straight line nor at a constant speed, verifying what Isaac Newton at that time called his curved orbit theory. Halley's comet, like the planets, revolved around the sun, and its path was influenced by the sun's magnetism. Its curved orbit was either a circle, an ellipse, a parabola, or a hyperbola, all of which occur when a cone is sliced through at different angles. At the same time that Halley discovered his comet, Newton was applying his laws of gravity to the paths of comets, planets and moons.

By the end of 1684 Isaac had mathematically determined the path of an object orbiting in space. He had applied Kepler's laws of planetary motion with his formula for centrifugal force. He mathematically proved the tendency of objects to recede from the sun reciprocally according to the squares of their distance from the sun. He used this inverse-square relationship, resting it firmly on Kepler's 3rd law regarding the mechanics of curved motion.[145]

Was it Halley, or someone else who spurred Isaac to calculate orbits? Halley, Hooke and Wren were familiar with Kepler's laws of planetary motion, but were unable to mathematically calculate a planet's orbit. Kepler's laws described the motion of planets around the Sun as such:

1. The orbit of every planet is an ellipse with the Sun at one of two foci.
2. A line joining a planet and the sun sweeps out equal areas (along the elliptical perimeter) during equal intervals of time.
3. The square of the orbital period of a planet is directly proportional to the Cube of the semi-major axis of its orbit.

It should be noted, however, that Kepler's laws are valid only for a lone planet that is not being affected by the gravity of other planets.

Such a phenomenon is a physical impossibility in the earth's solar system; therefore, Halley, Wren and Hooke were unable to mathematically calculate the orbital path of an object in space. All three of them agonized over their inability to calculate a formula for planetary motion.

But it was Edmund Halley who recognized the depth of Isaac Newton's genius and became singularly responsible for exhibiting it to the rest of the world.

CHAPTER 19

Universal Gravitation

• • •

"After Henry Oldenburg's death, Robert Hooke assumed some of the secretarial duties of the Royal Society.[146] Hooke had his own philosophies regarding the movement of planetary bodies, and in November of 1678 he wrote to Newton asking for his opinion about them:

1. All bodies [planets, etc.] have a gravitational power toward their own centers and may attract other bodies.
2. These bodies move in a straight line until bent by other bodies' gravitational powers to form the motions of a circle, ellipse, or other curved line.
3. That the gravitational power of bodies is greater toward nearer bodies.[147] ...

Upon returning to Cambridge after settling his mother's estate, Isaac responded to Hooke's letter, but declined to comment on his philosophies. Newton's occupation with family affairs and other matters had taken him away from philosophy for some time. He mentioned that he hadn't heard Hooke's orbital philosophy before, but suggested that Hooke conduct an experiment to reveal the earth's diurnal rotation.[148] In truth, Isaac's papers contained no similar concepts of circular motion before Hooke's letter.[149]

Though Isaac had demurred regarding Hooke's philosophy on planetary motion, the concept of gravitational power and orbital motion definitely piqued his curiosity. Isaac, therefore, did respond by sending Hooke a diagram of the path of an object falling toward the earth. Since prevailing thought indicated that bodies falling to earth would land westward due to the earth's rotation eastward, Isaac, for some inexplicable reason, sent Hooke a diagram showing the path of the object ending up at the center of the earth after a slight spiral motion.

Hooke quickly responded and kindly corrected Newton: "Under conditions of no resistance, a body let fall on a rotating earth would not fall to the center, but would rather follow a path resembling an ellipse."[150] Hooke called his orbital philosophy a "Theory of Circular Motions Compounded by a Direct Motion and an *attractive* one to a Center."[151] Hooke delighted in reporting to the Royal Society that he had corrected the esteemed Isaac Newton.

This time Newton knew he had erred. Though he didn't publicly acknowledge it, he never forgot his mistake. Drawing a path of a falling object without accounting for the earth's resistance was an oversight to say the least. Nevertheless, perhaps to show his extensive knowledge on the subject, Newton replied to Hooke's correction:

> *Yes, you are correct; the body would not descend to the center but circulate with an alternate ascent & descent; however, you are not correct about the ellipse in all situations, especially if gravity were not constant.*[152]

Isaac demonstrated his proficiency in orbital mechanics and mathematics to Hooke in four brief sentences. Although Hooke again responded, he demonstrated his confusion with Kepler's laws, accelerated motion and dynamics in general. He mixed a fallacious law of force with Kepler's fallacious law of velocities.

Newton did not answer a third letter from Hooke, and two weeks later received a fourth letter stating that Hooke had successfully performed the experiment suggested by Isaac to show the earth's rotation, but in that letter Hooke admitted that he nor anyone else had as yet mathematically calculated the path a body would follow while being affected by the inverse-square law. He again challenged Isaac:

> *I doubt not that by your excellent method[s] you will easily find out what that Curve must be, and its proprietys, and suggest a physicall Reason of this proportion.* [153]

Though Isaac again did not respond, he acted just as Hooke predicted. He did not start by investigating a body's path, however; he simply *assumed* the path and then mathematically demonstrated that an elliptical orbit around an attracting body located at one focus involves an inverse-square attraction. Newton's calculation of this elliptical rotation would soon become the well spring for his eventual fame and perhaps a recognition point for the growth of science and the era of the Enlightenment.

In essence, Isaac started with Kepler's law of areas and Hooke's philosophy of orbital motion by showing:

1. A force varies inversely as the square of the distance at two apsides of an ellipse.
2. The same relation holds true for every point on an ellipse.[154]

Proving elliptical motion was much more difficult than simply substituting Kepler's 3rd law into the formula for centrifugal force and assuming circular orbits. In fact, what Newton finally calculated is one of the two bases for the concept of universal gravitation.

Typically, Isaac revealed his calculations to no one; he put them into a drawer and contented himself with other interests, which undoubtedly included alchemy and theology. In the not too distant future, however, Newton would apply action at a distance to virtually all of the phenomena of nature. *There were unobservable motions in the cosmos among the particles of bodies.*[155]

CHAPTER 20

The Prize

• • •

"IN THE WINTER OF 1680–81 the sighting of a comet excited Isaac Newton. He and a few others recorded numerous observations of it from December 12 through March 9. The majesty of the heavens had again captivated Newton as it did when he was a school boy in Grantham. He even recorded observations made by others, including one received from Arthur Storer, the bully from Grantham, who had moved to the colony of Maryland in 1679 and had become an amateur astronomer. Customarily, Isaac collected these observations and recorded them under special headings in his notebook. ...

In 1682 Isaac met Edmund Halley and for the first time questioned him on his comet sightings. At about this time Isaac decided that comets traveled on curved paths, not rectilinear ones, and that comets were orbiting bodies, just like planets.[156] Newton and Halley would meet again in 1684 when Halley asked a question that would change Isaac's life forever; however, before the second visit Newton was quite busy. He was compiling manuscripts of his Lucasian Chair lectures for Trinity's library. He had lectured for over ten years, but hadn't deposited one lecture with the university as required under his Lucasian Chair obligations. Now with Humphrey Newton as his amanuensis, Isaac began fulfilling his duties. His work summarized Algebra and greatly advanced that science. Even Gottlieb Liebniz anonymously praised the work in the continent's science journal, the "Acta Eruditorum."[157] Although

Newton's work on Algebra was elementary, it became quite popular when published later under the title "Arithmetica Universalis."[158]

Newton also wrote a treatise "Matheseos universalis specimina" in which he elaborated on his method of fluxions. Newton's intent was to publish the correspondence between Leibniz and James Gregory in order to prove his priority over Leibniz's calculus, which Isaac had discovered was soon to be published. In the treatise Newton attacked modern analysts, including Descartes and Leibniz.

Halley, meanwhile, was busy trying to demonstrate the laws of celestial motion by using the inverse-square formula. Both Christopher Wren and Robert Hooke had already consulted Newton unsuccessfully about the same problem. Though they didn't get what they wanted, they unknowingly aroused the curiosity of the mathematical genius at Trinity. In January of 1684 Hooke, Halley and Wren were still unable to use Kepler's laws to calculate planetary motion mathematically. After a Royal Society meeting that month, the three of them discussed their dilemma:

Hooke said, "Gentlemen, I am confident that I will be able to demonstrate the laws of celestial motion from the inverse-square relationship between planets."

Halley responded, "I've already tried doing that, Robert. I haven't been able to come up with anything."

Wren asked Hooke, "Robert, do you have any proof to substantiate your statement?"

"I know I can demonstrate it."

Wren responded, "Robert, in my library I have a rare book worth forty shillings. Within two months, if anyone can prove celestial motion by using the inverse-square relationship, I will give my book as a prize in addition to any honors the winner will undoubtedly receive."

Hooke said, "Well, I know I can demonstrate it, but I will wait before doing so to give someone else a chance to come up with a solution."

Hooke then left the room, and Halley asked Wren, "Do you believe him?"

Wren shook his head sideways and said. "No. Hooke can't prove anything."

No one stepped forth within the two months –nor four months or six months. After seven months, Halley happened to be in Cambridge and seized an opportunity to call on Isaac Newton. After again discussing comets and concurring that comets traveled along a curved path, Halley posed a question to Trinity's mathematical genius:

"Sir, what do you think the curve of a planet's orbit would be supposing the force of attraction towards the Sun is reciprocal to the square of its distance from it?"

"It would be an ellipse."

Halley was shocked and asked, "How do you know?"

"I have calculated it."

"May I see it?"

"Certainly. I believe I placed it in one of these drawers a few years ago."

"A few years ago?"

"Yes –a few years ago."

Newton began rummaging through scratch papers in the drawers of his desk, but couldn't find the paper with his calculations. He looked up and said:

"Well, I must have misfiled it."

As Isaac searched he recalled his correspondences with Robert Hooke over four years ago, especially one in which he had incorrectly diagramed an object falling to earth. He looked up and said, "I will find it later. When I do, I will re-examine it and send it to you."[159]

Newton was not conducting any charade. The paper he had misplaced was found later among his papers; however, it also contained his faux pas, which Hooke had corrected and which Isaac preferred not to reveal.

Over the next three months Isaac recalculated, but was unsuccessful because he confused the axes of an ellipse with conjugate diameters.[160]

Characteristically, Newton never rested while a problem remained unsolved. He persisted and finally arrived at a correct recalculation, which he sent to Halley via Edward Paget, the Master of Mathematics at Christ's Hospital, a position which Newton helped Paget attain.

Although Halley had waited over three months, in November he got much more than he had asked for. Newton sent nine pages entitled *De Motu corporum in gyrum* [*On the Motion of Bodies in Orbit*]. Newton not only demonstrated that an elliptical orbit involves an inverse-square force on one focus, he demonstrated that an inverse-square force necessitates a conic orbit –which (below certain velocities) is an ellipse. Newton's treatise also proved Kepler's laws and broached the subject of dynamics by calculating the trajectory of an object meeting resistance while traveling through a medium.[161]

Halley couldn't believe his eyes. He was looking at something so immense that it could start a scientific revolution. He thought to himself:

> *The scientific world must witness this treatise. It must be published. Isaac Newton has demonstrated beyond any doubt an order of the planets, the structure of our entire planetary system. He has found secrets of our universe and how divinely it is structured within Kepler's laws and the unerring laws of nature. Furthermore, he has proven it mathematically. I am witnessing a prize for the ages.*

Halley immediately arranged a second trip to Cambridge in an attempt to get Newton to publish his treatise.

CHAPTER 21

The Principia

• • •

"Before Halley arrived in Cambridge, he pondered about what approach he would use to persuade Newton to publish his remarkable achievements. From information he had gathered from Royal Society members, Newton eschewed publishing and tended toward avoiding disputes. He also had a very sensitive nature. Again Halley reflected:

> *How do I persuade him to publish? Should I emphasize bringing new truths into the world? Should I caution him that others are seeking solutions to the same problems and that he must establish his priority? He must at least print his "De Motu" in the "Transactions." The world will be the better for it. ...*

Halley visited Isaac Newton late in November of 1684. He was invited in to Newton's apartment and was soon sitting across from him. The two men engaged in small talk before Halley said:

"Mr. Newton, your treatise is the most revolutionary document I have ever seen. I have come to ask you to present it to the Royal Society."

"Mr. Halley, please be at ease. I have been thinking along similar lines. In the past I have been averse to releasing my work, but I have since changed my mind. I *will* continue to be cautious about publishing at large for obvious reasons; however, I would be comfortable allowing the society to see my recent efforts."

"Mr. Newton, I am so relieved to hear you say that. I was fearful of another response."

"I can understand that, Edmund. I'm sure my reputation has preceded me. However, you must also understand that "De Motu" is not a finished work. Although I am most receptive to having it published, it is only an introduction to much more. However, you will have to wait for a complete manuscript. "

"May I inquire as to how long that will be?"

"I'm not really sure. I can only promise to give the manuscript my undivided attention."

After waiting until December 10, Halley decided to report his November visit with Newton to the Royal Society. He revealed that the Lucasian Professor had written a preliminary treatise on the orbiting of planets and had promised an expanded manuscript. Since Isaac had not yet forwarded this expanded work, Halley asked Secretary Aston to register "De Motu" immediately.

Meanwhile, in Cambridge, Isaac Newton was in his element. Orbital motion had consumed him and would not let him rest. He was again on a quest —perhaps even more challenging than past ones —especially if one were to witness his behavior as observed by his roommate, Humphrey Newton:

> ...he eat very sparingly, nay, oft times he has forgot to eat at all. When I have reminded him [he] would reply, 'Have I[?]' & then making to ye Table would eat a bit or two standing. ...at some seldom times when he designed to dine in ye Hall, would turn to ye left hand, & go out into ye street, where making a stop when he found his Mistake, would hastily turn back, & then sometimes instead of going into ye Hall would return to his chamber again.[162]

At times Humphrey watched his roommate take a walk, suddenly come to a standstill, turn himself around, run up the stairs to his desk and start writing without pulling up a chair.[163]

Isaac Newton had stayed inside Trinity since May of 1683. But beginning in August of 1684, he was in a creative euphoria totally divorced from alchemic experiments and theological study. He never left Trinity's confines until April of 1686 except for some family obligations in Woolsthorpe in the Spring of 1685, when he was absent for a total of six weeks. He had become absorbed in finding the principles of mathematics in nature, including space, where he was making some of his most unique philosophical discoveries.

While Halley waited for Newton's expanded treatise, Isaac was collecting data and calculating. He was discovering new truths and didn't know how long it would take. After promising John Flamsteed, the Royal Astronomer, a copy of "De Motu," Isaac began asking him for information:

"Can you provide me the distance from the foot of Perseus to its two stars? Can you give me information regarding the paths and velocities of the comets of 1664 and 1680? Can you give me information on the velocities of Saturn and Jupiter as they approach each other?" (Newton was attempting to prove that Saturn decreases its orbital speed as Jupiter approaches, and then accelerates after it passes.[164])

Flamsteed, still a proponent of the "ether" theory, replied, "I believe you will find Kepler to be correct in this regard. When these two planets are nearest to each other, they are separated by a distance four times the radius of the earth." Despite Flamsteed's doubts, he sent the information Newton had requested.

Newton did not respond to Flamsteed's skepticism, and in September of 1685 he asked for more information on the comet of 1680 and for something else:

"Would you send me information on your observations of the tides in the estuary of the Thames?"[165] It appeared that Newton was still collecting information about gravity.

In the midst of his extensive research, Isaac Newton was still fulfilling his lecture requirements at Trinity. However, his lectures were from his drafts of the *Principia*, as were the drafts he deposited in Trinity's archives. The problem was that no one in attendance understood what he was talking about. Furthermore, his lectures and drafts were all in Latin. Professor Newton lectured to the walls when no one was present --and refused to review any of that material in succeeding weeks. His superiority complex was never more evident.

In the fall of 1684 Newton's expansion of "De Motu" was getting more and more involved. Though the world didn't know it yet, what Isaac accomplished in the autumn and winter of 1684-85 would change western science for centuries. At this time he launched the science of dynamics. Though his first version of "De Motu" used the term *gravitas*, later versions incorporated the term *centripetal force*, a term which Newton originated:

> *My calculations reveal that the centripetal force by which our moon is held in her monthly orbit is to the force of gravity at the surface of the earth very nearly as the reciprocal of the square of the distance from the center of the earth.*[166]

By the spring of 1685 Newton had reinterpreted Kepler's Third Law. He found that the sun attracted all planets in proportion to their mass, and that the concentric orbits of Jupiter's satellites demonstrated that the sun attracts both them and Jupiter in proportion to their mass –and that *Jupiter and its satellites attract the sun in return*. Isaac logically concluded: "Every body in the solar system attracts every other body." [167]

Newton was now expanding "De Motu" into a systematic demonstration of universal gravitation. *And the medium he used was the first and noblest of sciences:* <u>Geometry.</u> He never explained why he cloaked **Principia** in classical geometry; however, thought patterns of *calculus* can be seen behind it.[168] (Euclid could not have made such geometrical ramifications.) Soon Newton mathematically calculated correlations of bodies, including the moon and the apple, to inverse-square relationships in the solar system. To geometrically demonstrate a sphere's attraction to another sphere was a primary principle on which the law of universal gravitation rested.

But Newton needed to go farther. The solar system consisted of more than just two bodies in motion. So Newton expanded his study to *three attracting objects*. From conclusions reached by studying three bodies, arguments could be made for a system of many bodies. In 1685, as far as scientists knew, there were six planets and the sun, and three of the planets had satellites. All of them, according to Newton, attracted one another. Newton started by writing six pages, then fifteen, then nineteen. He coined three new terms to further define quantities of centripetal force: *absolute, accelerative* and *motive*. Regarding many bodies revolving around a greater one, Newton wrote:

> *The orbits described will approach nearer to ellipses, & the descriptions of areas will be more nearly uniform if all the bodies mutually attract & agitate each other equally in proportion to their weights and distances. And if the focus of each orbit is placed in the common center of gravity of the interior bodies than if the innermost body were at rest and were made the common focus of the orbits.*[169]

Newton received a side benefit from analyzing three-body systems. He not only explained how their orbits followed Kepler's laws, he also discerned certain perturbations, as in the orbits of the moon.

By the end of 1685, Newton had accomplished miracles, but he wasn't close to finishing his treatise. For better or worse, **Principia** was primarily for the *Virtuosi*, the accomplished mathematicians. Probably no one else would understand it. The final product would consist of three books and an introduction, all of them perfect in form and content, as was true of every one of Newton's final products. Newton was the "perfect mechanic;" he did everything with perfect accuracy. Unfortunately, however, perfection sometimes takes time, and by the end of 1685, Newton hadn't given Halley anything. In fact, it wouldn't be until August of 1686 that publication would start. In its final form, **Principia** would consist of three books:

I. Book I – "Dynamics for bodies operating in idealized conditions" (No friction, No resistance)
II. Book II – "The Motion of Fluids and their effect on the motion of solid bodies suspended in them"
III. Book III – "Forces of Gravity on the celestial phenomena" (Bodies tend to the sun and to each other.) --From these forces, the mathematical calculations of the motions of the planets, comets, moon and sea.

In this third book, Newton returned to his lifelong desire to unify the spiritual and the temporal by combining terrestrial and celestial motion into a single formula.

Hooke and Halley may have given Newton the impetus to start his world-changing journey, but the first shoulders he stood on were Kepler's laws of planetary motions and Galileo's laws of the motions of bodies on earth. Both were separate laws –and both were incompatible with each other. Galileo said that the circular motion of planets is self-perpetuating, i.e. gravity on earth is not related to planetary motion. Kepler said that planets were driven by invisible spokes. But Newton would soon introduce some new contributions in his **Principia**, his *"Principles of Mathematics"*:

1. Centripetal Force --and the absolute, accelerative and motive quantities of the same.
2. Mass: the measure of a body's resistance to acceleration irrespective of volume.
3. Force: what is needed to change the motion of a body.
4. Influence of Force: Leave a moving body alone and it will go on indefinitely. The force on a planet is a deflecting one, not a propelling one.

5. Universal gravitation.
6. Cause of tides.

---And the list goes on.

In 1686, prior to presenting Halley with his masterpiece, Newton told him about a paper he had written in the 1660's:

"I tried to calculate how much the centrifugal force of the earth's rotation decreases gravity. But ...to do this business right is a thing of far greater difficulty than I was aware of. "[170]

Although Halley didn't realize it at the time, Newton was actually explaining the difference between "De Motu" and the *Philosophiae Naturalis Principia Mathematica* –his **Principia**.

To Isaac Newton, the universe was a colossal machine made up of components of mass, position and extension: a precise, harmonious, rationally ordered whole with mathematical laws binding each particle of matter to every other particle.[171] Newton had now discovered laws proving that mankind inhabits a preeminently ordered world. His Pythagorean power in mathematics and geometry plus his scientific methods had surpassed traditional thought and mundane assumptions.

At this stage of his life, Isaac Newton was in the process of contributing more than any other person in world history to the establishment and acceptance of a rational world view. Furthermore, he had provided the most valid evidence to understand the earth, the celestial bodies – and human existence.[172]

Newton's closest friend was also contributing something to the world. When King Charles II died on February 6, 1685, Charles Montague wrote some verses of poetry which were recited at the king's last rites and made Montague a favorite of the royal family.

CHAPTER 22

Resurgence of 'The Beast'

• • •

"Puritan concepts, like those ingrained in Isaac Newton, had managed to survive in England despite the exhuming and beheading of Cromwell in 1661 and the destruction of all records of his Protectorate. In fact, Puritanism had spread to the American colonies, especially in New England, where Puritans established Harvard University and would soon found Yale. Similar Protestant sects also sprang up in other countries, including France, where Henry IV had invoked the *Edict of Nantes* in 1598 in order to prevent violence and protect Huguenots from persecution in that Roman Catholic kingdom. ...

Both Huguenots and Puritans disapproved of kings, popes and others dictating what people should believe. These two sects not only abhorred the "divine right of kings," they believed in consulting the *Bible* directly and educating themselves rather than allowing others to think and interpret for them. Both sects believed in local church government, not government from afar. They elected their own representatives or "presbyteries." They believed in hard work and direct communication with God.

The kings of England and France had abided Protestantism until the current year 1685, a year that brought cataclysmic change. First of all, England's Charles II died early in February, and his brother James II, a professed Roman Catholic, assumed the throne. On the morning of February 9, Isaac Newton and the Trinity University faculty, resplendent in their robes, gathered in Cambridge to proclaim James II King of

England. After the proclamation, which Newton didn't particularly relish, he returned to his apartment instead of joining the vice-chancellor and other university officers in the Master's Lodge to drink to the king's health.

While the entourage in the Master's Lodge raised their glasses, the mayor, aldermen and other town officials gathered at the Great Gate directly below Newton's window to herald James II as King of England. Alderman Samuel Newton read the proclamation.[173]

Isaac watched the proceedings from his window and did not express any opinions at the time. He continued to work on **The Principia** but must have thought it a catastrophe to have a Catholic king. Later on, Newton would strongly address his aversion to James II.

Meanwhile, across the English Channel, another historical event was taking place. King Louis XIV of France suddenly rescinded the *Edict of Nantes*. All religious and political freedoms of the Huguenots were rescinded, and Roman Catholicism became the religion of France. All Huguenots were to convert to Catholicism or leave the country without their children, who were to be raised as Catholics in orphanages. The revocation of the 87 year-old edict was the worst tragedy to the Huguenots since the Saint Bartholomew's Day Massacre of 1572, when thousands of Huguenots throughout France were dragged from their homes and murdered by mobs. The Huguenots blamed that tragedy on the mother of King Charles IX, Catherine de Medici, who in 1572 plotted with Roman Catholic leaders to assassinate the popular Huguenot leader, Gaspard de Coligny. The assassination failed, however, and the royal family and the church hierarchy feared retaliation. Catherine de Medici convinced King Charles that the Huguenots were going to attack the palace in an effort to kill him. Therefore, Charles issued the following order against all Huguenot leaders:

Kill them all so that not a single one be left to reproach me. [174]

Coligny was murdered first, then all well-known Huguenots in Paris. Soon enemies of Huguenots throughout France went on a killing spree. For twenty-six years Huguenots lived in a state of fear until 1598 when King Henry IV invoked the *Edict of Nantes*, which gave Huguenots territorial and religious freedom.

The seaport of La Rochelle, from which 18 Knights Templar ships had escaped religious tyranny in 1307, became a center for Huguenot Calvinism, and from the pulpits of La Rochelle sermons railed against the French Catholics for their antipathy toward Huguenots. However, upon the advent of Louis XIII to the throne of France in 1610, continuous attempts were made to erode the *Edict of Nantes*. Beginning in 1621, the king attempted to blockade the port of La Rochelle, but English ships were able to penetrate the blockade and deliver supplies to the Huguenots. A Treaty of Montpelier temporarily ended hostilities in 1622.

In 1625 the Huguenots again rebelled, but the conflict ended when the king's forces captured the Île de Re' in La Rochelle's harbor and ousted the English who had landed there. The battle for this island may have started the Anglo-French War. In any event, Louis XIII and his minister, Cardinal Richelieu, had now made it their priority to subdue La Rochelle. In 1627 they initiated a siege of the city. They constructed a seawall to stop British ships and prevent escape by the Huguenots. Thirty thousand troops surrounded La Rochelle, which had about 30,000 inhabitants. All attempts to rescue the besieged Huguenots failed.

On October 28, 1628 the city capitulated. Fourteen months of starvation, disease and cannonade, had reduced La Rochelle to 5000 Huguenots. The casualties far exceeded the number of Christian Cathars who were burned at the stake at Montsegur in 1244.

Louis XIV continued to dismantle the *Edict of Nantes*. In 1660, he instituted *dragonnades* --quartering troops in residences. These troops intimidated families to convert to Catholicism, and Protestants were barred from holding public office. By 1682, Huguenot pastors were imprisoned (or worse) for speaking against Catholicism. Unfortunately, in August of this year, pastor Jean Desaguliers gave an ill-advised sermon, and an informant in the congregation reported it. Jean escaped to London, but his pregnant wife, Marguerite, was unable to sail.

England welcomed Desaguliers with open arms and gave him citizenship. In November, he was ordained a priest in the Anglican Church and sent to Guernsey, a haven for escaped Huguenots; but Jean was not given a rectorship due to an abundance of Huguenot priests.

On March 12, 1683, Marguerite Desaguliers gave birth to Jean Theophile Desaguliers, and in a few months decided to join her husband. She had one minor problem, however: *children were forbidden to leave France.*

With the aid of Huguenot minister Pierre du Prat and another minister's wife, Marguerite Desaguliers packed her possessions in a large trunk. She then gently placed Jean, Jr. in a medium sized barrel, which had small holes in the staves for ventilation. She had waited for four months in order for her son to become accustomed to sleeping through the night in the barrel. Then with the aid of Reverend Duprat and Marie Francoise de Mazieres, Marguerite rode in a carriage to the docks of La Rochelle where a ship was waiting. Fortunately, her baby did not wake up when she passed by the French troops who were inspecting passengers and luggage at embarkation.

Marguerite and her baby arrived safely in Guernsey. Her husband supported them by teaching in a school, a position that Reverend W. Douglas obtained for him. Mr. and Mrs. Desaguliers had escaped from France just in time; the *Edict of Nantes* was completely revoked by Louis XIV in 1685. Huguenot ministers as well as children were not allowed to leave the country. The Desaguliers family subsisted in Guernsey for nine years. They adopted the English forename, John, for their son who would forever be known as *John Theophilus Desaguliers* (pronounced *day-za-gulee-ay*). John became proficient in English and Greek on the isle of Guernsey. In 1692 the family moved to London, where Jean Sr. became a lecturer for a Huguenot church on Swallow Street. In 1695, the Desaguliers family received assistance from the Royal Bounty Fund and moved to Islington, three miles north of London, where Reverend Desaguliers established a French School. John Jr. was educated at this school by his father.

In 1685, the year of the revocation of the *Edict of Nantes*, Newton was laboring intensively on **The Principia** while maintaining his Lucasian Chair responsibilities. In fact, one student by the name of Charles Montague attended some of his lectures. Although Montague was unable to understand much of what Isaac was talking about, he was fascinated by the superior intellect of the Lucasian professor and attempted to grasp everything he could. After the lectures he even asked questions.

Soon a close relationship developed between professor and student; they had much in common. Montague even formed a philosophical society at Trinity in 1685, the same year that King Charles II gave him a Master of Arts Degree and a Fellowship by royal mandate. With his close relationship to the king, Charles Montague would become a useful friend of Isaac Newton's.

CHAPTER 23

Nearer the Gods

• • •

"ISAAC NEWTON CONTINUED TO EXPAND "De Motu" but had considerable difficulty deriving orbital motion from the interaction of inherent force with centripetal force, which diverts inherent force from maintaining motion in a straight line. Eventually, on his third revision, Isaac reconstructed his dynamics and inserted the term "impressed force," which changes uniform motion and the state "of resting." He had now implied a *dynamic* identity to *uniform motion* and *rest*.[175] Consequently, Newton added two additional laws to the two laws of force regarding *Inherent Force* and *Impressed Force*:

Law 3. Motions of bodies in a given space are the same, whether the space is at rest or moves in a straight line (the principle of *inertia*).
Law 4. The mutual action of bodies does not change the state of motion or *of rest* of their common center of gravity. (Newton is extending inertia to bodies which he considers "unities" or planetary families.) ...

The crux of Newton's dynamics lay in the relation between inherent and impressed force –or the relation between "the innate essential force of a body and the force brought to bear, or impressed, upon it."[176]

Following his last revision of "De Motu," Newton had placed dynamics into its final form. The principle of inertia allowed him to treat change of direction in the same terms as change of speed. He was able to recognize uniform circular motion and uniformly accelerated motion in a straight line. Never before had these two motions been treated dynamically the same. Once Newton had adopted the principle of inertia, the rest of his dynamics fell into place.[177] Of course, in order to perfect his treatise, new terms had to be added such as: "quantity of motion," "quantity of matter," the "time dimension," the "force of inertia," "inert matter," and "active matter."

Newton proved most of his concepts mathematically, and the first stage of his work on the *Principia* was the creation of his dynamics. In fact, at about the same time that Samuel Newton was announcing James II as King of England, Isaac Newton was proving that all bodies in the world attract other bodies. And it wasn't long before Isaac mathematically correlated the earth's attraction with the motions of the moon and the acceleration of gravity. *Thus was born the concept of universal gravitation.*

By the summer of 1685 Newton had developed so many new principles, he divided his treatise ("Book I" of **The Principia**) into two books, and began expanding "Book II," in which he used Flamsteed's table on tides. However, in computing the forces of the sun and moon that produced the tides, Isaac had to revise his calculations at least three times. In "Book II" he also suggested that the principle of universal gravitation could also account for other phenomena in addition to tides; for example, he demonstrated that comets came under the laws of orbital motion, just like planets.

Finally in August of 1685, Newton gave Halley a developed system of dynamics and a universal principle of gravity that applied not only to all bodies in the solar system, but to all matter in the universe. Up to this time Halley hadn't received anything from Newton since DeMotu in November of 1684. Now, almost a year later, Newton handed him a treatise that proved the principle of universal gravitation.

Halley was astonished to say the least, and his admiration of Newton increased dramatically. From then on, as Newton expanded

The Principia, Halley would call it, "Your incomparable treatise;" then, "Your divine treatise." Finally, upon receipt of a finished product, Halley wrote "An Ode To Newton" with a Latin phrase, "Nec Est Fas Poplius Mortali Aggredanza Divos." (Nearer the gods no mortal may approach.)[178]

But in the fall of 1685, Newton's first two books of **The Principia** were not yet a completed "divine treatise," because he kept expanding them into an investigation of all terrestrial and celestial motion that completely refuted DeCartes' theories.[179] As Isaac honed his dynamics he came to realize that the two major laws of force in "De Motu" were applicable throughout the universe, and that spheres attract just like their component particles –a principle he found "very remarkable."[180] Nevertheless, as far as the inverse-square law was concerned, Isaac also found that a third body in the mix always prevented a perfect elliptical orbit. Only two major laws of attraction, the inverse-square law" and the "direct distance law" were consistent with Newton's mathematically-ordered universe. Isaac realized again that the mechanics God applied in creating the cosmos were far superior than his own.[181]

In truth, Newton completed "Book I" of **The Principia** during the winter of 1685-86. As he was working on it, he sent a letter to Halley explaining that he was dividing that book in two. "Book I" dealt with motions of bodies in space free of resistance, but "Book II" would introduce resisting media.[182] He mentioned that he was giving the book to Humphrey Newton to copy; therefore, Halley would receive it soon. On April 21, Halley told The Royal Society that Newton's treatise was almost ready for the press. One week after Halley's announcement, Dr. Vincent delivered the first book manuscript to The Royal Society, to whom it was dedicated. But Newton still had much work to do.

Unfortunately, in the spring of 1686 The Royal Society had not been conducting business for want of a presiding officer. When the Society convened on May 19, Halley, now employed as a clerk for the organization, moved that it print **The Principia**. Though it was still without a presiding officer, the Society passed the resolution and ordered that ..."Mr. Newton's *Philosophiae naturalis principia mathematica* be printed forthwith in quarto..." –and that Halley take charge of the publication. Halley accepted the responsibility, despite the fact that he and the Society both had monetary problems. Halley had recently lost an income due to his father's death. He was supporting a young wife and family on a salary of 50 pounds per year as a clerk for The Royal Society.

Nevertheless, in his next letter to Newton, Halley informed him that despite the absence of a presiding officer, the Society decided "so excellent a work ought not to have its publication ...delayed." However, in the second paragraph of the same letter, Halley informed Newton of another matter that struck the Lucasian professor like a lightning bolt:

"There is one thing more that I ought to inform you of, viz, that Mr. Hook has some pretentions upon the invention of ye rule of the decrease of Gravity, being reciprocally as the squares of the distances from the Centers. He said you had the notion **from him**, though he owns the Demonstration of the Curves generated thereby to be wholly your own; how much of this is so, you know best, as likewise what you had to do in this matter. Only Mr. Hook seems to expect you should make some mention of him in the preface, which it is possible you may see reason to prefix. I must beg your pardon that it is I, that send you this account, but I thought it my duty to let you know it, that so you may act accordingly; being in myself fully satisfied, that nothing but the greatest Candour imaginable, is to be expected from a person, who of all men has the least need to borrow reputation." [183]

After reading the letter, Newton's face reddened. Clenching the letter in his fist, he said to his roommate:

"That damned Hooke is at it again!"

Humphrey Newton replied, "What is Hooke about, sire?"

"According to Halley, Hooke wants an acknowledgement in **The Principia** that he discovered the Inverse-Square law."

"But that is not so, sire! Hooke has told you nothing that you did not already know. Swounds! Mr. Hooke has tried these tricks before."

"I was actually going to mention 'the very distinguished Hooke' in my discussion of comets. Now this pretender of invention will be fortunate to have even his *name* mentioned."

Talking to Humphrey did not appease Isaac. He immediately sat down with pen and ink to write Halley a history of his relationship with Robert Hooke. Incomprehensibly, no other part of Halley's letter was mentioned except for thanking him for relating Hooke's wishes and requesting of Halley that "a good understanding" of the Hooke controversy be kept between them:

> *I did not mention Hooke in 'Book I' because I owed nothing to him. I have mentioned him in part of the work not yet sent; however, I owe nothing to him regarding the inverse-square law. I suggest that you consult Sir Christopher Wren about a conversation we had in 1677.*[184]

Upon receipt of Newton's letter, Halley breathed a sigh of relief. Hopefully, the inverse-square crisis was over. He sent a proof of "Book I" to Newton for approval with a flattering comment to heal any wounds that might still be open:

I have proof-read the sheet, but may have missed some errors. When it has past your eye, I doubt not but it will be clear from errata.[185]

Newton's reply would again give Halley a bolt out of the blue. It had been three weeks since Newton's last letter, just enough time for Hooke's claim to fester and finally erupt. Newton now wrote every detail of every conflict he ever had with Hooke –including a time concerning projectiles "descending hence to ye [earth's] center & [thence] conclude me ignorant of ye Theory of ye Heavens."[186] Isaac devoted 200 words to just this one episode with Hooke. He spent 70 words explaining his brief answers to two of Hooke's letters and his ignoring of a third.

In this same letter, Newton went into a history of his prior knowledge of the inverse-square relation. He wrote, "Even if I had obtained the inverse-square law from Hooke, Hooke only guessed at it, whereas I had demonstrated its truth."[187] Finally, at the end of the letter, Newton wrote, "I have decided to suppress 'Book 3'. Philosophy is such an impertinently litigious Lady that a man had as good be engaged in Law suits as have to do with her. I found it so formerly & now I no sooner come near her again but she gives me warning."[188]

Before Newton sealed the letter, however, Edward Paget entered the room exclaiming, "Robert Hooke is making a stir and demands that justice be done!"

Newton replied, "Justice? I will give him *Justice!*"

Isaac now became more enraged than ever. He began writing a postscript to his letter that ended up being longer than the letter itself. In it he repeated his entire complaint but added much more:

> *All Hooke has done is publish Borelli's hypothesis under his own name, and now he claims to have done everything but the drudgery of calculation. Now is not this very fine? Mathematicians that find out, settle & do all the business must content themselves with being nothing but dry calculators & drudges & another that does nothing but pretend & grasp at all things must carry away all the invention as well of those that were to follow him as of those that went before.*
>
> *…Should a man who thinks himself knowing, & loves to shew it in correcting and instructing others, come to you when you are busy, & notwithstanding your excuse, press discourses upon you then make this use of it, to boast that he taught you all he spake & oblige you to acknowledge it & cry out injury & injustice if you do not, I believe you would think him a man of a strange unsociable temper. Mr. Hooks letters in several respects abounded too much wth that humour wch Hevelius & others complain of …*[189]

When Halley received Newton's last letter and read his emotionally-charged sentiments, he realized that nothing riled Isaac more than a person seeking acknowledgements without the achievements to deserve them. Newton mentioned Hooke's claim three times, but instead of giving any type of recognition, he edited his draft of the final book by deleting all references to Hooke except one, which concerned the observation of comets; however, *"the very distinguished Hooke"* was reduced to only *"Hooke."* Of considerably more importance was Halley's reaction upon reading of Newton's decision to "suppress Book III." He almost had an aneurism. Halley could not abide such a threat and promptly replied:

My Dear Friend,
Your great work is without doubt your own and no one else's. You need not give acknowledgement unless you deem it worthy. You have created a masterpiece and the Royal Society stands with you and no one else.

I urge you not to consider suppressing any part of your work, there being nothing which you can have compiled therin, which the learned world will not be concerned to have concealed. I have done as you have suggested and spoken to Mr. Wren, and Mr. Wren's account of the conversation with Hook is wholly in your favor. I too had met with Hook and Wren in January 1684 and nothing in that meeting is to your disadvantage.

Granted, that later in a coffeehouse, Hook boasted of having given the invention to you, but I found nothing thereof appearing in print —not even in the books of the Society. The Society have a very great satisfaction in the honour you do them, by your dedication of so worthy a Treatise.[190]

Sir, I must now again beg you, not to let your resentments run so high, as to deprive us of your third book, wherein the application of your Mathematicall doctrine to the Theory of Comets and several curious Experiments will undoubtedly render it acceptable to those [who] call themselves philosophers without Mathematicks.[191]

The calming, cajoling words of Halley did the trick, and the crisis passed. When Newton returned correspondence two weeks later, he expressed regrets about his lengthy postscript and his threats to suppress Book III. He even proffered some measured positive comments about Hooke; however, he continued to firmly deny Hooke's claim regarding the inverse-square law:

"I, alone, found the inverse-square law, and I did not guess at it like Mr. Hooke. I developed it in a way that mathematicians appreciate." [192]

Although Newton did return Hooke's name to the manuscript regarding celestial bodies, it was mentioned only parenthetically "as our countrymen Wren, Halley and Hooke have also severally concluded."[193] Of course, Hooke's name was placed last. Before **The Principia** went to press, however, Halley –forever the conciliator-- placed his name behind Hooke's.

But Newton's mind was constantly preoccupied with Hooke's claims, and he continually pointed out instances of Hooke's contentions with specific dates to prove that Hooke was never the first inventor. One instance was found in a letter Newton had found while obviously still searching for evidence from past correspondence: Newton had proved in 1673 that he understood duplicate proportion, and in 1674 Newton pointed out Hooke's published admission that he didn't know by what proportion gravity decreased.[194]

Yet Newton's one mistake continued to haunt him, and in a letter to Halley in late July he wrote:

"In short as these things compared together shew, that I was before Mr. Hook in what he pretends to have been my Master so I learnt nothing by his letters but this [...] that bodies fall not only to ye east but also in our latitude to ye south ... And tho his correcting my Spiral occasioned my finding ye Theorem by wch I afterward examined ye Ellipsis, yet am I not beholden to him for any light into yt business….."[195]

After his July letter, Newton's tirade against Hooke subsided. But Halley still received nothing resembling Book III, and became quite anxious. Halley had no idea what would be forthcoming from Mr. Newton and mused over the Hooke controversy:

Why does Isaac protest so much? His position regarding the inverse-square law is quite secure, as I have told him at every opportunity. I firmly believe the better course is to give Mr. Hooke credit for even a meager contribution. Far from being injurious, such generosity would only enhance Isaac's reputation.

In his correspondence with Hooke in 1679 and 1680, Isaac focused only on gravity below the earth's surface and completely ignored Hooke's comments on orbital motion, which was fundamental in their exchange. Clashes with adversaries always seem to grow more heated at each exchange when each participant is dogmatic in his opinions. Newton had clashed with Hooke on two previous occasions, and perhaps this last charge of plagiarism was just too much for Isaac to bear. I doubt not that he will ever forget it, let alone forgive it. It will not matter one farthing on the bigger issue... that Newton has discovered universal gravitation and his name will be forever etched in stone as the man who proved it. Such a great discovery will be etched on my mind and that of many others, but also etched upon my mind is the weakness of such a talented, lonely genius who, though unwilling to take opinions and criticisms from inferiors, is nonetheless still tormented by them.

But I also find fault with Mr. Hooke. Though he rarely understands what he claims, he nevertheless claims he does. The inverse-square law entails a general mathematical system of the universe; yet, Mr. Hooke treats it as an object he believes he has discovered, and which Newton has stolen. He is as strong-willed as his adversary, and I sincerely doubt that the two of them will ever speak to each other again.

Halley did not realize that his thoughts were prophetic; Isaac Newton and Robert Hooke never spoke to each other for the rest of their lives.

It was not until 1759, long after Hooke's death, that the French scientist Clairaut gave the following acknowledgement: "Hooke's examples serve to show what a distance there is between a truth that is glimpsed and a truth that is demonstrated."[196]

In 1672 Newton had withdrawn from the world due to the merest ignorant criticism of his paper on colors. But now in 1686 under much more serious criticism, Isaac responded quite differently. Halley had predicted that **The Principia** would be the greatest discovery of nature since the world's creation, and Isaac Newton did not dispute him. Isaac may have made some idle threats, but he refused to sabotage his masterpiece. Now that the dispute with Hooke had subsided, Isaac rededicated himself to his **Principia**.

CHAPTER 24

The Crown Jewel of the Enlightenment

• • •

"Isaac resumed work on The **Principia** by expanding *Book II* with an attack on the theories of Descartes', especially the physical causes of resistance. He wrote that 'the quantity of matter is proportional to density' and 'the force of inertia, to the quantity of matter.' By proving that inertia was a source of resistance and that 'aether' was not, Isaac successfully replaced Descartes' philosophy on these subjects. ...

Isaac then conducted experiments on sound. He manufactured pendulums to measure the speed of sound, which he calculated at a velocity somewhere between 920 and 1085 feet per second –a remarkable measurement considering that he used pendulums to measure echoes. Clocks had yet to develop beyond a minute hand.

Finally in June of 1686 Newton wrote to Halley: "Book III wants ye theory of comets."[197] He was obviously wrestling with the influence of gravity on comets. But by the end of 1686, Isaac had accomplished another breakthrough. He found that "comets moved in a path resembling the perimeter of a slice through a cross-section of a cone, their foci being the center of the sun, their orbits resembling parabolas, which can be used [to describe their orbits] without sensible error."[198] Newton went on to calculate that comets return at regular intervals; consequently, he began plotting the curve of the Great Comet of 1680-81.

When Halley received Newton's information on comets, he also began painstakingly plotting the comet of 1682, which he predicted would return to earth in about seventy-five years. Halley's prediction proved to be correct; the comet was observed on Christmas day in 1758, 116 years after Newton's birth, and bears Halley's name. Isaac Newton, however, was the first to prove that comets revolve around the sun –and the proof is in **The Principia**.

In March of 1687 as Newton sent "Book II" to London and began final edits to "Book III," a small cabal of seven Royal Society members, including Robert Hooke, decided to inspect Halley's books in an effort to oust him. Hooke had now become an embittered man, and Halley suspected him of leading the effort. The books were in good order, however, and only six of thirty-eight members voted against Halley. Halley never reported Hooke's conspiracy to Newton for fear of evoking him into another writing tirade.[199] However, Halley did tell Newton that "Book II" would be printed in seven weeks and asked that he send "Book III" immediately so the printer could print all three books together.[200]

"Book III" contained Newton's most acclaimed scientific discovery: the law of universal gravitation --*Newton's Law*. "There is a power of gravity pertaining to all bodies proportional to the several quantities of matter which they contain."[201] In other words, every particle of matter attracts every other particle with a force proportional to the product of the masses and inversely proportional to the square of the distances between them. Newton's Law screamed out to the world: *no celestial body is more important than any other. All matter, from the largest star to the smallest corpuscle, obeys the same constant principle.*

Perhaps Newton's greatest discovery was that the entire universe was a colossal machine created with an intelligence that even he was unable to fathom. He had trouble scientifically calculating orbits if the orbiter is affected by other bodies than the body being orbited. In other words, if more than two or three planets are in a planetary unit, Newton had trouble making exact calculations. All planets' gravitations create minor disturbances in orbits and revolutions. Even with his unmatched analytical skills and his use of calculus, Newton could not calculate orbits of multiple planetary units to perfection. And *perfection* was Newton's *modus operandi*.

Even the moon had special irregularities of motion. Though it was affected by the earth, the sun also visibly disturbed the moon's orbit, and Newton by his complex calculations succeeded in formulating major disturbances in the moon's orbits and in the orbits of other planets. He calculated that the earth's density was between five and six times the density of water (later proved to be five and one-half). He proved that tides arise from the actions of the sun and the moon and applied the law of gravitation to prove that the moon attracted water more than the earth as a whole. He found that the earth is more attracted to the moon when water is farthest from the moon —especially at perigee, when the moon is nearest the earth.

Newton proved that planets are flattened at their poles because spinning bodies swell at their circumferences and subsequently shrink at their axes. Newton's universe truly was a "colossal machine," a precise, harmonious, rationally ordered whole, and that mankind truly inhabited a preeminently ordered world. His Pythagorean power in using numbers, especially his use of Geometry in **The Principia**, and his precise scientific method held sway well above the tradition, error, and mundane understanding of the past. Isaac, more than any other human being to inhabit planet earth, had presented a rational, objective explanation of the universe with evidence to explain terrestrial and celestial motion and existence.

On his own, Halley undertook publishing **The Principia.** On July 5, 1687 he sent some copies to Newton for distribution to booksellers and his friends at Cambridge. He also sent copies in Isaac's name to many members of The Royal Society. He placed the name of Samuel Pepys, President of The Royal Society, on the title page and wrote some verses in the prefix. One verse, "An Ode to Newton" contained the following:

> *He unlocked the hidden treasures of truth…*
> *Nearer the gods no mortal may approach.*

When asked about his unprecedented contributions to mankind, Newton answered, "If I have done ye Publick any service… 'tis due to nothing but industry and patient thought."[202]

Although he may not have known it, Newton had started a scientific revolution. Natural Philosophy (Science) had been placed on a firm foundation. The world had received correct new light. Physics and Astronomy had produced something other than the formerly unquestionable –and untouchable—ecclesiastical beliefs that were forced upon the world with punishments for any who would question them --as Galileo could have attested.

Regrettably, many educated men had trouble understanding **The Principia** –including most of the professors at Trinity University and most mathematicians in Scotland. Yet John Locke, who had been accused of "radicalism" by King Charles II and had fled to Holland, set upon mastering **The Principia**. Though not a mathematician, Locke wrote a flattering review in March of 1688. His was the first review published on the continent. Soon other reviews were published giving high praise to Newton.

Meanwhile, Robert Hooke continued to pursue the justice he felt had been denied him and attempted to ride the coattails of Isaac Newton. It appears that a desire existed to merge his own account with that of the victor after such a great intellectual feat. His failure and Newton's triumph was still the stuff of high drama.[203]

Despite all the praise, Newton was dissatisfied. He still couldn't explain *gravity*. In any event, his work on **The Principia** had been consummated. He could now return to alchemy and find the secret to matter and life itself.

As Humphrey Newton observed, "I've never met anyone like Mr. Newton. I believe I am witnessing the supernatural in action within my own chambers."[204] It wasn't long before everyone in England looked upon Isaac as nothing short of a miracle –after all he was born on Christmas! By the 1690's Europe had practically made Isaac an idol. After a French mathematician, the Marquis de l'Hopital, had read **The Principia**, he asked John Arbuthnot specific questions about Isaac Newton, including "Does he eat, drink and sleep? Is he like other men?"

Arbuthnot responded, "He converses cheerfully with his friends, assumes nothing and puts himself upon a level with all mankind."[205]

Newton was the crown jewel of the Enlightenment, but he was no loyal subject. By the time he had published **The Principia**, King James II had reigned almost two years. On March 11, 1687, Isaac Newton finished editing his masterpiece and immediately turned his attention to dethroning King James, who seemed intent upon returning "The Beast" to England.

At this moment in world history, Isaac Newton had uncovered more scientific facts, more light, than anyone before him.

PART 2

From Reclusion to Involvement

• • •

"Moshe, you have indulged me in a biographical narrative about Isaac Newton's life, but as yet I have not focused entirely on his religion. I'm sure you know that one must know a person's history to know his soul. If you have studied psychology, you are aware of this fact."

"I understand, professor, but I admit to feeling like I did when I was reading whale cetology in <u>Moby Dick</u>."

"Be assured that you will soon hear more of Isaac's theology, including his strong opinions about the most powerfully organized religions in Europe and England. In fact, Isaac publicly opposed King James' mandates to appoint Catholics to college leadership positions. I have already mentioned that Isaac knew more about scripture and its origins than anyone on the planet. Besides opposing Athanasius's Trinity, he was of like mind with John Locke in opposing a theocratic state. ..."

CHAPTER 25 OF THE
PROFESSORS NARRATIVE

Thwarting the Beast ...

• • •

IN MID-FEBRUARY OF 1687, BEFORE Newton had completed *Book III* of **The Principia**, Humphrey Babington paid him an unannounced visit. After Newton invited him in he asked,

"Professor Babington, what brings you to my humble chambers? 'Tis good to see you!"

"Likewise, Professor Newton. To be candid, I've come on university business," said Babington.

"I fear I haven't been involved in university affairs for some time, Humphrey. I've been engaged in scientific matters."

"So I have heard, Isaac; so I've heard."

The two men walked into the parlor and Isaac said, "Professor Babington, I'd like you to meet my amanuensis, Humphrey Newton; Humphrey Newton, Dr. Humphrey Babington."

Humphrey Newton said, "It's a pleasure to meet you, sir."

"My pleasure also, Mr. Newton. Are you two related?"

"Isaac said, "Not that I know of."

Humphrey Newton said, "If you gentlemen don't mind, I must excuse myself. I have some work to catch up on."

Humphrey Newton left the room and Isaac said, "So what type of university business brings you here, Dr. Babington?"

"King James' mandates."

"Ah yes, I've heard about them. Apparently the King is filling vacant fellowships with his Catholic friends. It's bad enough that England's universities are steeped in patronage, but mandating appointments of Catholic fellows is to me an affront to England."

"But now it's being used for more than just fellowships, Isaac. The King is mandating appointments of *Masters* for our universities and exempting them from taking oaths."

"*Masters without oaths*? That is contrary to law. Masters as well as Fellows must take an oath to 'detest and abhor popery.'"

"Not if a royal order is made to dispense with the oath. You of all the men at Cambridge are quite familiar with such a royal dispensation. Am I not correct?"

"Aye, ye speak the truth, but I was not appointed a master of a college. Where are these letters mandates being sent, Humphrey?"

"Well, they started at about the same time that James II was crowned. He began filling fellowships with Roman Catholics in almost all of the universities. Then about three months ago, Edward Spence, a professor at Jesus College, gave a speech satirizing the Catholic Church. The King heard about the speech and forced Spence to recant publicly before the Senate House. Spence's mind has not been the same since. Then to add salt to his wounds, the King issued a mandate to appoint Spence's prosecutor, Joshua Bassett, to be Master of Sydney Sussex College."

"Sydney Sussex? That is one of two bastions of Puritanism in England. It is one of the two foundations of Protestantism."

"Yes, and King James also issued a royal order that Bassett not be given vows to abhor Popery. Furthermore, Bassett has been appointed to the caput, and is now one of four men who control the senate, which governs our colleges."

"Humphrey, this is worse than I had imagined."

"There is more, Isaac. James II has appointed Obadiah Walker as Master of University College, and Samuel Parker as President of

Oxford –both Catholics. When twenty-five fellows at Oxford resisted, the King summarily dismissed all of them. Some administrators still protested against installing Parker, but the rest of them voted him in by a single vote majority. The fellows of Oxford then locked the door of the president's residence. Parker had to break down the door to get in.

"Now these letters mandates have reached Cambridge, Isaac. *Trinity College is being threatened.* You may recall when the King mandated that the Ambassador of the Emperor of Morocco be given a Master of Arts degree without taking the oath of supremacy."

"Yes, but the Moroccan was not a resident, nor even a Christian. This was just an honorary degree, not a legitimate one."

"Well, the King is now extending this authority. He has just given us a mandate to make Father Alban Francis, a Benedictine monk, a Master of Arts at Magdalene College in Cambridge without taking any class work or oaths. You may recall that it was Father Francis who carried the mandate to Sydney Sussex for Joshua Bassett. Father Francis intends to reside in Cambridge and vote on university matters. I will wager my Doctor's Degree that King James has other Catholics in the wings to follow Father Francis."

"Well, if we are to save this university from papal decrees, we must take a stand immediately. James II bears a remarkable resemblance to Louis XIV of France; we can ill afford a suppression of religious freedom in England."

While Isaac & Professor Babington discussed Trinity's fate, Dr. John Peachell, the current Master of Magdalene College and Vice Chancellor of Trinity, pleaded with Chancellor Albemarle to speak to King James about withdrawing his mandate to appoint Father Francis. Albemarle acceded but the King rejected his appeal. Then the university's senate drafted a petition against the mandate; however, Joshua Bassett, the King's appointee to the *caput* vetoed it.

On February 19, 1687 Isaac Newton sent his own letter of protest to the Duke of Albemarle, Chancellor of Trinity College:

Worshipful sir, our university cannot accept a letter mandate from the King to give Father Alban Francis a Master of Arts degree without an oath of supremacy.

University law dictates that the Oath of Supremacy must be given to those who receive degrees. His Majesty needs [to] be advised that appointments to teaching positions at the university require such an oath before any appointment. No man need suffer for neglect of it.[206]

Despite Newton's differences with the Church of England, he used Anglican law against the King –especially the one requiring oaths—all the while keeping within his own breast the fact that he too had circumvented church law in the past. For the first time in his life, Isaac Newton placed himself in the forefront of a political movement.[207] In fact, due to Isaac's urgings, on February 22, "unsolicited opinions" were sent to Vice Chancellor Peachell that "it would be illegal and unsafe to admit Father Francis without oaths."[208]

Meanwhile Father Francis had been traveling between Cambridge and London listening to the most recent news and reporting it to the king. After two days of "unsolicited opinions" the king again sent his mandate to Cambridge with an accompanying statement that if the senate refused to accept it, "they would refuse *at their peril.*"[209]

Upon seeing the king's words, Master John Peachell was beside himself. He wrote to Samuel Pepys, one of the king's advisors, that he was suffering the displeasure of the king after giving him nothing but loyalty during his reign. Many fellows from Trinity also felt the wrath of the king and sympathized with Peachell. They felt that to refuse the king's recommendation would be to their own prejudice.[210]

By March 11, Newton had written his last words for **The Principia**, and ironically on the same date, the senate, knowing Isaac's views, designated him and John Billers to again convey to the vice chancellor that it would be "illegal and unsafe" to give Father Francis a Masters Degree without his "oath of submission."[211] In the next two weeks, Isaac openly vented his case to the vice chancellor while others at Trinity remained cautiously silent.[212] But on March 27 Newton deemed it prudent to visit Colsterworth "to attend to some landlord matters" --as well as to escape the charged political climate.

As April rains began, King James became furious. Seeing his letters mandate being ignored, he summoned Peachell and other university representatives to appear on April 21 before the Court of Ecclesiastical Commission. Without Newton's presence, the senate selected him, Dr. Babington and six others to accompany Peachell before the court. When Newton returned to Cambridge approximately one week before the court proceedings, he was surprised to find Babington and Humphrey Newton waiting for him in his apartment.

Humphrey Newton said, "I am glad to see you sire. Dr. Babington has been waiting for you with urgent news."

Dr. Babington said, "Yes, and I am also glad to see you."

Isaac responded, "You have important news?"

"Yes, the king has ordered John Peachell and some representatives from Trinity to appear before the Ecclesiastical Commission on April 21. You and John Billers have again been selected as two of the representatives."

"I expected as much. It's a rare day indeed when a king's mandate is refused. Quite frankly, I am glad I have spoken my piece and that we have the king's ear. The time is long overdue to stand up against the king's attempts to erode our universities one brick at a time.

"Humphrey, ... I'm going to need you to transcribe some legal documents. We haven't much time before this hearing.

"Dr. Babington, let's see if we can nip this weed before it overtakes our garden."

For four days Newton devoted his best efforts in preparing arguments to defend against the king's chief justice and successfully thwart the king's mandates. On April 18 the representatives met with Vice Chancellor Peachell in one of Trinity's board rooms to discuss the case. After opening the meeting, Peachell said:

"Gentlemen, I have received a proposal from the Chancellor of Ely that, with your approval, I will submit to the king. The paper is a compromise; if we agree to admit Father Francis, the King must agree that his appointment will not be a precedent for the future. Is anyone against this compromise? It will preserve our institutions for the future and avoid the wrath of the king for the present."

None of the representatives spoke. Then Newton suddenly stood, turned back and forth two or three times, walked up to a university administrator next to the fireplace and said to him, "This is giving up the question!"

The administrator pointed to the table of delegates and replied, "Why don't you tell them?"

Isaac returned to the table and spoke his mind:

"Gentlemen, if we approve this compromise, the door is open for Rome again to conquer England. Whether the king agrees to it or not, he will not abandon his purpose. Our universities and our country have enjoyed a freedom from Popery for 140 years." By this time Newton had become visibly impassioned. "Do not open our doors to a beast that will usurp this freedom!"

After further deliberation, the representatives agreed to reject the compromise. Seeing strong passion from a man who had previously demonstrated only a passive countenance had shocked and riveted the other delegates. Newton, and Newton alone, had convinced them to change their minds. From that time on, the fellows at Trinity desisted from scratching out Newton's diagrams on Trinity's walkways.

None of the men in that board room had seen this side of Isaac Newton. They probably didn't know Newton's "raison de etre," nor that Roman Catholicism was his "beta noire."[213] Newton's entire life was centered on religion, not science; and his beast was the church which had willfully perverted Isaac's cherished scriptures. Newton, a master of scripture, selected the "Book of Solomon" to support him:

> *The wicked flee when no man pursueth, but the righteous are bold as a lion.*

Quite frankly, Isaac had little to lose. Since he had eschewed ordination, no higher office was available to him. He could oppose the king without fear of reprisal, and fortunately –up to this point—*King James II had no idea who Isaac Newton was* nor had he an inkling of the intelligence and fortitude of the man spearheading the movement against him.

On April 21 the Cambridge delegates appeared before thirty-eight year old Chief Justice Lord George Jeffreys. A large throng had gathered, primarily to see Jeffreys, whom Charles II had once characterized as having "..no sense, no learning, no manners, and more impudence than ten carted street walkers."[214] Without a doubt, Jeffreys was ruthless, coarse and intimidating. After Monmouth's rebellion, he was known to have taken bribes and sold people into slavery. He had also withdrawn from Trinity in 1663 without a degree.

The first item on Jeffreys' agenda after calling the commission to order was to cross-examine Peachell:

"Are you a subject of the King?"

"Yes."

"Are you an obedient subject?"

"Yes."

"Were you not appointed by the King of England to your present high position?"

"I was appointed by the university upon the King's recommendation."

"Does our King have the province under the law to command universities to appoint Fellows and Masters?"

"Yes …under the law."

"…Then why have you not obeyed the King's command?"

"Your Lordship, May I take a short recess before answering, both for our safety and your lordship's honor?"

"Why yes, Mr. Vice Chancellor, for your own safety, my lords are willing that you should take all the care you can; but for what concerns our *honour*, do not trouble yourself. We are able to consult that without any interpretations of yours."[215]

The day ended with little progress being made by either side. The commission convened again on April 27, and John Peachell read Newton's statutory objections as an answer to Jeffrey's last question as to why he hadn't obeyed the king's command:

> *...All Masters should be proficient in their major study.*
> *The Senate must first approve all appointments made by the Crown before said appointments are granted...*

Jeffreys interrupted, "You have not mentioned that the King can divest you of your office without senate approval. Are you aware of that, sir?"

"Yes," answered Peachell.

"Is that what you wish, Dr. Peachell?"

"No, your honor."

"Well, it appears to me that you and your delegation seem to wish it."

Humphrey Babington rose to speak, but Jeffreys barked, "When you are vice chancellor, you may be allowed to speak!"[216]

Newton started to stand up, thought better of it and wrote in his notes:

> *A mixture of Papists and Protestants can neither subsist happily nor long together...*
> *'tis not their preferments but their religion which men of conscience are concerned for.* [217]

The Ecclesistical Commission continued to meet. Finally on May 9 Jeffreys opened the meeting and stated, "Dr. John Peachell, please rise."

After Peachell arose, Jeffreys continued, "Dr. Peachell, you are hereby discharged as Vice Chancellor of Trinity University and as Master of Magdalene College. ...You may be seated.

"Members of the Trinity delegation, you are to report to the Commission on May 12 to hear my decision regarding your positions."

The representatives from Trinity agonized over their fate for four days. On May 12, they appeared before Chief Justice Jeffreys, who addressed them:

"Gentlemen, you cannot be but sensible –as must the world— to how pernicious and obstinate your university has shown itself in refusing the King's commands, which ought to be obeyed. Though your guilt is not as great as Dr. Peachell's, my lords understand well the sly insinuations in the papers he has submitted to this court. I can only advise you that in the future, your best course will be a *ready obedience*. Therefore I shall say to you what scripture says, 'Go your way and sin no more,' lest a worse thing come unto you." [218]

Jeffreys closed the hearing, and Trinity's representatives were summarily dismissed. Although Newton knew whom he was up against, the King and his cohorts didn't really know who was leading the opposition, even though Isaac was at the Ecclesiastical Commission hearing. Although the King had discharged Peachell, he did not succeed in granting Father Francis a Masters Degree --primarily because of Isaac Newton's zeal.

Isaac returned to Trinity and resumed his low profile. His correspondence at that time, except to wayward tenants, is unknown. It is known that in September he took on his third student, Robert Sacheverell, whom Isaac had carefully selected with more than tutelage in mind. Sacheverell was the son of William Sacheverell, a member of

Parliament who had led the movement to prevent James II from assuming the throne. Newton also rekindled his close relationship with Charles Montague, who was a rising political figure known to be opposed to King James II.[219] In fact, Montague had co-written a burlesque "The City Mouse and the Country Mouse" based on Dryden's "The Hind and the Panther." The play was a phenomenal success, and Montague had become a very wealthy man. Although Newton had to maintain a low profile after the Ecclesiastical Commission, he nonetheless began associating with men who, like Montague, were planning a revolution against the king.

By the end of 1687, as the people of England abided arbitrary rule by King James II, they anxiously awaited a succession by one of his two Protestant daughters, namely Mary, the wife of Prince William of Holland. It became a vain hope, because in six months, James II's second wife bore a son, James Francis Edward Stuart III. Upon the birth of a Catholic successor to the throne of England, James II ordered celebrations throughout the kingdom.

But James II's strategy to return England to Catholicism had reached its high water mark. Formidable and able adversaries were now organized against him. King James had unknowingly confided with one of them, his daughter Mary's husband, William III of the Netherlands, better known as William of Orange. William III and Isaac Newton were both encouraging James' opponents. In fact William III, grandson of the ill-fated Charles I, had been planning an invasion of England since April of 1688 and had sent Parliament the following message:

I will come and rescue the nation if invited.

Since the birth of James III virtually guaranteed a Catholic successor to the throne, the Bishop of London and six of his peers met William III in Holland on June 30, 1688. They invited him on behalf of Parliament to rescue England. Although the revolution had begun, most people knew that it had started when one man, a reclusive professor of mathematics at Trinity College displayed the courage to stand up against King James' mandates and his cronies.

In September of 1688, James II learned that an amphibious invasion from Holland was on its way, and Parliament was turning a deaf ear to it. He immediately issued a royal decree stating that he would do nothing "inimical" to the Church of England. In October he restored Peachell to his mastership and allowed Sydney Sussex to dismiss Joshua Bassett as Master of the College. He then dropped his mandate to grant a Masters degree to Father Alban Francis, even though the order had already been disobeyed for over a year.

Unfortunately for James II, the fence-mending came too late. On November 3, the first of William's 600 ships passed by an enthusiastic crowd gathered atop the white cliffs of Dover. The banner of the flagship displayed the words "Religione of Libiertate –Je Maintiendrae,"[220] meaning, "I will preserve freedom of religion." By mid-December his troops were approaching London without meeting resistance.

On December 24, 1688 King James II fled London by yacht and landed in Calais, France on Christmas Day. The King's wife, Mary of Modena, had previously fled England disguised as a laundress on December 10. Louis XIV of France, the Huguenot suppressor, gave them his palace at St. Germaine En-Laye, where they resided until they died. In 1690 James II attempted with French troops to lead an Irish revolt against William, but was soundly defeated at the Battle of the Boyne. It would be up to James Francis Edward Stuart III, eventually known as The Old Pretender, to regain the throne of England for the Stuarts.

Although James II and his wife had escaped to France, his Chief Justice, Lord Jeffreys, didn't fare as well. Disguised as a sailor, he stowed away on a ship that was waiting for a favorable wind to sail for France. It was a long wait, so Jeffreys, a hopeless tippler, slinked ashore to the Red Cow Tavern for a drink. Unfortunately, a former defendant, whom Jeffreys had mistreated, recognized him. Jeffreys was arrested and imprisoned in the Tower of London where he died of alcoholism within four months. He was laid to rest at the Tower next to Monmouth and his followers, whom Jeffreys had sent to the gallows by the score.[221]

William of Orange entered London the same day that James II landed in France. Isaac Newton had much cause to celebrate on his forty-sixth birthday. It was almost as if the spirit of Oliver Cromwell had returned with his Parliamentary Army to rescue England from another despotic Stuart king. But it would only have been Cromwell's *spirit* which returned. His body had been carved to pieces by Charles II.

CHAPTER 26

A Man of the World

• • •

"By January of 1689 almost all of England knew the name 'Isaac Newton,' and not just as the author of **The Principia;** Isaac had also become famous for opposing King James and the Ecclesiastical Commission. At the onset of 1689 the university nominated Newton and two other Fellows for Cambridge's two seats in the new National Convention. In a close election Newton and Robert Sawyer were winners and Newton immediately set out for London. On January 17 all three of Cambridge's nominees dined with none other than William of Orange, whom they all agreed was much more intelligent than James II.[222] Newton's friend, Charles Montague, who had also been elected to the convention, attended the dinner with Isaac. ...

The year 1689 and the advent of a new government introduced a new Newton; he seemed to change from a cocoon into a butterfly over night. After gaining a modicum of fame, Isaac commissioned England's leading artist, Sir Godfrey Kneller, to paint his portrait. But what was even more astonishing is the fact that Isaac Newton, a man who had hardly published anything before **The Principia,** released a pamphlet: "The Cambridge Case for Refusing to Admit Alban Francis, a Benedictine Monk, to the degree of Master of Arts, without taking Oaths." Isaac had obviously compiled a detailed record of the hearings and the documents relating thereto.[223] And he also wanted the world to know his aversion to James II and Catholicism.

On January 22, an atypical Newton settled in with Charles Montague and other convention delegates to enact new laws for a new government. The convention was divided on a bill stating that the Crown was vacant due to James' "abdication." Then a blacklist was distributed showing the names of 150 delegates who opposed the "abdication" bill. After that distribution, the bill passed; Newton and his friend Montague had voted for it, of course. William and Mary were then elected and proclaimed monarchs on February 15.[224] After the proclamation, Newton, resplendent in his professorial robe, participated in the grand procession through London. Two months later, the official coronation took place.

Soon the convention passed a Bill of Rights and laws to protect Englishmen and Parliament from abuses by the throne, such as levying taxes, raising an army, or making laws without the approval of Parliament. A bill also passed to exclude Catholics from the throne. The convention then voted to convert itself into England's Parliament.[225] At this time, Charles Montague and other friends of King William were considering Newton for a royal patronage office. A provost position was suggested, but King William was constrained from using "letters mandate" due to Parliament's new laws restricting methods that were used by King James II. Nevertheless, Parliament did grant Newton an appointment as tax commissioner, a position awarded only to leading citizens.

By May of 1689, Isaac was exhibiting a new personality; he was not the isolated hermit of the past twenty-three years. He even associated with people of prominence such as the Duke of Lauderdale, the Earl of Westmoreland, Francis North, Thomas Tenison (the future Archbishop of Canterbury), and the bishops of Ely and Lincoln.[226] In June of 1689, Christiaan Huygens of the Netherlands visited Isaac, and then John Locke, who had left the Netherlands to return home after the Glorious Revolution. Newton eagerly met with these two icons of the Enlightenment. On June 12 he was also introduced to a twenty-five year old brilliant Swiss mathematician by the name of Nicolas Fatio de Dullier, with whom Isaac seemed to demonstrate an immediate bonding.[227]

While Newton was in Parliament, he represented his university well, always keeping Trinity's vice chancellor John Covel advised. A new oath of allegiance was now an important issue facing the universities, especially St. John's College, where churchmen, including John Billers, who had sat with Newton against Father Francis, had already sworn allegiance to King James. No one objected to insisting on an oath for first-time oath-takers, but many who had sworn allegiance to King James objected to taking a new vow of allegiance to William III. Newton did not take umbrage with these objectors because his major concern was the oath against Popery, which the objectors had already taken. Therefore, he felt that a bill requiring oaths for only *new preferments* would pass, and in March he assured Covel it would. [228]

But at the end of March, the House of Lords approved a bill requiring oaths from everyone. Isaac promptly wrote to Covel, "They outvoted us yesterday by about 50 votes."[229] Nevertheless, twenty fellows from St. Johns refused to swear allegiance to the new king, and these twenty succeeded in keeping their fellowships until 1717, when only six of them were still alive.[230]

While in Parliament, Newton also drew up proposals to inhibit letters mandate, to give all university libraries a copy of every book published, and to restore the rights of university preachers.[231] Newton's bills failed to reach Parliament's floor; however, some bills on religious issues did get voted on. There were three bills, but only the first one became law:

1. To tolerate worship by dissenters –*except Catholics* and *Those who deny the Trinity*.

Newton was concerned about the second exception in this bill and talked to his friend Charles Montague about it:

"Charles, I know Parliament is naturally concerned about Catholics threatening the sovereignty of the state, but *Arians threaten no one*. The passing of this bill simply proves the contempt that our fellow legislators have toward non-Trinitarians. Parliament obviously considers them the scourge of the earth."

"Isaac, the absence of debate on this part of the bill shows me why you have kept your religion to yourself. The entire country –and Parliament-- obviously is Trinitarian. And if you are *not* one --and I am sure you aren't-- you have been wise to remain silent. Fortunately, the new law applies to 'public worship,' and since there are no Arian churches, you can maintain your personal beliefs. I would go as far as to say that if you simply take Communion at times, you will be safe. You can simply refuse the sacraments of the Anglican Church on your deathbed."[232]

Isaac repied, "I have long abided the Church of England. Fifteen years ago I was prepared to forsake my fellowship –and even my chair and my livelihood-- than be ordained in the Anglican Church as an offspring of *The Beast.*"

During the remainder of Parliament, Newton made no large impressions, but he was undoubtedly a changed man. While in London he developed many friends and received many encomiums for the feats that undoubtedly had vaulted him into Parliament --the Parliament that was the most important in English history. Except for one brief interlude a century hence, no future English King or Queen ever defied Parliament –or even tried. Yet --except for casting votes-- while Newton sat in that august body, the only words Isaac spoke after the *anti-Trinitarian* bill were to an usher: "Please close the window."[233]

Outside of Parliament's chambers, however, Newton socialized with the rich and the famous, the *virtuosi*. Twice he met with Christiaan Huygens at the Royal Society and then visited him on July 9 at Hampton Court. They had much to discuss: light, motion, optics, colors, etc. On July 10, Huygens escorted Newton and John Hampden, a leader in Parliament, to see King William in order to procure a college mastership for Newton. They did not succeed, and Huygens returned to Holland in August. His correspondence with Newton ceased.[234]

Early in 1689, Newton began what is perhaps his closest "soul" relationship, his friendship with John Locke. It's ironic that the Newton of the 1670's had shunned exchanging letters with Gregory, Huygens, Collins and Leibniz; yet, in 1689 he embraced corresponding with John Locke –undoubtedly because of their mutual interests and beliefs. Locke had already read and digested Newton's **Principia** and had published a laudatory critique of it throughout Europe.

But the subjects these two men discussed most were *religion and government*, and Newton confided his religious beliefs to Locke more than he had ever done to anyone. John Locke's revolutionary views on government and religion closely resembled Isaac's. In fact, these views were later embraced by the founding fathers of the United States of America

CHAPTER 27

Birds of a Feather

• • •

"IN 1689 JOHN LOCKE MADE a special effort to meet Isaac Newton at a weekly gathering of philosophers at the salon of Lord Pembroke in London. Newton became familiar with Locke during their joint efforts to oust James II and because of Locke's published praises of **The Principia**. Isaac was eager to meet an Englishman who not only helped to plan the Glorious Revolution, but was also averse to some church practices. In fact, Locke had participated in a failed attempt to oust James II soon after his coronation. ...

In the 1660's, John Locke had been a friend of the Earl of Shaftsbury and had been active in British politics. Unfortunately, in 1679 Shaftsbury became involved in a plot against Charles II and was imprisoned in the Tower of London. Predictably, Charles II suspected that Shaftbury's friends were part of the conspiracy, so Locke fled to the Netherlands, which had become a haven for Protestants.

In 1679, William of Orange welcomed Locke with open arms. William endorsed Locke's ideas regarding basic human rights. Locke also advocated that if any government did not protect these rights, the people had the right to change the government. It may have been this type of reasoning that justified William's Glorious Revolution –especially when the British Parliament and men like Isaac Newton were unhappy with James II. Locke became quite close to Prince William, and when William's wife Mary sailed to England, Locke escorted her.

Naturally, Newton was eager to meet this pillar of human rights, and in September of 1689 Lord Pembroke introduced Isaac to Mr. Locke at Pembroke Hall. After the introduction, Newton asked Locke, "Are you the gentleman who published the review of **The Principia** on the continent?"

Locke replied, "Yes, and you will now find my review in England also, Mr. Newton."

"I am most grateful to you, sir. And as a token of my appreciation, may I give you the most updated version of **The Principia** with my latest corrections and my signature."

After accepting the book, Locke replied, "My sincerest gratitude, Mr. Newton. I will cherish your gift always."

"Now, Mr. Locke…"

"Please use my forename, sir."

"Very well, if you will do likewise. Now, Mr. ..uh.. John, how were you able to write a critique of my book when it is known that you are not schooled in mathematics?"

"I was in Holland and consulted Christiaan Huygens, who assured me of your mathematical accuracy; therefore, I only had to address your excellent discoveries."

"I see. Well, I am nevertheless pleased that you have endorsed it and that you did not have to concern yourself with its mathematics. Quite frankly, **The Principia** is the result of years of study, calculation, determination and hard work."

"I recognized that at once, Isaac."

"Is it true that you are also writing something?"

"Yes, I am writing an "Essay on Human Understanding," and "Two Treatises on Civil Government."

"May I inquire as to their content?"

"Certainly, Isaac. I believe the human mind is born blank until the world is described to it through our five senses until knowledge is acquired. That knowledge is then perfected by reflection, causing us to think and create ideas on space, time, infinity, and so on. I believe science is created because our senses produce ideas that represent reality. I contend that our original state is happiness, which is characterized by reason and tolerance. In this natural state all people are equal and independent and have no right to harm another's life, liberty or possessions."

"And this is undoubtedly in your essay on human understanding."

"Yes, it is. My treatises on civil government begin with the premise that all people are equal, and that we are endowed with certain God-given rights, including life, liberty and property. Our natural state is happiness, and we should remain in that state as equals –equally independent and respectful of each other's happiness and independence. I believe that governments should respect the natural law, and that they should establish checks and balances to assure and protect our natural rights.

"I furthermore contend that if any government violates these rights, it is the right of the governed to change their government. The pursuit of happiness and pleasure –if conducted rationally— leads to cooperation. Eventually, private happiness and the general welfare coincide. My treatise advocates broad religious freedom; but religion, however important to an individual, *is not to be the basis for government*. States are formed when individuals grant others the power to enforce morality, and to execute laws and punishments. But churches are voluntary associations, which aren't based on people relinquishing political power; therefore, churches have no right to prosecute or persecute. They are associations that people have the right to join or leave freely.[235] Ethical Christianity is not compatible with religious dogma that demeans or harms other human beings. I'm essentially saying that governments must have the consent of the governed. Reasonable Christianity is loving God and one's fellow man."

Newton interrupted, "John, it appears you are suggesting that some organized churches do not practice reasonable Christianity?"

"I suppose I am, mainly because of their ex-communications, suppressions and punishments. To me, some churches practice 'unreasonable Christianity'."

"John, you and I have much in common. Will you be here next week? I have some very private research to show you, and I would prefer not to mail it. We can carry on our discourse with more freedom when we meet in person."[236]

The two men met again at Pembroke in a week. Newton spoke first: "John! I am glad to see you."

"And I, you. Last week you mentioned some unknown research. I am eager to see it."

"And I have brought it. Are you familiar with the Council of Nicaea?"

"Yes, in the fourth century. Is that the council that voted to make Jesus God?"

"Aye, the very same. And I have done enough research to prove beyond a shadow of a doubt that scripture was corrupted to make him so."

"Not a scintilla of doubt?"

"None! Here are my findings."

Newton handed Locke a volume of papers starting with quotations by Dionysius and continuing with some of the changes to the scriptures made by Athanasius and his followers establishing Trinitarianism as the foundation of the Christian church. Newton had never shown this evidence to anyone.[237] After briefly perusing the document, Locke looked up and said, "If this work be true, it doth appear the current basis of the Trinity is built on a corruption."

In the fall of 1690, John Locke moved into the home of his close friend, Damaris Masham, wife of Francis Masham of the Oates Highlaver Parish near Harlow in Essex. Newton's letters to Locke at Oates indeed broached subjects he had pursued in isolation for over twenty years.[238] Locke wholly concurred with Newton's findings. The two men were truly of like mind, not just intellectual peers who were gifted with extraordinary wisdom and intelligence. Newton trusted Locke implicitly and vice versa, and rarely had Newton trusted anyone before. Together they seemed to lay a groundwork for reasonable government and theology.

It wasn't long before Locke and Newton gained the attention of the literate world. These two men began to change the thinking of world educators, philosophers, scientists, and civic and religious leaders. They became the leaders of the <u>Enlightenment</u>. Their writings and revelations continued to influence people for centuries. Locke and Newton may have influenced principles which would be found in the laws and constitutions of future nations.[239]

Isaac Newton had now become so bold that he promised to send Locke more material from his notebook on theological studies. On October 28, 1690, he apologized to Locke for taking longer than expected to compose this material.[240] Finally, on November 14, 1690, Isaac sent *"An historical account of two notable corruptions of Scripture, in a Letter to a Friend."*[241] The two corruptions, *1 John 5:7* and *1 Timothy 3:16*, were of course the most serious according to Isaac. *John 1* has the passage that states Christ is equated with God. Newton wrote that *1 John 5:7* made sense without the disputed passage but no sense with it: "Before the corruption, three bore record in heaven: the Father, the Word and the Holy Ghost, and *these three* are one. However Athanasius inserted *the Son* in place of *the Word*."

Later in November of 1690, Isaac sent a third letter to Locke citing twenty-six additional passages that had been corrupted in order to bolster the concept of the Trinity. At the conclusion of this letter Newton wrote:

> *...and to the shame of Christians, ye Catholicks are here found much more guilty of these corruptions then the Hereticks... . The Catholicks ever made ye corruptions (so far as I can yet find) & then to justify & propagate them, exclaimed [railed] against the Hereticks & old Interpreters, as if the ancient genuine readings and translations had been corrupted.*[242]

Newton continued in his third letter to Locke:

> *In disputable places [of the **Bible**] I love to take up wth what I can best understand. Tis the temper of the hot and superstitious part of mankind to like best what they understand least. Such men may use the Apostle John as they please; but I have that honour for him as to believe he wrote good sense, & therefore take that sense to be his wch is the best: especially since I am defended in it by so great authority.*[243]

The "new" Isaac Newton had now become so bold that at the end of his November letter he asked Locke to forward his treatise on corruptions of scripture to one of Locke's friends in the Netherlands to be published anonymously in French. The two men continued to correspond, not only on the Trinity, but also on prophecies and miracles. In January of 1691, Newton stayed an entire week with Locke at Oates. However, one year after this visit Newton thought better of publishing his ...*Two Notable Corruptions of Scripture* and asked Locke to stop the publication. It was a good decision, because the publisher had found out who the author was. Fifty years later, the manuscript was found in the Remonstrants Library in Amsterdam *with Newton's name on it.* Had the manuscript been published in 1692, Newton would undoubtedly have been ostracized from Cambridge and society.[244]

In May 1692 Locke visited Newton in Cambridge. Again the conversation turned to religion. Isaac said to John, "I'd like to know more about your thoughts concerning religion, John. I fear that we have fairly exhausted discussing my religious views, and I would truly desire to know your thoughts on the subject."

"Since you have inquired, I should be pleased to tell you that my thoughts center about the mutual toleration of Christians in their different professions of religion. I answer you truly that I esteem toleration as the mark of the true church. Whatever people boast about the antiquity of places and names, the pomp of their outward worship, the flaunting of others of their discipline and all of the orthodoxy of their faith, ... these things are marks of men striving for power over one another than of exemplifying Christ. Verily, I believe if one is destitute of charity, meekness and goodwill toward all mankind ---even to non Christians— he falls short of being a true Christian himself.

"Allow me to elaborate. I believe that a church is a voluntary society which one should be allowed to leave if it is not helping with his salvation. To me, the business of a true religion is not striving for power or empire; the role of a church is to guide its members in their war against their own vices and other superfluities of life. To me, a church exemplifies holiness, not violence or persecution. The pretense of religion should not be a cloak for covetousness, plunder, ambition, or harm to others.

"To force someone to believe in something he doesn't believe in is absurd and an offense to God. And if a religion makes slaves of men's minds to convince their followers to destroy life, health, liberty or property, I think it should be banned or reformed.

"Nevertheless, I don't believe in a civil power interrupting a religious ceremony of free men, *unless* that ceremony violates civil life and civil law, such as killing or sacrificing human beings or plundering their property. These acts place the security of nations and people in jeopardy. The state must harbor no prejudice nor allow injury to any law-abiding man. The laws of toleration must guarantee a civil peace, and the state must regulate that peace."[245]

Newton asked, "What about atheism? An atheist may condone peace and may not violate any civil laws?"

"Isaac, I think that atheism is a danger to the civil order. The taking away of God dissolves everything. To not recognize nor appreciate the perfect arrangement of our universe and its natural laws is to believe in a void. It ignores creation and life itself, which man cannot create. Although I advocate tolerance of religious beliefs, I do not tolerate or condone atheism nor any religion that disrespects life. If one can be so ignorant to deny that *something* created our universe, he is to be pitied, but allowed to keep his natural rights to believe or not believe whatever he wishes. Nevertheless, he should not *publicly* worship emptiness, nor should he be permitted to remove or recommend removal of a trust in God by man or nation.

"Isaac, since you have asked for my personal thoughts, I have some opinions about certain organized religions. When I see men persecute members of their own flock with fire and sword for sinning; when I see them express their love and desire of salvation by inflicting torments and cruelty in the name of charity and love; when I see men deprived of their estates, maimed with corporal punishments, starved in prisons, and even killed, I say if all of this be done merely to make men convert to a religion and thus procure their salvation, why then do they allow whoredom, fraud, incest, rape, malice, deceit, hypocrisy and other like enormities to predominate so much and abound amongst them and their flock. These and such like things are certainly contrary to the glory of God, to the purity of the church, and to the salvation of souls.

"Why then does this burning zeal for God, for the church and for the salvation of souls gloss over moral vice and wickedness without even a chastisement?[246] Individual responsibility is paramount in my philosophy. Individual conscience is a conscience built upon reason and education –and I must add 'virtue,' Isaac, because education without virtue can make one a clever devil. The legitimacy of any civil government is based on trust and confidence. If a civil government violates that trust, the people have a right to rise up against that government."[247]

Although Newton and Locke did discuss some alchemy, especially after Robert Boyle's death in 1691, religion, government and natural philosophy dominated their correspondence. The two men gleaned much from each other. After reading Locke's essays, Newton placed Locke above all other "Master Builders of the Age."[248] Isaac Newton also supported Locke's ideals by relating the laws of the universe to the laws of governments and societies. Both men believed that reason needed to be applied to government, religion and society, especially after so many new truths had been recently revealed to the world.

In four more years Locke published his essay *The Reasonableness of Christianity* with the following words that Newton undoubtedly agreed with:

"Reason is the candle of the Lord in men's minds, …gullibility is not piety. Accepting a book on blind faith, without even knowing the author, is profound superstition. How can it honor God to say that faith overrides reason? Is not reason also God-given? Faith convinces us of nothing if it is in direct contradiction with knowledge.

"Yet in some things knowledge is yet unattained; for example, what is 'heaven' or 'immortality of the soul' –or for that matter, 'immortality.' Opinions on matters like these are based on one's faith or beliefs. No one should object to revealed truth; however, if one must decide whether something is a divine revelation or not, reason must prevail. Religion must not be discarded but purified of irrational elements and placed on a rational foundation. Nothing should be more intrinsically rational as religion."

History eventually labeled Newton and Locke's era *The Age of Reason* with good cause; they were truly enlightening the world.

In this last decade of the 17th century, Newton was also developing friendships with gentlemen of considerable intellectual ability, who had similar theological leanings.

CHAPTER 28

A Flood of Followers

• • •

"AT ABOUT THE SAME TIME John Locke and Isaac Newton became friends, another natural philosopher and future disciple of Newton's appeared on the scene. Christiaan Huygens introduced Isaac to Nicholas Fatio de Duillier, a twenty-five year old Swiss mathematician who had very impressive credentials; in fact, he was elected into the Royal Society on his first application.[249] ...

Before he met Newton, De Duillier had traveled throughout Europe and had established ties with Huygens in Holland, Leibniz in Germany, de l' Hopital and Cassini in France, and Bernouilli in Switzerland. Fatio was proficient in Greek, Latin, Philosophy, Mathematics, Theology and Astronomy. He achieved fame at age 22 when he informed Prince William of Orange of a French plot to kidnap him. Prince William accordingly rewarded Fatio handsomely with a professorship, a house in The Hague, and a yearly stipend of 1200 florins.[250] De Duillier however, fearful of French retaliation, asked to be sent to London in 1687 until "the Prince of Orange was in full power of these Kingdoms."[251]

Fatio was proposed and elected to the Royal Society on June 22, 1687, but did not attend a meeting for a year. He met Newton on June 12, 1689 at a Royal Society meeting where Huygens was giving a discourse on light and gravity.[252]

As with Locke, Newton shared some private information with de Duillier, and was so impressed with Fatio that he actually resided with him at times. According to de Duillier, Newton was "the greatest mathematician ever to have lived, and the most worthy gentleman he had ever met."[253] Fatio became a "Newtonian" and soon abandoned his Cartesian beliefs.

Though twenty-two years younger than Newton, Fatio saw himself as an image of Isaac Newton; in fact, some of the Royal Society members called Fatio "an ape of Newton."[254] In 1690 he wrote "The True Physical Cause of Gravity" and asked Newton, Halley and Huygens to sign a copy of his treatise. Newton later advised the youthful upstart that his signature did not mean that he approved the content.[255]

It appeared as though de Duillier may have sought to gain favor in the scientific community by a close association with Newton. In a letter to Huygens, Fatio wrote, "I know of no one who so well and thoroughly understands a good part of **The Principia** as I do."[256] The statement seemed to be an indirect derogation of Halley. Huygens wrote in the margin of the letter, "Happy Newton."[257] Fatio also wanted to edit the second edition of **The Principia** in order to correct some matters he had mentioned to Isaac. He had written to Newton that his edition "would be easier to read and comprehend."[258] It became obvious to Huygens and Newton that Fatio had quite an ego.[259]

On January 27, 1690, Parliament was prorogued, and in one week Newton returned to Cambridge. On February 26, Fatio read his hypothesis on gravity to The Royal Society. Robert Hooke described it as "Not sufficient" in his diary, and later described Fatio as "the perpetual motion man."[260] De Duillier was so active, he even tried to procure a government position for Isaac. At the end of February, de Duillier wrote to Newton, "I did see Mr. Lock above a week ago, and I desired him that he should speak earnest of you to my Lord Monmouth [about a position]. He promised me he would do it. Mr. John Hampden and I are planning to visit you soon in Cambridge."[261]

Newton responded, "It is unnecessary for you and Mr. Hampden to come to Cambridge. I am planning to come to London in a week or so."

Fatio then wrote, "I expect any day to receive a copy of "The Treatise of Light" that Huygens wishes to give to you. I will keep it until you ask for it. It being writ in French, you may perhaps choose rather to read it here with me."[262]

Newton left Cambridge on March 10 and spent one month at Fatio de Duillier's apartment in London, where he read Huygen's "Treatise on Light." At the same time, Fatio labored at revising "Proposition XXXVII, Book II" of Newton's **The Principia** and procuring a government position for his idol, an objective he had mentioned in his February 24 letter. Unfortunately, Hampden had grown out of favor with the king, so another connection was needed. Hampden, Fatio and Huygens had seen the king in July of 1689, but were unsuccessful in obtaining a provost position for Newton.

In June of 1690, Fatio returned to the Netherlands to spend some time with Huygens in The Hague. After returning to England in September of 1691, he and Newton visited each other on many occasions until February 14, 1693. Always in perpetual motion, de Duillier continued to correspond with Huygens and Leibniz, who learned much about Newton's mathematics, gravity and light from Fatio's letters. During his many visits with de Duillier, Newton taught him much about theology and alchemy –almost all of which were digested and adopted by Fatio, though he had little interest in them before meeting Isaac Newton. [263]

Because de Duillier was a foreigner with few connections in England, he was now relying on John Locke to help secure a government position for Newton, who was quite receptive to obtaining such a position. Trinity College had not been faring well financially and had paid no dividends in 1688, 1689 and 1690.[264] Isaac had heard from Henry Starkey that positions in the Mint "were very good places, and that the incumbents make them as good as they please themselves."[265] Apparently Fatio's entreaty for Locke to contact Lord Monmouth encouraged Isaac to write to Locke, "I am extremely much obliged to my Ld and Lady Monmouth for their kind remembrance of me."[266]

From September 1691 through 1692, Newton received many self-absorbed letters from de Duillier. For example, in November of 1691, Fatio wrote:

> *I have Sir almost no hopes of seeing you again. I have caught a cold coming from Cambridge that spread to my lungs and caused some kind of rupture in the 'upper left lobe'. Thanks to you my soul is quiet, but my head [has] something out of order and the powders [medicine] have proved insignificant. If I am to die, would you accept my eldest brother into your care?*
>
> *Your most affectionate and faithful friend to serve you,*
>
> *Fatio* [267]

Newton responded quickly with more pathos than he had ever before expressed:[268],

"My Dear Friend, please obtain a physician before it is too late. I will provide money if you need it. I will be glad to make acquaintance with your brother, but it would be to your brother's advantage if you were to bring it about."[269]

On November 22, Fatio wrote that the crisis had passed, *and described in detail every aspect of his malady.* Newton now realized that his genius friend was not only egotistical, but hypochondrial. (Fatio actually lived sixty-one more years!) Nevertheless, his cold had persisted and he decided to go to Switzerland. Newton sent him a letter that a change of air might be good for him.

In truth, de Duillier had a second reason for traveling to Switzerland. His mother had died and left him an inheritance. While in Switzerland he wrote asking if Newton wanted him to return to England, and in the same letter, did some Biblical interpreting. He equated metaphorically the *Serpent of Eden* with the Roman Empire, *Adam* with the clergy, and much about "The Prophecies." Newton replied, "Please be cautious about indulging in too much fancy in some things, but there is much in what you say about *The Prophecies*." [270]

Correspondence between Newton and de Duillier continued during the first half of 1692. They discussed living near each other and with Locke at Oates. They wrote on alchemy –specifically the effects of mercury on gold –a subject Isaac had already exhausted. Fatio remarked in May of 1692 that his health had returned due to a "secret remedy," which he wished to market after getting a physician's degree. He disingenuously hinted that Newton could be a partner, but 100 to 150 Pounds would be required. Newton visited Fatio two times in May and June, but was not enamored with the remedy. Fatio soon abandoned his commercial "dream," and correspondence from Isaac soon discontinued. In September of 1694 Fatio told Huygens that he hadn't heard from Newton for seven months.

Some historians have mentioned a possible sexual relationship between these two men, even though Newton had taken vows of chastity. Although few people really knew Newton, most considered him dispassionate and celibate. On the other hand, Fatio seemed rather effeminate.

More Newton admirers sought him out in the 1690's. When Robert Boyle died in 1691, he bequeathed money to Trinity College to fund eight lectures per year "to prove Christianity above all other notorious infidels." [271] Richard Bentley, a twenty-eight year old Trinity Fellow, was selected to give "The Boyle Lectures" in London's most prestigious churches. Historian Trevelyan considered Bentley to be second in intelligence at Trinity only to Newton.

Bentley had already consulted Newton in order to better understand **The Principia**, and was now communicating frequently with him in preparation for the Boyle lectures. Isaac titled Bentley's sermons "A Confutation of Atheism."[272] In Bentley's sermon of October 1691, he stated that a Divine Providence exists "as proved by the evidence of design in the universal laws revealed by Isaac Newton in **The Principia**."[273] Bentley consistently inserted Newton's beliefs in the Boyle Sermons: "**The Principia** proved God's existence and immutability –an absolute confutation of atheism by natural law."[274] According to Bentley, Newton believed that an intelligent agent had framed the universe.

Isaac Newton loved the Boyle Sermons and attended almost all of them, as did many of his followers. The lectures drew crowds that surpassed all expectations, and Newton was pleased that so many people listened to the doctrines that he espoused about the existence of God and the infiniteness of the universe. *If God hadn't aligned the planets they would all gravitate toward a center and form a single spherical mass.*[275] Of course, Newton had another argument regarding the church's definition of the Deity, but decided to discreetly "let it sleep until the principles on which it is grounded be better received."[276]

In 1690, David Gregory, another great mathematician came to live in London. Gregory had been lecturing on **The Principia** in Edinburgh and had drawn the ire of civil and religious leaders in Scotland. Gregory had written many flattering but sincere letters to Isaac Newton, who knew the mathematician as a professor as well as a lecturer on "infinite series" and **The Principia**. The two men soon became good friends.

In 1691 Edward Bernard resigned as Savillian Professor of Astronomy at Oxford, and Newton recommended Gregory for the position. Gregory's major competition for Bernard's chair happened to be Edmund Halley, who was endorsed by The Royal Society. Newton had committed to Gregory prior to knowing that Halley wanted the same position.

Interestingly, applicants for chairs at Cambridge and Oxford needed approval from the Church of England, and Richard Bentley, the Boyle lecturer, was assigned to interview all applicants. Halley was an outspoken Deist, and though Newton had cautioned him about public criticisms of religion,[277] he frequently ridiculed orthodox Christianity. Furthermore, Newton had carried on extensive correspondences with

Gregory, Locke, de Duillier, Bentley and others, but had not communicated much with Halley from 1687 to 1695.

In describing Halley's religious views, a story is told of a Scotsman who traveled to London just to meet the man [Halley] who had less religion than Gregory.[278] The fact is that both Halley and Gregory were "Newtonians" and not just Arians. They believed that most organized religions of the world were using corrupted scriptures, and two of these corruptions were the foundations of almost all of Europe's churches.

Quite expectedly, Halley's interview with Bentley was a disaster. As a consequence, the church rejected Halley's nomination, and the Savillian Chair fell to David Gregory –even though Fatio de Duillier boasted that he could have gotten it had he applied.

During the 1690's, Isaac Newton gathered some very talented young men around him. His correspondence with them during the seven years after **The Principia** exceeded everything he wrote in the twenty years before it.[279] Truly, the fame resulting from **The Principia** and his contributions to the "Glorious Revolution" marked a turning point in his life. Now he was actively communicating with a youthful generation of natural philosophers who looked up to him. He was their idol, a man who had discovered, proved and disseminated truth. He had the greatest mind they had ever known.

Before 1690, William Whiston, a Cambridge undergraduate, had listened to Newton's lectures on **The Principia**, but had difficulty understanding them. Therefore in 1690 he decided to master that treatise. In 1694 he sent his manuscript, *New Theory of the Earth*, to Isaac. Whiston reported to some people that the manuscript met with Newton's approval. Whiston also discussed theology with Newton, because he soon became a spokesman for views identical to Newton's –including anti-Trinitarian orthodoxy.[280]

By the end of 1694 Newton had almost as many disciples as Jesus Christ. And by 1704, Newton would be the primary reason that three university chairs were filled with three of them: David Gregory, Edmund Halley, and William Whiston.

CHAPTER 29

Madness

• • •

"In 1693 Isaac Newton displayed some unusual behavior, yet his youthful entourage continued to idolize him. Those who were closest to him noticed some irrational –perhaps even paranoid—conduct. Some of them believed that certain external events may have contributed to this conduct. For example in 1692 Humphrey Babington died, one of Isaac's oldest and dearest friends. Then in August of 1693, Newton's half-sister Hannah requested aid and comfort from Isaac because her husband had died and left her with three children to support. …

Many people thought that Isaac was succumbing to the rigors of being famous. He had been making many public appearances and mentoring many followers. Still others thought that Isaac was heart-broken when Fatio de Duillier departed for Switzerland. It was a wrenching break-up. Although Newton was an avowed celibate, he may have sinned in thought, which to an ingrained Puritan was equivalent to doing the deed. Unlike de Duillier, Isaac eventually recovered. Some people thought Newton was on the verge of a nervous breakdown when a fire in his apartment destroyed many of his most valuable, irreplaceable papers.

Whatever the reason, Isaac began to behave like a man possessed. He sent no answer to Hannah in her hour of need; yet in September, just after her sorrowful appeals, he sent two strange letters to other people; one to Samuel Pepys and one to John Locke. To Pepys he wrote, "I haven't eaten nor slept well for twelve months, nor do I have a consistency of mind. ...I must withdraw from your acquaintance and see neither you nor the rest of my friends any more."[281] On September 16 Isaac sent a letter to Locke "...begging your forgiveness for wishing you dead."[282]

Regarding his mental state, Newton told Mr. Millington of Magdalene College that he had a distemper that "much seized his head and kept him awake," and that he had not slept one hour in fourteen days --"and five days not at all." He even accused his loyal admirers of conspiring against him, and referred to conversations that had never occurred.[283] He was obviously sick in mind and heart.

On October 15, 1693 Locke wrote Newton, "I am more ready to forgive you than you can desire it." He quickly planned a trip to Cambridge, but before he left, Isaac's affliction had passed.

Historians have not come to terms on the exact cause of Newton's mental disturbance, though some wrote that it was the fire that destroyed a considerable amount of his life's work. Many wrote that the malady was caused by mercury and lead poisoning from his alchemical experiments. However, after 30 years of having been exposed to mercury, Newton displayed no symptoms, such as tremors or tooth loss.

Few historians have attributed Newton's behavior to letters that had been circulating for some time among his peers --especially between Leibniz, Gregory, de Duillier, Huygens and John Wallis-- concerning claims of authorship to mathematic formulae that Isaac had previously calculated. Some publications by Leibzig and Gregory, which alluded to their priority on certain discoveries, were very disturbing to Newton, especially some papers by Leibniz on *differential calculus.* Throughout Newton's life he had reacted strongly to anyone claiming priority on something that he had already created or discovered.

A strong argument for Newton's madness was his ultimate failure to achieve the intended purpose of his alchemic experiments: to find the link to life and matter, a basis for natural order –a divine cause. When he found nothing to prove that elemental particles became flesh and bone, that there was no balance between sea and shore or the orbiting planet and the fixed star, he might have lost his God-given confidence.

Furthermore, having solved many of nature's mysteries, for the first time he had found imperfection in his mechanical philosophy.

Exhaustion also may have been a factor in Isaac's mental state; after all, in the early 1690's Isaac had stretched himself to the limit with intellectual excitement. He was under an acute state of tension until the summer of 1693.[284] Whatever the cause, Newton's madness of 1693 definitely affected his creative work, and some thought it would mark the end of it.

CHAPTER 30

Leibniz

• • •

"IN THE FALL OF 1691 Newton composed a defense of his priority over Leibniz regarding calculus. De Duillier had just returned from the Netherlands, and Isaac spent one week with him. Whether or not Fatio had brought information from Holland to spur Newton into defending his priority is unknown. It is also unknown what the two of them discussed; however, before the year ended, Fatio and Newton were writing feverishly about Newton's priority in inventing calculus –and never before had Newton seriously addressed the issue. ...

Newton sent the first salvo in a letter to Gregory in November of 1691 per Gregory's request to publish a general paper on "*Quadratures.*" Gregory said he would disguise the paper as a letter sent to Newton for Newton's editing "since ...I know that ye have such a series long ago." [285] Naturally, Gregory did not reveal that he had deduced binomial expansion from two quadratures that John Craig had copied from Newton's papers.

When Newton responded, he not only spelled out his own earlier discovery of the series, but also mentioned the letter Craig had sent to Gregory about the plagiarism Gregory thought had been carefully secreted. Gregory was so embarrassed he didn't publish his paper for two years, taking great care not to mention Craig and pointing out that Newton had developed the series before he did.[286]

Newton's final letter to Gregory in 1694 gave a complete description of his fluxional method, "De Quadratura Curvarium" ["The

Quadrature of Curves"]. The letter was almost superhuman. First, it discredited Gregory; then it demonstrated Newton's unparalleled intelligence, which was superior to anything mortal that Gregory had ever witnessed. Newton presented rules showing how from any trinomial one could find the simplest binomial of equal area. He then developed the quadrature of polynomials by series expansion.[287] Newton's letter was actually a full-scale disclosure of his fluxional method and affirmed him as the titan of modern analysts.[288]

When Gregory read Newton's letter of masterful mathematics – especially regarding series expansion-- he was awe-struck and wrote a memo stating that Newton "develops that matter astonishingly."[289] Newton's letter was also a masterwork for expertly disposing of Gregory's pretentions to greatness. Leibniz, however, to whom the treatise was really addressed, would be another story.

If priority concerns had caused Newton to suffer a fit of madness in 1693, he had suddenly recovered with a display of genius comparable to what he had exhibited in **The Principia**. But this time he not only demonstrated his unmatched skill in mathematics, he also showed a remarkable expertise in dealing with adversaries.

Although Newton had created his fluxional method in 1665, ten years before Gottfried Leibniz published *Differential Calculus*, in 1677 a feud festered between them over who had invented calculus. At this time Leibniz had already gained fame as a genius among natural philosophers on the continent and in England. In fact, his book **Hypothesis Physica Nova** was the subject of a spirited debate in one of The Royal Society's meetings. Most society members extolled Leibniz's book; however, Robert Hooke characteristically rejected it.[290]

As far back as February 1, 1672, Leibniz had visited The Royal Society to personally demonstrate a calculating machine he had created --although Robert Hooke, without proof of course, claimed he had built a similar but better one. At this same meeting Hooke had also denigrated Newton's reflecting telescope.[291] Of course, in 1672 both Newton and Leibniz were not yet well-known.

After Leibniz's demonstration of his calculator, he applied for membership in The Royal Society before returning to Paris. After arriving in Paris, Leibniz wrote to Secretary Oldenburg about Robert Hooke in a manner resembling something that would come from Isaac Newton's pen. He first assured Oldenburg that he had indeed invented the calculating machine prior to Hooke, but if Hooke had any advice to give, he should impart it. Then Leibniz let his hair down:

"If he [Hooke] does this, I shall praise his good spirit in public; if he does not, he will do something unworthy of his nation, and unworthy of the Royal Society."[292] However, Leibniz did not reveal that his calculating machine was actually an improvement of one developed by Pascal, a fact that Newton would later pounce upon to attack Leibniz's character in a future predictable and notorious dispute over who had invented calculus.

The calculus dispute gestated slowly. Unfortunately, Isaac Newton had never divulged his fluxional method until his letter to Gregory in 1694, even though he had previously corresponded to Leibniz. John Collins, however, did correspond with Leibniz regarding the status of mathematics in England. In these letters he mentioned Newton's name four times, especially in material concerning the squaring of curves and in solving geometrical problems through infinite series.[293] Collins prudently thought it best not to inform Newton about his letters to Leibniz –including the mentioning of Isaac's name.

After writing to Leibniz at least four times, Collins began to have second thoughts about what he had divulged to the German genius. Significantly however, whether intentional or not, Collins had established a written record of priority for some of Newton's mathematical discoveries. Leibniz also communicated Newton's findings to Huygens; consequently, Europe began looking to England as the authority and ultimate word regarding mathematics.[294]

Leibniz's *"annus mirabilis"* came in 1675, and despite centuries of debate that questioned how he had developed calculus, the fact is indisputable that he invented calculus on his own –independently-- but ten years after Isaac Newton did it. Newton wrote to Leibniz in June and again in October of 1676. Both letters were later used in evidence in the priority dispute that eventually occurred at the turn of the century, when Newton had also developed the cunning of a first-class trial lawyer. At that time Newton labeled his 1676 letters *Epistolia Prior* and *Epostolia Posterior*.[295] Unfortunately, Isaac's letters expounded on infinite series and squaring of curves, but avoided all mention of *fluxions* [calculus]. Nevertheless, he informed Leibniz that he had something "of great moment" by stating:

> *From all this it is to be seen how much the limits of analysis are enlarged by such infinite equations; in fact by their help analysis reaches, I might almost say to all problems ..... Yet the result is not altogether universal unless rendered so by certain further methods of developing infinite series... But how to proceed in those cases there is now no time to explain, nor time to report some other things which I have devised.*[296]

Meanwhile, Collins began publishing some of James Gregory's mathematical discoveries in his "Historiola," which alluded to Newton's fluxional treatise, "De Analysi," that Collins had received from Newton in 1669. Newton was convinced that information from the "Historiola," combined with his own letters, were enough to provide a path for Leibniz to follow in order to develop "Calculus." In truth, Leibniz never saw "Historiola" until he visited London in October of 1676, one year after he had independently developed calculus.

In August of 1676, relations between these two giants were still being conducted on a fairly high plane. In Leibniz's letter of August 27 he wrote, "Newton's discoveries are worthy of his genius."[297] However, Leibniz also baited Newton with many questions that revealed his own progress in a vain hope of bringing Newton out of his shell. Leibniz employed this technique later in life by the use of "challenge problems" sent to Newton and others.

In the fall of 1676, when Leibniz visited Collins on his way from Paris to Hanover, Collins told him about Newton's mathematical secret, *fluxions*, and allowed Leibniz access to his vast files. Leibniz spent almost all of his free time copying excerpts from Newton's "De Analysi" and Gregory's "Historiola" regarding the expansion of series. Of note, however, is that Leibniz took no notes –at least none that we know of-- on the calculus located at the end of "De Analysi." Perhaps he had already mastered the subject.[298] Newton never learned that Collins had shown his files to Leibniz until long after Collins had deceased --of course Leibniz's lips were sealed regarding his reading of Collins' files.[299]

Epistolia Posterior reached Leibniz in June of 1677, eight months after Newton had written it. However, instead of revealing his fluxional method, Newton provided only a clue to it in the form of an anagram: *6accdae13eff7:319n404qrr4s8t12vx*. A translation of the cipher is believed to be "given any equation involving any number of fluent quantities, will lead one to find the fluxions, and vice versa."[300] Newton wrote the solution to this anagram in his "Waste Book" and never revealed it to Leibniz nor placed it in his **Principia** eleven years later, when enmity between Newton and Leibniz reached its peak.

Leibniz was pleased to receive *Epistolia Posterior* and immediately began composing a letter to Oldenburg in response, first praising Newton and promising to write to him. However, once Leibniz started writing, he couldn't restrain himself. He filled ten pages with diagrams, calculations and the basis of his differential calculus.[301] On July 12 Leibniz wrote a second letter to Oldenburg asking to be informed of all important developments "not only in geometry, but in other areas likely to appear in the '…Transactions'." [302]

When Oldenburg read Leibniz's second letter he must have thought, "This is a man who must be unhappy with his peers at Hanover. He appears to be a lonely man whose genius is not appreciated. Sadly, he will undoubtedly receive a similar experience in England." [303] Oldenburg responded to Leibniz's letter in August accordingly: "Do not expect a timely reply from Mr. Newton. He is occupied with other matters."[304] What the Royal Society Secretary failed to mention, however, were Newton's most recent words to him: "I hope this [Epistola Posterior] will so far satisfy Mr. Leibniz that it will not be necessary for me to write any more."[305]

If Oldenburg had any intention of changing Newton's mind, he never had the opportunity to do so. The long-time secretary of The Royal Society came down with a severe fever at the end of August and died within a few days. His copies of Leibniz's letters were given to Newton; however, they did not induce Newton to publish his "Fluxions" nor open up a dialogue with Leibniz on the subject. The lack of action by Isaac Newton undoubtedly helped to cause a dispute of world-shaking proportions. Nevertheless, Leibniz had to bear much responsibility. He made a decision not to admit having acquired knowledge from Collins of Newton's priority in developing fluxions.

Eventually, when all was finally said and done, more accusations were said by these two men against each other than were true. Nevertheless, rumor and suspicion reigned, and two brilliant mathematical minds became like two poles of a magnet rejecting each other. Only the death of Leibniz finally put an end to the antipathy. Throughout the dispute, however, Newton appeared to have an advantage because of the cadre of disciples who ardently rallied behind him and levied a deluge of bias against Leibniz. Leibniz, unfortunately, was a lonely, uncomely, unappreciated German who was simply not as politically connected as the famous Lucasion Professor from Cambridge.

In the final analysis, undergirding Newton's refusal to publish or discuss his most cherished discoveries lay an ego that, like his intelligence, was unmatched on the planet. Perhaps Newton thought that a mind like his could not be duplicated, and only upon his death should works of his caliber be revealed for posterity. As Halley had written, Newton was closer to God than any mortal –and Newton may have believed him.

Yet, in 1684 Newton had received correspondence from David Gregory, who had inherited the chair of mathematics at the University of Edinburgh from his uncle James. David stated that, depending on John Wallis' progress on a "Treatise of Algebra," he was considering publishing a paper on infinite series as a sequel to his work on geometric measurement. Upon reading David Gregory's comments, Newton would undoubtedly have been unnerved. It is possible that such comments could have contributed to Newton's madness. One could imagine the thoughts that raced through Newton's mind as he rationalized:

"Is it possible that fluxions (calculus) is no longer the property of mine alone? Surely my own friends would not steal my work! Gregory and Wallis have always been on the level with me. Is it possible that they have achieved this level of mathematics on their own? It is unthinkable that these two men could rival my own achievements. Apparently Leibniz is not alone in threatening me mathematically; it appears that John Wallis and David Gregory have joined him."

On December 18, 1691, Fatio de Duillier wrote to Christiaan Huygens:

> *It seems to me from everything that I have been able to see so far, among which I include papers written many years ago, that Mr. Newton is beyond question the first author of the differential calculus and that he knew it as well or better than Mr. Leibniz yet knows it before the latter had even the idea of it, which idea itself came to him, it seems, only on the occasion of what Mr. Newton wrote to him on the subject. Furthermore, I cannot be sufficiently surprised that Mr. Leibniz indicates nothing about this in his "Leipzig Acta," Leibniz's publication on differential calculus.*

In February, Fatio wrote to Huygens again to state that Liebniz had published his "Acta..." *after* Newton's letters "without rendering to Mr. Newton the justice he owed him. ...I cannot prevent myself from feeling very strongly that their difference is like that of a perfected original and a botched and very imperfect copy. ..."[306]

In 1693, John Wallis offered his "Opera" publication to whatever Newton wanted to insert, and after much prodding, persuaded Newton to send the precis' of his "De quadratura," which contained information about Leibniz and some calculations of fluxional equations. The precis' mentioned that in 1676 Newton had already developed fluxional analyses, but he didn't place it in his published papers before 1690.

Huygens sent part of Fatio's letters to Leibniz, but not the remarks concerning Newton's priority. All of Europe, including Leibniz, waited in anticipation for Newton's articles in Wallis' *Opera*. In fact, Leibniz wrote a gracious letter to Newton in March of 1693 seeking philosophical correspondence and praising Newton for his "knowledge of Mathematics and of all nature," and for **The Principia.** At the letter's end Leibniz apologized for his long silence.

Newton didn't respond until October. He also apologized for the delay, but also warned Leibniz of the impending Wallis' *Opera*, in which Leibniz's name would be appearing.[307]

It is little wonder that in 1693 Newton's mind became troubled with priority threats and other problems –not to mention the high levels of mercury that were later discovered in his system. Newton's own letters mentioned symptoms resembling mercurial poisoning: sleeplessness, digestive upset, loss of memory, paranoid delusions, etc.[308]

As we know, Newton recovered in 1694 and began work on perfecting his lunar theory. However, correspondence with Leibniz had ceased.

CHAPTER 31

Moonstruck

• • •

"In the year 1693, another climax occurred in Newton's intellectual activity. It was an attempt to solve the mystery of the moon's orbit, which was a three-planet problem that continued to perplex him. Otherwise, Isaac engaged in no new theories or investigations. He seemed satisfied in perfecting his previous accomplishments. ...

However, mathematically solving the orbiting of a moon in a three-planet grouping continued to elude the Lucasian professor from Cambridge. In fact, he is quoted as stating to John Machin, another of his disciples: "My head never ached but with my studies of the moon."[309] To bring the moon's orbit under some quantitative treatment within the theory of gravitation in **The Principia**, Newton needed observations of the moon from the Royal Observatory and its astronomer, John Flamsteed. Consequently, on September 1, 1694, Newton and David Gregory decided to call on Flamsteed at the Greenwich observatory.

As the two men travelled by coach to visit the Royal Astronomer, Gregory asked Newton, "May I relate to you what information I have about Flamsteed and the Royal Observatory?"

"Certainly," said Isaac.

"In June of 1675 Charles II appointed Flamsteed as Royal Astronomer, and Christopher Wren as the architect for a Royal Observatory. Within two months a cornerstone was laid with the inscription 'Risum Teneatis

Amici,' which, as you know, translates 'May this keep you laughing, my friends'."

"Quite an interesting inscription," said Isaac.

"I agree. It is also interesting that Flamsteed was assigned the responsibility of installing all instruments, even though he was not a man of means. I have heard that he has documented over 20,000 observations of the stars, including perhaps some of the moon."

"I hope he has made some calculations regarding the moon's orbit."

"I'm not sure, but we might want to ask him."

When the carriage arrived, Flamsteed came out to greet his visitors and escort them into the observatory. After a brief tour he asked, "Pray, what has prompted such distinguished gentlemen to visit me?"

Gregory answered, "As you may know, Isaac's **Principia** is inconclusive concerning a mathematical theory for the moon's orbital path. We have come to you for assistance."

Newton added, "If you would be willing to provide me with exact observations of the moon's distances from the earth and the sun at different times and seasons, I might be able to calculate a lunar theory that might also apply to other three-orb systems in the universe."

Flamsteed responded, "I have always admired you, Mr. Newton, and I am honored that you and Mr. Gregory have personally asked me to assist you. I'm also quite pleased that you didn't bring your friend Edmund Halley along with you; I doubt very seriously whether I could do business with an irreligious libertine like him."

Newton asked, "Then you will help us?"

"I will, under the following conditions. Whatever you obtain from the information I send you must be given to me first, before publication. Also you must not give my observations to anyone else. I am writing a catalog of the fixed stars and I do not want information that could appear in my catalog to be released prematurely."

Newton said, "I can accept those terms, John, especially if your observations will be numerous and will be performed expeditiously."

"I will do my best. However, I have some health problems. I also frequently meet with other obligations in addition to my star catalog and my duties as Royal Astronomer."

Gregory stood up, took Flamsteed's hand and said, "Then we have an agreement. Thank you, John."

Newton also arose and shook the Royal Astronomer's hand. Newton and Gregory bade their farewells and were soon in their carriage on the return trip to Cambridge.

Newton said, "David, I wonder what Flamsteed would do if he knew *my* religious preferences?"

"I doubt that he will judge you as harshly. He hates Halley because Halley criticized his 'Table of Tides' ten years ago. Flamsteed and Halley actually had worked together from 1670 to 1676. They had a falling out about a year after Flamsteed was appointed Royal Astronomer over Halley."

"That explains a lot."

"You and Flamsteed have much in common, Isaac. You both have Puritan backgrounds, and you both dislike Robert Hooke; however, I think Flamsteed's major interest is becoming one of your peers. He is much like Robert Hooke in that regard."

Newton said, "I am sure that we will soon discover his level of expertise."

Newton was happy at the outset of his relationship with Flamsteed. The Royal Astronomer promptly mailed many observations of the moon, and with these first observations, more were promised as Newton needed them. In October of 1694, after having examined many observations, Newton wrote: *I believe I could set right the Moon's Theory this winter.*

In December Newton also wrote to a friend:

A little more diligence in making frequent observations this month and another month or two hereafter will signify more towards setting right the Moon's theory then ye scattered observations of many years.[310]

Unfortunately, Flamsteed's agenda was not the same as Newton's. After all, the Royal Astronomer had a star catalog to complete –and reliable observations of the moon depended on its relationship to the fixed stars[311] and not just the sun. Consequently, it wasn't long before Newton became impatient and requested more observations. Flamsteed responded by moralizing –a strategy he employed in almost every letter with statements such as:

I have to visit my church for Christmas. This is my first task. You know me not so well as I hoped. ...My Saviour, his Apostles and the Scriptures permit me to give you a truer character of my selfe. I was never tempted with covetousness. ...I am, I profess, a friend to frugality; sparing my time is precious to me.[312]

In almost every letter Flamsteed denounced Halley, and Newton began to tire of the moralizing and the denunciations. To be perfectly honest, Isaac owed a deep debt of gratitude to Halley for publishing **The Principia,** and Flamsteed was in large measure a contributor to Newton's headaches over the theory of the moon. Forty-two letters were exchanged between Newton and Flamsteed during this period of "working together." And all this time Flamsteed praised only himself, and leaped at every chance to criticize others.[313]

During this time, Halley was also working on a theory of the moon's orbit, and he wrote to Flamsteed in order to obtain some lunar observations. Of course, Flamsteed denied his request, so Halley decided to pay a personal visit to his former rival for the Royal Astronomer's job. After Halley arrived he was subjected to much verbal abuse before being allowed to take a few notes. Afterward, Halley told Newton that he had met with Flamsteed, and Newton expressed the hope that a dialogue had begun between the two adversaries. Unfortunately, Flamsteed remained recalcitrant and never mentioned the Halley meeting.

In the meantime Newton continued to request additional data from the Royal Astronomer, whose plate suddenly seemed to be quite full. In one letter Isaac alluded to some "faulty observations"[314] and Flamsteed predictably responded that most of his observations were "quite accurate." By now Newton had decided that a third body other than the earth and sun was affecting the movement of the moon, and he was quite baffled –so much so that he attempted to induce Flamsteed to send more observations by offering him money. Flamsteed took the offer as an insult --he wanted to be Isaac's peer, not just a paid employee; in fact, he accused Halley as the instigator of the offer and renewed his attacks on Newton's friend.

Thankfully, Halley never entered the fray nor responded to the brutal attacks. Flamsteed, however, had found another opportunity to moralize and to criticize. He was so displeased about Newton offering him money, he wrote a letter to Robert Hooke:

Isaac doesn't know me well.

A few days later he wrote to Newton:

Pray…lay by any prejudicall thoughts of me, which may have crept into you by mailtious suggestions" of a "maliltious false friend." He [Halley] possest the malice and envy of a person from whom I deserved much better things. …All the return I ever expected … is only to have the result of their [your] Studies imparted as freely as I afford them the effect of mine or my paines.[315]

Newton must have bristled at these remarks. At an earlier time he probably would have sent a fiery response and terminated the correspondence.

But Isaac needed the observations from Flamsteed; therefore, on this occasion he tried reconciliation. In a December 20 letter he wrote:

> *What you say about my having a mean opinion of you is a great mistake.*
> *I have defended you when there has been occasion, but never gave way to any insinuations against you. ...Let all this pass.*[316]

However, in February of 1695 Newton warned Flamsteed that only if his observations were published in conjunction with an accomplished lunar theory would Flamsteed be assured of a place in history.

By April of 1695, Newton had almost lost his patience. He became more irritable with Flamsteed's observations and wrote:

> *I have set the moon's theory alone at present, and intend to start over once I obtain better observations. ...I reccon it will prove a work of about three or four months. And when I have done it once, I would have done with it forever.*[317]

The Royal Astronomer, who had desired some measure of fame by being associated with Newton, reacted to Newton's negative comments by relaying some uncomplimentary rumors about Isaac—especially a rumor that he had died. When Isaac heard the rumor it was his turn to be offended. Flamsteed had been sniping at Newton over Isaac's choice of Samuel Newton over Flamsteed's choice for the Savilian chair of Mathematics. Therefore, when Newton received some erroneous calculations of the moon's positions while still stewing over the false rumor about his premature demise, he vented his spleen in a June, 1696 letter to Flamsteed:

> *I want not your calculations but your observations only. Pray send me first your Observations for the year 1692 & I will get them calculated & send you a copy [of my calculations]. But if you like it not, then*

I desire you would propose some other practicable method of supplying me with observations or else let me know plainly that I must be content to lose all the time & pains I have hitherto taken...[318]

Newton's letter was a knife to the heart of Flamsteed, who wanted to be a colleague. But Newton wanted a dependable, productive and obedient observer –a pure and unemotional technician, not a calculating thinker. Flamsteed replied to Isaac by sending a list of his recent observations along with Isaac's letter, which had a note on the back: "I contend it."[319]

Another major reason for a deteriorating relationship between Newton and Flamsteed was that Newton had found the Royal Astronomer incapable of philosophical discourse. For over a year Newton had asked Flamsteed to adjust his observations for atmospheric refraction. To help Flamsteed, Isaac developed a table of refractions and sent it to him. Flamsteed then asked for the foundations which Newton used to compute it. At first Isaac said that the theorem was too intricate to put in a letter, but after Flamsteed insisted, Newton sent him not only the table but "the ground of it."

After giving Flamsteed the complicated formula by which he calculated his refraction table, Newton found that Flamsteed was incapable of mathematically discussing it. Newton then found that Flamsteed hadn't even read Book II of **The Principia** and couldn't even discuss the density of atmosphere at different heights. Later, when Isaac tried to discuss his equation of lunar parallax, Flamsteed could not understand the vectorial analysis on which Newton's lunar theory rested.[320] Newton now realized that Flamsteed was incapable of understanding what he was trying to do --and he let the astronomer know it:

I believe you have a wrong notion of my method in determining the Moons motions. ...the vulgar way of approaching by degrees is bungling & tedious.The method wch I propose is first to get a general notion of the equations to be determined & then by accurate observationsto determin them. [321]

The method used by Newton was foreign to Flamsteed and no doubt contributed to the reason Newton wasn't sending him corrected parameters based upon existing theory. All of this contributed to Flamsteed's suspicions that Newton was violating his promise. After Newton asked Flamsteed to send raw observations without calculations, the entire enterprise became tenuous.

The last straw occurred when Flamsteed heard a story circulating around London by Richard Bentley that the second edition of **The Principia** would not have the lunar theory because Flamsteed was not providing correct observations. When he told Newton what he had heard, Newton sent a furious letter, which all but sealed the fate of his studies of the moon. The letter documented most of the experiences Newton had encountered during his enterprise with Flamsteed and actually admitted that without correct observations he had despaired of the Moon's Theory as something impracticable and had mentioned this to a friend who had called on him.[322]

Upon reading Newton's letter, Flamsteed thought he was now being ostracized. He hurriedly sent more raw data on July 13 followed within a week by a letter totally capitulating to Newton's demands. In the letter Flamsteed asked for no other reward than to see the result of Newton's efforts, and if Isaac thought "not fit to favor me ...I can easily be contented."[323] Newton sent a conciliatory reply offering to help squelch the Bentley rumor and expressing concern for Flamsteed's health. He even sent a headache remedy for the astronomer's migraines *–but nothing else.*

Newton's last letter to Flamsteed was in September of 1695. He told the astronomer that he was leaving on another type of "journey" and had no more time to devote to the theory of the moon. He also told Flamsteed not to wonder about his silence. But the astronomer did wonder, and after a void of four months sent a letter asking Newton if he had come to any "uncontestable principles." The letter's final plea was "Please let me know."[324] Newton did not respond.

For all practical purposes, 1695 was the end of Newton's work on the "Theory of the Moon." In Newton's mind the effort was a failure;

nevertheless, he did define a number of new inequalities, which he drew up in two different forms: "A theory of the Moon" and a scholium that he inserted at the end of the lunar theory in his **Principia**.[325]

Disappointed at what he thought were two wasted years, Newton again turned his attention toward seeking a patronage appointment in government. He obviously discounted any ecclesiastical advancement at Trinity. Any such appointment would involve taking Holy Orders. However, Isaac had another motive for wanting to leave Trinity. The college had been in a financial crisis since 1688, and Newton was quite concerned about his livelihood.[326]

1695 was indeed an eventful year. Isaac's friend, Charles Montague, was elected President of The Royal Society and was also given the responsibility of making new coins for the nation. In November of this year a story began circulating in London that Isaac Newton was to become Master of the British Mint.[327]

CHAPTER 32

A Lifelong Stint at the Mint...

• • •

"The 'journey' Newton mentioned in his letter to John Flamsteed had begun well before September of 1695. During the last weeks of that month, Isaac's whereabouts were never disclosed, but neither Newton nor Halley ever denied that Isaac went to London and met with Charles Montague, the Chancellor of the Exchequer and a member of the Privy Council. Obviously, something was afoot. Not only had Newton forsaken his correspondence with Flamsteed concerning studies of the moon, he had concluded his alchemical experiments. ...

While Isaac was in the middle of changing occupations, Halley told him that a comet which appeared in 1682 had also appeared in 1531 and 1607. With help from Flamsteed's observations, Newton confirmed Halley's discovery. Halley published his findings in The Royal Society's "Transactions." The society named the comet "Halley's Comet" for posterity.

In November of 1695, John Wallis heard a rumor that Newton was to be Master of the Mint. At this time the Whigs were back in power and Charles Montague, Isaac's friend, was in a position to find a government position for him. During the winter, rumors of Isaac taking a post at the Mint became so numerous that on March 14 of 1696 Isaac asked Halley to quell them. But before Halley could act, Isaac received a letter from Montague appointing him Warden of the Mint. Although Warden was a step lower than Master, according to Montague it paid "up to 600 Pounds per year" and demanded "not much business requiring more time than you can spare,"[328] Newton promptly sent his acceptance of the position on March 23. He was eager to depart Trinity and escape its ecclesiastical environment.

There was one other consideration that may have been a factor in Montague's selection of Newton to be Warden of the Mint. The Royal Society, which proudly boasted of having Isaac Newton among its members, had recently selected Charles Montague as its president –with Newton's encouragement. Montague may have been returning the favor.

After having resided at Trinity for three and one-half decades, Newton gathered up his possessions, and before the month's end, permanently vacated the university. In fact, during that March he resided in London most of the time. After having been Trinity's greatest scholar and mathematician, Newton left the religious environment to become a secular man, so secular that he retained his fellowship and his chair –*and their incomes*— without performing any commensurate duties. In fact, he made a complete physical break from his alma mater and did not correspond with anyone at Cambridge for the rest of his life.

Being Warden of the Mint did not turn out to be the sinecure, snug position Montague had portrayed; Isaac's work ethic wouldn't let it. He recognized a definite challenge in his new position. In truth, the Mint was in a mess. Counterfeiting and "clipping" had become rampant. Furthermore, when William of Orange became king in 1689, England had adopted a policy of resisting French and Roman Catholic expansion by placing a large army on the continent and building up Britain's navy. Unfortunately, King William's war placed a financial strain on the British Empire that was greater than any previous war.

Before Charles Montague made Newton the Warden of the Mint, he invited Isaac to visit him at his Office of the Exchequer. After Newton arrived, Montague opened the conversation.

"Isaac, Parliament passed a recoinage act two months ago in order to avoid a devaluation or even bankruptcy. But England has another serious problem. Unscrupulous 'moneyers' are clipping off the edges of our silver and copper coins to make counterfeit coins or sell the clippings. At this time the average weight of silver coins turned in to us for recoinage is only 54% of their original weight. Almost all of the coins now in circulation are old hand-made coins that are either half their legal weight or counterfeited from lead, copper, tin and brass.[329]

"The French solved their clipping problem in 1639 by manufacturing coins with a machine developed by Pierre Blondeau. Their new coins had a firm, ridged edge that virtually eliminated clipping. Unfortunately in England, moneyers' kept this machine out of the country until Charles II ordered its use in 1661. Full-scale production of milled money with Blondeau's edging process began in December of 1662,[330] but the new coins quickly disappeared from circulation because we didn't recall the old ones. Consequently, new coins found their way to goldsmiths who melted them down and sold the metal to Holland or the Far East, where they garnered a better price. I would estimate that since 1672 over two million pounds have been lost in illicit bullion trade.[331] Frankly, why would anyone pay for goods with new coins when the old coins with half the silver would accomplish the same purpose?

"Isaac, the monetary system of England has become ludicrous. Counterfeiters and clippers are melting and coining incessantly. The goldsmiths and coiners are making large profits at public expense, and our country is on the verge of bankruptcy."

Newton said, "John Locke and I believe that a financial collapse would bring about another Stuart restoration. The Jacobites are watching us closely."

"They probably are, Isaac. But I'm hoping the new act will rescue us. Old coins are being recalled and melted down for re-minting. Our new coins are being produced by Blondeau's machines and will have identical weights and precise markings. Holders of hand-made silver coins –including counterfeits— have until the second Saturday in May to turn in their coins for new ones. We have imposed a tax on hearths to pay for the re-coinage. Unfortunately for the poor people, only those who pay a hearth tax or make loans to the government can turn in clipped money at face value."[332]

Fortunately, Montague had selected a perfectionist with a herculean work ethic to be Warden of the Mint. His original intention was to offer Isaac a "plum" because previous wardens allowed salaried assistants to operate the Mint. In fact, Montague did not even expect Newton to resign his chairmanship nor his fellowship at Trinity. Nevertheless, on April 20, 1696, Newton signed Trinity's Exit and Redit Book for the last time.[333] He had a new calling, and Isaac Newton did nothing halfway. As it turned out, Isaac left the ecclesiastical climate none too soon.

750,000 people lived in London, one-tenth of England's population. It was a town full of laborers, beggars, prostitutes and professional criminals. Public hangings were commonplace. Counterfeiting was a treasonous offense, and those convicted of treason were hanged to the point of death, cut down, disemboweled, and then mercifully beheaded and quartered. Hanging was also the penalty for clippers, but they didn't have to endure the gruesome amenities given to those convicted of counterfeiting.

London was also the home of a large middle class of law-abiding respectable citizens and an upper class of wealthy merchants, bankers and politicians. These two classes enjoyed a city where beauty, grace and culture thrived.[334] Beautiful buildings, many designed by Christopher Wren, occupied areas destroyed by the Great Fire. Nearly 60 churches with elegant spires dotted the city's landscape –especially St. Pauls. But the most formidable structure was the Tower of London, built during the reign of William the Conqueror and later refurbished by Christopher Wren.

The London Mint and the warden's residence were housed in the Tower of London. However Newton quickly found that living there was untenable. The noise and smoke from forges operating twenty hours a day, the smell of horse manure, and the noise from soldiers and horses were too much to bear. By August, Isaac purchased a house close to Parliament on Jermyn Street near the St. James Church in Westminster. He also purchased a sedan chair in which he travelled through London's streets dangling his arms out the side widows.

Although the Master and Comptroller of the Mint were in charge of coinage, they had long ago passed their duties to the Warden, who, in turn, delegated the coinage to clerks. But now, because of the "Recoinage Act," Newton recognized the need to strengthen the Warden's authority. Thomas Neale, current Master of the Mint, was tied-up as Groom-Porter to the King and a creator of lotteries --the source for most of his wealth. Therefore, Neale had relinquished his Mint responsibilities to his assistant, Thomas Hall. Hall and his deputies, in turn, were more than happy to turn over the leadership at the Mint to Isaac Newton, whose reputation had preceded him. The expert of the cosmos certainly would be able to untangle problems that had been generated by mere mortals.

On May 2, 1696 Newton took the oath given to every official at the Mint, in which he promised not to reveal the secrets of the "rounding and edging" process. By this time the Mint was already deeply immersed in recoinage and in debt for unpaid wages and new machinery. Working hours had expanded to twenty hours a day in two ten-hour shifts, six days a week; yet, old coins poured in at a rate that swamped the Mint. After the proclamation in January for people to turn in old coins, the Treasury had taken in coins worth over one-third of a million pounds.[335] However, new coins were painfully slow getting into circulation.

To increase production and aid in the distribution of new money, five country branch Mints were established throughout the kingdom. The responsibility of operating these extra Mints was given to Hopton Haynes, a ten-year clerk at the Mint.[336] In a gesture of reciprocity for publishing his **Principia**, Isaac also arranged to appoint Edmund Halley as the deputy comptroller of the Chester Mint.

The Treasury was to stop accepting coins at "nominal value" after the second Saturday in May. So on the day before that deadline, people flooded the Treasury from dawn until midnight with their coins. Armed guards were needed to contain them.

Newton's skill in mathematics, organization and categorizing –not to mention his intelligence and moral upbringing—were gifts that made him a perfect administrator for the demands of the Mint. Recoinage just happened to be another historical occurrence in which Newton played a principle role. The other ones were of course The Glorious Revolution and the Enlightenment.

In fact, the efforts and administration required for recoinage may not have been accomplished by anyone other than Isaac Newton. When he arrived at the Mint, new coins were so scarce that people couldn't carry on their necessary transactions for daily living. The few new coins being issued were being hoarded in expectation of devaluation.[337] The Mint was working at a frenetic pace. Besides its hours of operation, fifty horses turned ten mills operated by 300 men. Nine great presses struck between fifty and fifty-five times per minute, and produced up to 100,000 pounds per week. By the end of the summer of 1696 2,500,000 pounds had been coined primarily due to Newton's careful studies of the Mint's operations, especially the workmen's diligence.[338]

In 1697 production at the Mint was temporarily hampered when Newton and Lord Lucas, the lieutenant governor of the military at the Tower, engaged in a war of words over who had jurisdiction over the Mint. The storm finally subsided and recoinage continued at its previous pace; nevertheless, tension with the military lasted until Newton's death. Newton also took umbrage at many of the financiers of the city. Even though recoinage strained the country's finances, financiers and goldsmiths left no stone unturned in trying to fleece the government. Two respected goldsmiths offered to melt clipped money for 12.5 pence and half a farthing per one pound troy until Newton found that other goldsmiths charged 7.5 pence and half a farthing and still returned a profit of one pence per pound.[339] No one topped Newton's analyses and studies. He seemed more than adept in his role at the Mint.

At the Chester Mint, however, Halley didn't fare as well as Newton. It appears that Halley's clerk, Edward Lewis, was a pawn for the deputy master of the Chester Mint and was committing fraud. After Halley dismissed Lewis, all hell broke loose between the deputy master and Halley. But when the deputy master tried to abscond with all employees' salaries for the last quarter of 1696, Newton entered the fray. Incomprehensibly, Thomas Neale, Master of the Mint, defended the deputy master and opposed Newton in a debate before the lords commissioners. Although Neale was an expert debater, Newton soundly defeated him.

The dispute with the Master was an indication of the discord Newton faced. In 1696 Newton reported that the Warden's salary did not support the authority of his Office.[340] In June of 1697 he said, "The Warden is... by his Office a Magistrate & the only Magistrate set over the Mints to do Justice amongst the members thereof in all things."[341] And again in 1697 Newton said, "The Warden's authority was originally designed to keep the other officers of the Mint in the duty to the king and his people. Nor do I see any remedy more proper and more easy then by restoring the ancient constitution."[342]

Newton never succeeded in remolding the constitution of the Mint, so he tried another approach: he would make himself master *in fact* if not in name. He amassed Mint history and its operations. He collected proclamations and warrants dating back to King Edward IV, and he became an expert like no other on the inner workings of the Mint. He made multiple copies of everything. He relied with confidence on himself alone and advised other officers, "trust not the computation of a single Clerk nor any other eyes then your own."[343]

Now, as Newton occupied himself in a more secular climate, he had less fears about losing his employment because of his religious convictions –especially his discoveries concerning the Trinity. In the confines of his home or within the Tower of London, he was not among religious heretic hunters, even though news of them reached his ears. One incident in the summer of 1697 was very upsetting to Isaac. An eighteen year-old student by the name of Thomas Aikenhead was hanged in Edinburgh for denying the Trinity. As sorry as Newton was for the fate of that youngster, he realized the same fate could be his were his beliefs made public.

By the completion of the recoinage in 1698, Newton was for all practical purposes the Master of the Mint without having the title. Even the Lords Commissioners asked Newton to draw up the final accounts of the country mints, a task normally assigned to Master Thomas Neale. If the truth were known, Neale's records were in horrible shape up to and after his death in 1699.

At the end of recoinage, the Mint and its subsidiaries had recoined 6.8 million pounds from 1696 to the summer of 1698 –almost twice the total coins produced in the previous thirty years.[344] Unfortunately, through no fault of Isaac's, the new silver coins again went into the melting pots of the same goldsmiths who attempted to overcharge the Treasury for legal melting. Not much of the recoined silver remained in circulation.[345]

Perhaps Isaac's biggest claim to fame at the Mint was a job he didn't bargain for. It fell upon the duties of the warden to apprehend and prosecute coiners and clippers. In fact, the warden had been assigned a second clerk because the first one was engaged entirely in the pursuit of criminals.[346] Counterfeiting had taken the place of clipping after the recoinage, and at the outset, Newton wanted no part of catching and prosecuting perpetrators. He felt that the job belonged to the Solicitor General.[347] Newton had already had some bad experiences in prosecuting for men's estates. Because the estates of defendants were normally forfeited to the warden to finance the pursuit of coiners, jurors did not believe the testimony of paid prosecution witnesses. Isaac felt that the vilifying of witnesses was a reflection on him.[348]

However, Newton did not succeed in delegating law enforcement duties to the Solicitor General, so he jumped into them with both feet –as usual. In fact, he devoted an inordinate amount of time and energy to prosecuting coiners and clippers and getting witnesses. He collected most of the evidence and attended all of the trials. He is even credited with the Act of 1697, which made it illegal to make or repair tools for coining.[349]

Isaac was relentless in finding witnesses and pursuing counterfeiters. He collected as many as fifty-eight depositions in only two months.[350] He took depositions in taverns and in prisons. His contacts included beggars, thieves, prostitutes and murderers, many of whom were mentally deranged. Were it not for Christopher Ellis, younger brother of Comptroller Charles Ellis, Isaac could easily have been killed. Ellis had been appointed by the Treasury in the fall of 1696 to help Newton detect and prosecute coiners, clippers, and counterfeiters.

Regardless where Newton's prey fled, with the help of Ellis, Newton found them. He went after the rich and poor, the baron and the peon. None of them possessed Newton's strong moral compass, and, though Isaac himself stayed within the law, his assistants may have bent it to get testimony. Evidence supports the fact that he deferred to a Higher Authority on many questionable legal matters. His instincts served him well in governing his most difficult decisions.[351]

Though he had agents operating in eleven counties, Newton took a personal role in pursuing and prosecuting over one hundred counterfeiters.[352] Coiners had never seen a prosecutor so relentless, and they soon began to despise him. One coiner, Francis Ball, wrote that he would have been out of Newgate had it not been for Newton. Ball told his brother, Samuel, "If ever King James came again I would shoot the Warden." Samuel answered, "God dam my blood so will I ..."[353]

Many criminally-minded officials at the branch mints were also doing their utmost to undermine the great recoinage. For example, Isaac Hayes, the Deputy Comptroller at Exeter, had embezzled 1,100 pounds. Unfortunately, he couldn't be prosecuted because he had sailed to Madagascar at the request of Parliament to negotiate with pirates. Frankly, he was well-suited for this type of company. Hayes died in that foreign land in 1701, and the Treasury had to write off his embezzled money. Even Anthony Redhead, Neale's deputy at the Norwich mint, went to prison because of incorrect accounts.[354] But one coiner, William Chaloner, was a worthy adversary for Isaac Newton, and Isaac devoted much time and effort pursuing him and eventually convicting him of treason.

On March 22, 1699, Edmund Halley visited Newton in London to witness Chaloner's execution. Halley, asked Newton about Chaloner's crimes, and Isaac, though normally a man of few words, answered Halley in detail:

"Edmund, the lords justices had sent William Chaloner to me for questioning in the summer of 1696. I accordingly collected Chaloner's life history before the interrogation. When only a pauper, Chaloner had taken up coining in 1690 and in a short time became a wealthy gentleman. An artist among counterfeiters, he had written a book on a new method of coining. Edmund, I think Chaloner is the most dangerous man I have ever met --probably because he plays both sides on the street of respectability. For example, he would write Jacobite propaganda and then, for a reward of 1,000 pounds, turn in the printers he induced to print it. He actually prided himself on having "funned" the king out of one thousand pounds. He then did the same thing to a bank for 200 pounds. But, Edmund, his deception was not fun for the men Chaloner turned in. They were hanged! Under the guise of respectability, he even gave me one of his associates to help me pursue some coiners. But when I caught these coiners, *they informed on Chaloner* --under duress of course. So then the scoundrel simply arranged to "hang them out of the way" before they could testify against him. Chaloner's funning was always fatal to someone.

"However, the rogue's downfall started in 1697 when he actually attempted to fun Parliament. In testifying before a Parliamentary committee investigating abuses at the Mint, Chaloner said he had a way to improve coinage and eliminate counterfeiting in the process. Against my wishes, Chaloner was installed as a supervisor in the Mint in order to oversee the process. Unfortunately, after getting inside the Mint, he tried to fun the government again with his old Jacobite printing scheme.

But I had already told the lord justices about Chaloner, and when they heard Chaloner's charges against the printers, they became suspicious and decided to investigate further.

"In August of 1697 I provided enough evidence to have this rotter imprisoned for his bogus coining operation. And since I am a justice of the peace in all of the local counties, I did not allow him bail. I am sure that if Chaloner had known that I had been gathering evidence against him on a regular basis, he would probably have gone underground and not tried his latest funning scheme against the printers.

"Nevertheless, he had the audacity to petition Parliament and claim that I was trying to destroy him because of his previous testimony against me about abuses at the Mint. Charles Montague, James Vernon and William Lowndes were appointed by Parliament to investigate Chaloner's petition. But despite the evidence against him, Chaloner secured his release from prison by buying off Thomas Holloway, the chief witness against him. Chaloner immediately whisked Holloway off to Scotland, where British law couldn't touch him.

"I'm certain that Chaloner didn't know we were still watching him, because after he left prison he embarked on another counterfeiting caper, the forging of malt tickets, which are used to pay the duty on malt. But Montague and Vernon were carefully watching Chaloner's new counterfeiting scheme. In fact, it was James Vernon, not I, who issued the warrant for his arrest. Chaloner was much too dangerous to be at large. Edmund, I was determined to produce enough evidence to convict him. I even placed spies in Newgate to report everything Chaloner said and did.

"A month or so later I got word that Thomas Holloway had returned from Scotland, so I took him into custody. Counting Holloway, I had fifteen witnesses to testify against Chaloner. In one day, despite acting insane and producing a large contingent of defense lawyers, Chaloner was convicted of high treason. His wealth had produced the best defense imaginable —even a petition for pardon that went all the way to King William. When Chaloner realized that he was going to be given the ultimate execution for the crime of treason, he fainted. He obviously had never considered that the naïve government he had fooled in the past could convict him and impose the most horrific and barbaric execution imaginable."[355]

On March 23, 1699, William Chaloner was executed for counterfeiting. Isaac Newton and Edmund Halley watched the barbaric proceedings. Chaloner was drawn on a sledge, hanged to the point of death, disemboweled, mercifully decapitated, and then quartered; a gruesome penalty for a meager ten years of "funning."

Afterward, Newton said to Halley, "Had Chaloner squared his actions by the dictates of morality and virtue, he may have been a useful member of society; however, as he followed only the dictates of vice, he was as a rotten member cut off."[356]

During Newton's first three years at the Mint, Peter the Great, Tsar of all Russians, traveled incognito to England to meet the author of **Principia Mathematica**. On February 5, 1698 Isaac gave the tsar a tour of the Mint and explained the details of minting new coin and the purpose of recoinage. Apparently Peter was so impressed he made a second visit before returning to Russia. Two years after his visit he initiated a process in Russia that closely resembled England's recoinage.[357] Unfortunately, Peter's visit to England was marred. His entourage literally trashed John Evelyn's splendid estate at Sayes Court, where the tsar had resided. Eventually, the Crown compensated Evelyn 350 pounds for the extensive damage.[358]

Many notable events took place during Isaac's first years at the Mint, and one of these occurred shortly after Isaac had moved from the Tower to Jermyn Street. Isaac's half-sister Hannah Barton, who had become financially burdened upon becoming a widow, persuaded Isaac in late 1696 to take her seventeen year-old daughter Catherine into his home. Frankly, Isaac needed someone to handle his domestic affairs anyway.

Sometime before January 29 of 1697, Catherine Barton moved into Newton's Jermyn Street house. Of all his blood relations, his niece was by far the most gifted. Due to Isaac's hosting of social events –he was no longer a recluse— Catherine's beauty, charm and entertaining conversation became known to many men, including some famous ones. She seemed to be fascinated with the opposite sex, which may have been another reason her mother placed her under Uncle Isaac's supervision. She added spice to conversation, and all the visiting gentlemen enjoyed her risqué humor –and her voluptuous appearance.

It was also on January 29th that Isaac received a letter from Johann Bernoulli, a professor of mathematics in Switzerland. The letter challenged Isaac to solve two mathematical problems, the first of which had been published six months ago in the *Acta eruditorum*. According to Bernoulli, no one had been able to solve the problem over the past six months – no one perhaps except Leibniz, who said he had solved it and asked Bernoulli to extend the time so other mathematicians would have a chance. Bernoulli, however, added a second problem before sending his letter to Newton and other mathematicians on the continent.[359] He offered no material prize, only the prize of "honor …to celebrate the perspicacity of an Apollo-like seer."[360]

The first problem challenged mathematicians to determine the curve at which a heavy falling body will descend most rapidly from a given point to a second point. The second problem was to find a curve having the same property that the sum of any two segments of a straight line drawn to intercept it –and raised to any power—will intercept it.

According to Catherine, her uncle "…did not come home from the Tower until four P.M. very much tired.[361] …He opened the letter, read it, and did not sleep till he had solved it, wch was by four in the morning."[362] Newton set down the answers to both problems and sent them to his close friend, Charles Montague, President of The Royal Society. In February, the answers were published anonymously in *Philosophical Transactions*

If the truth were known, Isaac had calculated solutions to these types of problems before 1684. The only reason he took twelve hours to rework them in 1697 is because of his long absence from mathematics.

Incredibly, he still took only twelve hours to solve what all but a very few were able to do in a lifetime. Although Isaac's answers were published anonymously, almost every mathematician knew the solver. Bernoulli, who had consulted with Leibniz before testing the savant from Cambridge, wrote to a friend, "The precision and quality bore the distinctive mark: *ex ungue Leonem* --from the claws of the Lion."[363] Both Bernoulli and Leibniz had mistakenly assumed that Newton's silence during 1696 meant that the first problem had baffled him. They had to retest him to be sure of their superiority.[364]

Newton was quite perturbed about being tested, and he rightfully suspected that Leibniz had a role in challenging him. To Isaac, the test was an attempt by Leibniz to prove the superiority of calculus over fluxions by proving that Newton could not solve a problem that probed the utmost recesses of calculus. Within twelve hours Newton proved Leibniz wrong by solving two of Bernoulli's tests. He even planned to challenge Bernouilli and Leibniz some day with a test of his own that would assuredly confound them. Leibniz, however, having been embarrassed by his failure to stump Newton, wrote to The Royal Society disclaiming any knowledge of the challenge submitted by Bernoulli. Newton, of course, scoffed at the disclaimer and again, despite his Puritan upbringing, began to harbor a grudge. If past behavior were any indication, Newton would not forget Bernoulli's test and would vent his spleen to someone —even if it were not to the person causing his distemper.

In his first year at the Mint Isaac met Hopton Haynes, who soon became another Newton disciple. At age twenty-four, Haynes was in charge of training personnel at the country mints. Newton maintained a patronage to Haynes and always provided him with important posts even after re-coinage. Referred to as "the most zealous Unitarian" by Richard Baron of the same faith, Haynes later said that he and Newton held the same religious views and should have started a new Reformation[365] to reform the corruptions that Martin Luther hadn't addressed.

Newton found that in London he could freely discuss subjects he couldn't broach in Cambridge. He was now waxing theologically with

Locke, DeDullier, Halley, Bentley, Whiston, Samuel Clarke, Hopton Haynes, and probably John Wallis and David Gregory --all of whom were thought to be Newton disciples. One or two of these disciples even published their unorthodox beliefs anonymously; however, as previously noted, Newton avoided publicizing his orthodoxy. He was cautious and practical. He did not wish to risk his livelihood and his fame by being identified as someone outside the religious norm.

By the time re-coinage declined, Isaac's niece had become quite popular. All gentlemen who met her seemed to fall in love with her. She was the only Newton relative who possessed some of his superior mentality. Unfortunately, at that time in the world, women had few opportunities to succeed or to find gainful use of their intelligence. Nevertheless, like her uncle, Catherine Barton found that material success bore a strong correlation to having wealthy and powerful friends.

As the eighteenth century approached, many English and Scottish natural philosophers had joined social and intellectual organizations such as The Royal Society, The Invisible College and some masons' guilds. Also before the turn of the century, John Locke's essay on tolerance began circulating throughout the kingdom.

In 1910 a researcher named Paul Hazard wrote that the precise historic era between 1680 and 1715 was the "European Crisis of Conscience." In Hazard's in-depth study he describes these "thirty-five years of the intellectual life of Europe as a time of change whose effects have lasted to the present day. Change was wrought during those years when certain men of genius, such as Newton, Boyle, Locke, Spinoza, Fenelon, Leibniz and Bossuet --to name only a few— addressed themselves to the task of exploring the whole field of knowledge in order to bring out the verities which govern and condition the life of man." [366]

It became true that in the closing years of the seventeenth century a new order had begun its course.[367]

PART 3

Fame And Its Fortunes

• • •

"Moshe, Isaac Newton is now approaching the last one-third of his life. His final 28 years seem to underscore the fact that he was a freethinker with religious principles that differed from the mainstream. Somewhat contrary to his many Puritan beliefs, he also determined that both God and Jesus Christ would not object to his enjoying the earth and its bounty. Isaac was now one of the 'rich and famous' and seemed happy with his station in life. Commensurate with his worldly success, one of Isaac's priorities was to safeguard his income and his reputation –within his concept of God's parameters, of course. ...

Moshe asked, "*His* concept of God's parameters? Are you saying that Isaac did not take his revered scriptures literally?"

"No, I'm not saying that, Moshe. Isaac still applied the scriptures to his actions –but only *correct* scriptures– as evidenced from history and his research. True to his beliefs since 1670, he just couldn't accept some doctrines of established, well-heeled Christian churches. He felt strongly about the messages of Jesus Christ before their editing in the fourth century; however, Isaac also believed that God's messages weren't simply messages of blind faith. They contained much *reason*, which Isaac believed led to true salvation. Newton still believed that God didn't want him to allow faith to override reason; he thought Jesus exemplified this as the way to salvation and true happiness. Jesus personified the Golden Rule, and Isaac definitely tried to apply that standard, despite his human weaknesses."

"But I thought you said that Isaac didn't believe in Jesus?"

"Au contraire. I said that he didn't believe Jesus was God. Isaac still believed that Jesus was a messenger *from* God and spoke the words and parables that were inspired by God. Now, as Newton approached age 60, he wanted to fine tune all of his life's works and beliefs. He didn't just want to tie up loose ends; he wanted to expand upon his discoveries. Moshe, the world had become Isaac's oyster, and he was taking advantage of that role in the belief that God was okay with it. Isaac had found his own 'true religion,' however he kept it confidential so as not to endanger his status in life. The great mass of humanity on earth had been indoctrinated in another theology, and they gave little quarter to 'non-believers.' In fact, Parliament passed the *Act of 1698* for 'The Suppression of Blasphemy and Profaneness,' which removed from public office anyone who denied the Trinity as defined in Anglican scripture.

"Isaac continued to have trouble applying the Golden Rule to those who criticized him or even hinted criticism. He demonstrated the intransigence of his past at times. He definitely had some personality issues. He incurred negative criticism by detractors, Robert Hooke and John Flamsteed, and by one of his disciples, William Whiston. I also found a letter by John Locke instructing his cousin on how to approach Mr. Newton, but I'll tell you about that later.

"Of course, I have developed my own opinions about Isaac's personality in these later years, and to be candid, my conclusions are the exception. To most biographers, Isaac was a mystery. What I have discovered, unlike Isaac's scientific findings, is certainly subject to criticism. You might call my conclusions conjecture, but to me they are as true as the Pythagorean Theorem. I envision conversations that definitely took place, and despite the absence of records, I am as positive about such conversations as I am of you sitting before me. True, the words may not be identical to those spoken, but the gist is there even if there is no written evidence.

"To Hooke, Flamsteed and others who primarily strove for recognition, Newton was the target of much wrath. But to those who respected

Isaac and knew him closely, he was a most congenial fellow. Isaac simply wanted respect. He didn't want anyone to cross him.

"The most startling revelation I have made, which has not been mentioned by biographers, is that Isaac Newton did find one disciple who seemed to convey Isaac's basic beliefs without offending church or state. He was a disciple who understood Isaac's deepest scientific revelations and his religious beliefs, and he conveyed them to men in the world who wanted to receive them. It was late in Newton's life that this one disciple, more than anyone else, started the proliferation of Newtonianism. Furthermore, in addition to a constitution and some ancient rules and landmarks, Newton's convictions regarding God and nature are disseminated orally to this day in almost every nation. This one Newton disciple also placed into fraternal rituals certain principles about friendship, morality and brotherly love, which Newton seemed to display primarily to those closest to him.

"Newton believed that the intent of the ancient philosophers and prophets was to improve one's internal character in order to attain immortality of the soul. He wished to teach *truth* about God, nature and the universe-- not to dispense myths or falsehoods. It is true that another of Newton's disciples took a more confrontational approach by publicly exposing corruptions in scripture and criticizing the 'credulous' established churches. But because most organized religions and nations were not very tolerant during Newton's time, that particular disciple paid dearly for openly asserting his views. In the seventeenth and eighteenth century many religious dissenters sailed to America to keep from being persecuted for practicing their religious beliefs.

"Moshe, let me start this era of Isaac's life with a conversation that I believe took place between Isaac and his niece in 1698 after the funeral of the Duchess Dowager of Manchester, Charles Montague' wife.

"Incidentally, Moshe, Isaac and his niece were both Capricorns, and Capricorns were known to be ambitious, cautious and practical. ...

CHAPTER 33

Capricorns

• • •

Upon returning home after the Duchess's funeral, Catherine Barton asked Isaac, "Uncle, was that portly man in the first pew of the church the Dowager's husband?"

"Yes, that was Charles Montague. Why do you ask?"

"Well, for one thing, he appears much younger than his wife."

"He is," said Newton. "She was more than twice his age."

"He smiled at me after the service, uncle," Catherine said demurely.

"He may have been smiling at me, Katy. He hasn't met you."

"I swear he looked at me and smiled, uncle."

"Well, perhaps he did. You are a very attractive woman."

"Why, thank you, uncle! Mr. Montague had people with him. He must be an important man."

My dear Katy, haven't I told you of him? He is my friend and my patron. It was he who arranged for me to be warden of the Mint. He is the First Lord of the Treasury, Chancellor of the Exchequer and a member of the Regency Council. He can even speak for the king in the king's absence. He rescued me from suffocating in the parochial climate of Trinity College, and I am deeply indebted to him."

"I can imagine. Is he a wealthy man?"

"Yes is, Katy; yes he is. And why, pray tell, do you ask?"

"He appears to me to be wealthy."

"Well, he has been quite fortunate. He became rich from writing *Country Mouse and City Mouse*. Of course, he also married a duchess and will inherit her estate."

"He wrote *Country Mouse and City Mouse*? I'm familiar with that. Isn't it critical of Dryden's *Hind and the Panther*."

"Yes it is. Dryden had defended the Catholic Church during James II's reign. Montague took exception to it, as did many Englishmen. He wrote his parody and became famous for it. Unfortunately, due to Montague's wealth and power –and some of his religious vitriol-- parliament seems to resent him. In fact, I think he will find it difficult to hold on to his government offices. Because of the turmoil surrounding him, he has recently resigned as President of The Royal Society. It would be a shame to lose him in Parliament. He's been an influential leader and a great help to me personally."

"He looks like a nice man. I hope I will soon have the occasion to meet him."

"You will in due time, Katy. It is sad that his success and his zest for life have evoked such accusations from the ministers. Sadly, Montague does little to ward off their slings and arrows; he ignores and sometimes berates his accusers as if they were inferior creatures."

Although Isaac had an enduring friendship with Montague, no such relationship existed with John Flamsteed. This fact became obvious in December of 1698. Newton had been pressuring Flamsteed to publish his studies of the stars, and when John Wallis asked Flamsteed for information on the Stellar Parallax to place in his upcoming "Opera," Flamsteed acceded. He wrote some information for Wallis in a letter which had a paragraph stating that Flamsteed had been "closely associated with the very learned Newton" and had even given him "150 places of the Moon." The paragraph also stated some things that Flamsteed planned to do for Newton in the future.[368] Flamsteed gave the letter to David Gregory, who was told to deliver it to Wallis. However, Gregory, who was seeking Newton's endorsement for a position, promptly reported the letter's contents to him. Gregory then asked Wallis not to print the controversial paragraph that contained Newton's name.

Wallis immediately wrote to Flamsteed that "an unnamed correspondent in London, who was a friend of yours and Newton's," had asked him not to print the contested paragraph. The Royal Astronomer did not get Wallis's letter until he had returned to Greenwich from London on December 31. He immediately wrote to Newton enumerating the pains, expenses, and time involved in doing Newton's bidding. He also said, "[Do] not envy me the honor of having said that I have been useful to you in your attempts to [develop] a *Theory of the Moon*. I might have added the Observations of the Comets and of the superior planets and refractions… but this I thought would look like boasting & therefore forbore it."[369]

Flamsteed heard nothing from Newton for the next three days, so he wrote a second letter. On January 7 he had still not received a response, so Flamsteed wrote to Wallis that Newton was apparently unconcerned and that the paragraph in question might stand."[370] Unfortunately, immediately after mailing his letter, Flamsteed received a letter from Newton dated January 6, 1699. Newton minced no words in severing his relationship with John Flamsteed. He objected to being "publickly brought upon ye stage" for what was perhaps "never fitted for ye publick."[371]

Newton continued his castigation:

"I do not love to be printed upon every occasion much less to be dunned & teezed by foreigners about Mathematical things… . It was I who advised Dr. Gregory to write to Dr. Wallis against printing that clause. ….You may tell the world all you want to about how great you are, but friends should not be published without their leave."[372] Newton then said that he hoped Flamsteed would "so order the matter so that I will not be brought upon the stage."[373] Flamsteed quickly wrote Wallis to remove the "Offensive *Innocent* Paragraph."[374]

A year passed before Flamsteed visited Newton again. Isaac answered the door at his residence and glared at his visitor. Flamsteed said, "I hope I have found you in good health."

Newton answered, "My health is satisfactory, thank you."

"I came by to invite you to Greenwich."

Isaac responded with a quick "What for?" and closed the door. Flamsteed then left a note, "Read *Jeremiah IX*, 1 – 9." Isaac knew the verse and did not take kindly to the note.

Four years would pass before Flamsteed would make another attempt to regain Isaac's favor. At that time he sent invitations for Newton and Christopher Wren to come to dinner at Greenwich, but both men refused.

By November of 1699, England's national debt had gone out of sight due to King William's War against France, whose king was intent on expanding French and Catholic rule throughout Europe and America. The ministers thought another reason for the debt was that Charles Montague had pilfered the public coffers. Montague didn't wait for the impeachment trial. In November he resigned from the House of Commons and all other government positions. At this time his relationship with King William was still strong, and within two months the King helped Montague by making him the Baron of Halifax, and as such he was admitted to the House of Lords. However, the ministers kept after him like hounds after a fox. Impeachment proceedings began in the upper house, but eventually Montague would be found innocent.

On December 23, 1699, Thomas Neale, Master of the Mint, died of natural causes. Although Montague had no authority over the Mint at this time, he had made provisions for naming a successor to the Master's position. Despite the fact that no warden had ever succeeded as Master of the Mint, on December 26 Isaac Newton was appointed Master effective December 25 to coincide with his birthday, which incidentally was two days after Catherine Barton had turned age 20. Like Isaac, Catherine Barton was a Capricorn and also possessed superior intelligence. But unlike Isaac, she had a zest for enjoying life that began to rub off on her uncle ever so gradually. Perhaps her enjoyment of life's pleasures was one of the reasons her mother sent her to live with Isaac.

Incidentally, in addition to being the first warden to become Master of the Mint, Isaac was the first master to be appointed for the duration of the king's pleasure, not for life.

On the day after Neale's death, a joint birthday party was held for Isaac Newton and his niece. Charles Montague was invited and was introduced to the pretty lady to whom he had smiled at his wife's funeral. Montague was noticeably enamored by Catherine's beauty, and after only brief conversation, became fascinated by her intelligence and charm.

Unfortunately, Montague was unable to start any type of romantic relationship with Miss Barton because shortly after her birthday party she contracted small pox, which was quickly diagnosed by her uncle. Isaac was deeply concerned that pustular eruptions of the pox would blemish Catherine's beautiful face. Since the established remedy for combating the pox and other contagious diseases was to quarantine the carrier, Isaac sent his niece to the Gyre's residence in Oxfordshire near Woodstock. Catherine would remain under the Gyre's care for the remainder of the year. She wrote twice to Isaac during this time. He responded tenderly on August 5, 1700:

> *I had your two letters & am glad ye air agrees with you & though the fever is loath to leave you yet I hope it abates, & yt ye remains of ye small pox are dropping off apace. ... I intend to send you some wine by the next Carrier wch I beg the favour of Mr Gyre & his Lady to accept of. My Lady Norris thinks you forget your promis of writing to her, & wants a letter from you. Pray let me know by your next how your face is and if your fevour be going. Perhaps warm milk from ye Cow may help to abate it.* [375]

In 1700, the 58th year of Newton's life, the Archbishop of Canterbury, Thomas Tenison, visited Newton at the Mint. He made quite a spectacle in his vestments as he departed his carriage and entered the Mint with his escort of clergy. Inside Newton's office after brief greetings and comments,

Isaac was taken aback as he heard from the Archbishop the purpose of his visit. Suddenly the exposure of Isaac's heterodoxy again was at stake.

"Doctor Newton, after studying the qualifications of many learned gentlemen, I have selected you to be the new Master of Trinity University."

Newton paused before answering, "Reverend Archbishop, I am humbled by your offer. It is indeed a singular honor to be selected to such a revered position, but with all due respect, I cannot accept the appointment. I have not taken holy orders."

"Isaac, we can easily correct that minor omission."

"I must still respectfully decline the offer, your grace."

"Why will not you? You know more than all of us put together."

"Why then," said Isaac, "I shall be able to do you the more service by not being in orders."[376]

Newton then recommended Richard Bentley for the position. Bentley had been a disciple of Newton's since 1691 when he and Newton collaborated on the Boyle sermons. Tenison soon asked Isaac to be one of the first nine trustees of the Golden Square Tabernacle, a chapel which the archbishop had personally endowed. Perhaps to avoid suspicion, Newton accepted the appointment. He also accepted one to serve on the commission to oversee the completion of St. Paul's Cathedral; however, after an argument with Archbishop Wake concerning the hanging of some pictures of Christ adorned with halos, Newton refrained from attending any further meetings of that commission.[377] To the world at this time, Isaac Newton was revered as a God-fearing Anglican.

During the year 1700, Halifax, formerly Montague, prepared to be impeached by the Ministers of Parliament; Catherine Barton spent the entire year recovering from small pox, and John Locke resigned as President of England's Board of Trade due to ill health. Last, but not least, Isaac severed all correspondence with the Royal Astronomer John Flamsteed.

It is worth noting that John Theophilus DeSagaliers turned 17 on March 12, 1700. His father had been teaching him in the family's school in Islington. Before the ex-Huguenot minister died in 1699, he knew that his son was a genius.

CHAPTER 34

Catherine Barton

• • •

"Before her 21st birthday Catherine returned from the Gyres with no apparent ill effects from small pox. Isaac invited some friends, neighbors and his assistant, Christopher Ellis, to a birthday party for his niece on December 23. When guests sat at the dining room table for a light repast, Christopher sat next to Miss Barton. During the dinner, he felt a hand on his knee. He looked at Newton's niece, who smiled wistfully at him without removing her hand. …

After the meal and some toasts to Catherine, the party finally broke up and only Ellis, Newton and his niece remained. Dr. Newton said, "I hope you two will excuse me; I have some work to do in my study. Will you be all right without me?

Catherine responded, "We'll be just fine, uncle."

"Good. Don't stay up too late, Katy. You need your rest. I'll see you tomorrow."

Catherine invited Christopher to sit on a red settee in the parlor. Once they were seated she again placed her hand upon his knee and smiled.

Christopher flinched immediately and asked," What if your uncle comes back?"

"Oh, he won't. He becomes most preoccupied with work. Nothing ever distracts him."

No one will ever know what happened in Newton's parlor that evening. All one needs to know is that British women in the 18th century were still quite Victorian, and for a lady to place her hand on the knee of a recent acquaintance was unheard of. Catherine Barton may have emulated her uncle by not abiding certain traditional habits, and to her, some of these were the current acceptable sexual practices. Like Newton, Catherine had a mind –and a body-- of her own.

Eventually, Christopher blubbered, "I hope you will forgive me, madam."

"For what? countered Catherine. We shared some enjoyment on my birthday. You have made me very happy."

"But…"

"No 'buts,' Mr. Ellis. I could tell you were enjoying yourself, and so was I. But I trust that you will never mention what happened between us this evening. If you do, I shall deny it. My uncle is most insistent that I maintain a good reputation."

"My lips are sealed, Miss Barton."

"Good. I thank you sincerely. Now the hour is late and I must retire."

Catherine escorted Christopher to the door. As she opened it she gave him a peck on the cheek and said, "Sweet dreams, Christopher."

On his way back to his apartment at the Tower of London, Christopher muttered to himself, "I don't believe what just happened. I must see her again."

Within the week Christopher and Catherine did see each other again at Newton's home. In fact, Christopher's heart skipped a beat when Newton again excused himself later in the evening. Unfortunately, believing that Miss Barton was of the same theological bent as her uncle, Ellis proudly announced to Catherine that he was not a traditional Trinitarian –never mentioning of course that her uncle was also an Arian. Immediately, Catherine exclaimed, "What? You are not a Christian?"

"Well, not exactly. I just don't believe that Jesus was God."

"Mr. Ellis, leave this house immediately. I will not allow myself to consort with an infidel. You are still my friend, but that is all. Good night, sir."

"But, I thought…"

"I don't care what you thought, Mr. Ellis. Good night!"

And that was the end of Mr. Christopher Ellis's hopes for a future with Miss Catherine Barton, a woman who seemed to steal the heart of every man who met her. To his everlasting chagrin, Ellis regretted mentioning his heterodoxy, which he thought Catherine shared with him.[378]

As intimated, other men also developed close relationships with Miss Barton, and one of them had a decided advantage. Unfortunately throughout 1701 he was extremely busy defending himself against being impeached. Halifax's pursuers left no stone unturned in attacking him. And if he were to be connected romantically with a woman eighteen years younger than he, his adversaries would consider burning him at the stake. The ministers were besmirching him every day in pamphlets that questioned his morals and his income. Indeed, Halifax had his hands full without adding fuel to the inferno already enveloping him.

Newton continued to support Halifax throughout his ordeals. In the past he had done much of Halifax's bidding, and the year 1701 was no exception. Isaac also did very little to discourage a budding relationship between his niece and Lord Halifax. Throughout the year, which was a busy one at the Mint, Newton was hosting social functions. Many notable men of Europe and England came to Newton's soirees and had the occasion to meet his niece, and all of them were well-entertained by her charms.

At one of these parties, Newton again excused himself as the evening waged on. Catherine remained in the parlor entertaining some gentlemen, one of whom was the writer Jonathan Swift. One of the other gentlemen ogling Miss Barton asked her, "Have you heard any recent gossip?"

Catherine answered, "Oh yes, I have heard much, Lord Somers. Are you sure you want to hear it?"

"Of course! We all do."

"Very well," said Catherine. "Perhaps you have heard that a certain lady of London, a daughter of one of our lords, was recently with child, but she pretended that it was only inflammation caused by gas, and told everyone so. Suddenly she disappeared for three weeks, but when she returned her tympany was gone. No wonder she married; she was so ill at containing." [379]

The gentlemen roared with laughter, of course.

On another occasion, many visiting gentlemen heard another of Catherine's stories:

> *"An old gentlewoman died recently. She had placed in her will that her sixteen pall bearers —eight men and eight maids—should be paid two guineas apiece, while the parson should have ten. There was one other stipulation: 'Each must swear to his or her virginity.' The poor woman still lies unburied —and will remain so until her general resurrection."*[380]

Catherine was indeed witty and charming. Although her theological views did not exactly conform to her uncle's, she had something else in common with him. Both of them harbored unorthodox views which, if released to the world, would be devastating to their reputations, and probably endanger their livelihoods. What is more singular is that they concealed their innermost convictions even from each other. Only trusted, like-minded confidants would ever be privy to their unorthodox views. The masses would forever be unaware of the inner workings of two profound minds.

If the people of England had known the mind of Isaac Newton, he may not have been twice elected to Parliament.

CHAPTER 35

Politics

• • •

"Like gauging the wind, as he once did in a jumping competition at Kings School, Isaac tested the water before entering a political contest. He had previously represented Cambridge as one of its two delegates during the Convention Parliament after the Glorious Revolution. Now in the fall of 1701 he would be asked by Lord Halifax to run for office again. …

In late September, Lord Halifax called upon Isaac at his Jermyn Street residence. Catherine Barton met him at the door and held out her hand, which he kissed enthusiastically. She escorted him to the library, where Isaac greeted him.

"Lord Halifax, what brings you to my humble abode?"

"I need you in Parliament, Isaac. Will you run again?"

"Do you mean as a candidate from London?"

"No, from Cambridge. I think you will stand a better chance of winning there."

"Pray tell, why do you want me stand for election?"

"The Whigs barely have a majority, and we could lose it in November. I'm confident that you can be elected."

"But you said that *you* needed me?"

"Yes, I do. Some of my Whig friends and I are undergoing a trial of impeachment. I need every vote possible."

"I see."

"Will you run?"

"Charles, if the political winds at Cambridge are still favorable, I will be happy to stand for election –and if I am elected, I will support you in your trials."

Lord Halifax grasped Isaac's hand and said, "Thank you, my friend."

On November 26, 1701, Isaac again won election to Parliament from Cambridge. He came in second in balloting to Henry Boyle, son of the venerable Robert Boyle. Although Newton managed to squeeze out more votes than his Tory opponents, the Tories gained seats in Parliament due to their strong support from the Anglican Church. Within three weeks after the election, Isaac resigned his fellowship and his Lucasian Chair at Cambridge. He recommended William Whiston as his successor, and the Trinity Trustees agreed with Isaac's choice.

Newton felt that it was a good time to resign his positions at Trinity. His office as Master of the Mint was affording him considerable income and his future looked promising, especially since the peace treaty at Ryswick appeared to end King William's War. Isaac was now not only receiving a salary but also royalties on every troy pound of coin minted. He also received 150 pounds per year for storing and supervising the sale of tin. Combined with income from his rentals, Newton was becoming a wealthy man. He made approximately 3500 Pounds in 1701 –much more than the few hundred he had received from his Trinity salaries or his position as Warden of the Mint.

Yes, Newton's future never looked more secure. Even in Parliament things were looking up. Though the House of Commons had impeached Halifax –despite Newton's vote-- the House of Lords voted to dismiss the charges. Halifax could now make a political comeback.

Unfortunately Newton's confidence was soon shaken. Although King James II had died in France, Louis XIV recognized James' son as King of England instead of King William. William immediately nullified the Ryswick treaty, and England was again immersed in war. Then on March 8, 1702, King William died, and Princess Anne, his sister-in-law, ascended to the throne. Queen Anne, like her sister, Queen Mary, was raised as a Protestant and had opposed her father, James II. To make matters worse for Isaac, coinage was down considerably.

Three weeks after William's death, Halifax again called on Newton at his residence. This time he gave Catherine a big hug upon entering the door. She said, "My Lord, what gives you cause to embrace me."

Halifax said, "Catherine, your efforts in supporting your uncle in the past election have not gone unnoticed. You have entertained many supporters and have contributed greatly to his reelection."

"Why thank you, sir."

"Is the esteemed savant in?"

"Yes, he is. Let me take you to him."

Halifax followed Isaac's niece, his eyes completely fixated on her firm, oscillating, beautifully proportioned hips. They reached the library door, and Catherine said, "Go right in. My uncle heard you when you came in, and he is undoubtedly expecting you."

Catherine gave Halifax a wink and walked away. His admiring eyes followed her for an instant. He entered the library and Newton said, "To what do I owe the honor of your visit today, Lord Halifax?"

"Queen Anne, Isaac."

"I am assuming that you are concerned about her politics. Is it so?"

"Quite. Have you heard anything in the House?"

"I am told the Queen dislikes political parties."

"Well, I can say assuredly that she dislikes one of the parties –ours!"

"You are certain of this?"

"Her closest friends are Duke and Sarah Marlborough, my staunchest adversaries. I have heard from reliable sources that all Whigs holding high government offices will be dismissed –including me. I'm referring to Lords Spencer, Somers, Russell and Wharton; all to be replaced by Tories."

Isaac said, "I should have suspected as much. She was reared in the high church and the Tories have always sided with the Anglican Church and the Crown instead of secular government and Parliament."

Halifax said, "She appointed Marlborough as General of the British Army and, as you know, he received the Order of the Garter two weeks ago. I personally have heard her say that she will favor those who are most loyal to the Church of England."

"This will not bode well for the parliamentary elections after she prorogues Parliament, Charles. John Locke will be most displeased with her theocratic dispositions."

"Will you stand for re-election again, Isaac?"

"Charles, I would prefer that another candidate be found. The current political climate at Trinity is not good, and I haven't time to solicit votes. The tides are not flowing in our direction, Charles."

"You're probably right, Isaac. Anyway, I am grateful for all that you've done in the past."

"I was happy to do so, Charles."

Halifax stood up and said, "Thank you for giving me some of your time."

Isaac escorted his guest to the front door and opened it. Halifax noticed that Catherine had entered the foyer, so he blew her a kiss before he left. Newton closed the door, and Catherine asked, "What was the purpose of Lord Halifax's visit, uncle?"

Newton responded, "He wanted me to run for Parliament again, but I refused. I have found that the political climate at Cambridge has changed. After the last election, one of the losing Tories published a pamphlet about Whig members of Parliament supporting candidates favorable to the New East India Company, in which many ministers were stockholders. In fact, Halifax introduced the bill to incorporate the company. I do not want to be connected with any alleged conspiracies."

But Newton didn't tell Catherine his second reason. Before becoming Queen, Princess Anne had addressed Parliament about the need for "religious conformity." And soon another pamphleteer at Cambridge brought up the issue of "hypocrites destroying the church by pretending to be true Anglicans."[381] The "hypocrites" were taking communion once a year in order to meet church membership requirements. Newton fit that stereotype and decided to assume a low profile. After all, his job was at the will and pleasure of the Crown. Far be it for him to place himself under public scrutiny by being a candidate for election.

Soon after Halifax's visit, however, the ministers presented Newton with an opportunity to gain the Queen's favor, and suddenly the clouds of despair disappeared. Isaac was asked to design and manufacture the coronation medal for distribution to dignitaries at Queen Anne's coronation on April 23. Isaac took advantage of the situation.

The medal he designed expanded upon William III's coronation medal, which depicted William as Jupiter, the King of the Gods and father of heroes. In Isaac Newton's medal he depicted Anne as the goddess Pallas Athena destroying a great Egyptian army. According to the Roman myth, Athena entered the fray in relief of Jupiter, who had wearied of the carnage. The Mint produced 300 gold medals and 1,200 of silver. Newton's efforts may have saved his Mastership.[382]

Nevertheless, Newton was a practical man, and in October of 1702 he decided to travel to Essex and the Masham estate to visit his seriously-ill friend, John Locke. Newton had a twofold purpose in mind. Truly he wanted to see Locke, but he also wanted to visit the Mashams, Locke's close friends. The Mashams were related to Abigail Hill, a relative of the Marlboroughs, who were the Queen's closest friends and advisors. The Mashams had lobbied for Newton in 1691 when he was seeking a government position. He just might need their support again.

But Newton primarily wanted to see John Locke on his 70th birthday. He found his friend in failing health, but Locke was pleased to see Newton and said, "Isaac, I am so happy that you took the time from your schedule to travel all the way to Essex. We have shared much together."

Newton said, "It's good to see you again, John. Yes, we have shared much."

Locke commented, "I'm sorry that my health would not permit me to stay in London and continue on the Board of Trade, but the air was too disagreeable. I wanted to pass my final days with my dear friends, the Mashams."

"I am of the opinion that you will have many days upon the land our God has given us, John."

"I earnestly hope so, but in the meantime, I have written a paper on St Paul's first two Epistles to the Corinthians. May I ask you to comment on it? I have observed that Paul never referred to Jesus as God. He said that God sent the Spirit of his Son into our hearts crying 'Abba! Father! We are all heir[s], *through God*,'[383] and he was including himself."

Locke handed Newton a rather lengthy commentary. Newton perused the first pages and remarked, "John, you have written a very long document. Would you mind mailing me a copy so I may examine it further?"

"Of course not, Isaac. I am pleased that you will give some of your time to it."

The two men then had a rather deep discussion on religion and politics. Locke said, "Isaac, when civil or religious authority runs contrary to the rights endowed by God and the consent of the governed, people have a right to inaugurate peaceful change. When the Jews were expelled in England and France due to their beliefs, God could not have been pleased. Why are sentences of death, imprisonment or exile given to those with a different theology of God when that theology does not threaten the lives or beliefs of others? Why can't all people have the right to pursue the truth without being oppressed or punished for such a pursuit. To speak freely against an entity that sanctions death and destruction to peaceful people is a God-given right. Entities resorting to such measures are not Godly nor reasonable. To hate others violates one of God's two greatest commandments. No one should be punished for upholding truth and righteousness.

"To me, Isaac, man inherits religions like a seed inherits a tree. A seed forms roots and becomes the same tree as its procreator. Though all trees have the same sun, earth, rain and nutrients; under their shaded covering they grow to be the same species of plant as their predecessors. Religions are similar. They all rely on God for their existence, yet they have roots handed down from the ideologies that have grown from the hoary founders before them. We also inherit roots, which are nurtured from birth. It is difficult to change how we are born and nurtured.

"Do you know what I think the world needs, Isaac? It needs a new world order, a type of ideology that is so true everyone can agree with it; one that does not demand allegiance solely to itself and doesn't declare war on peaceful, tolerant people of different theologies. All religions need to adopt basic commandments: to love God, the creator of the universe; and our neighbors, our fellow creatures. We do not need to *idolize* our own trees and the humans who have planted them. I long for a religion that respects life, creation, truth and harmony —what God wants us to respect. I long for a considerate world where all people respect their fellow creatures —or at least exist with them without malice. I do not want a world where murder, punishments and penalties are committed by religious sects in the name of God; nothing is more blasphemous.

"Isaac, let me know your opinions of my paper on Paul's Epistles"

The two men said their farewells. Isaac spent a short time with the Mashams and returned to London in November. Before his birthday in December he received the document Locke had promised; however, due to other matters, Isaac did not immediately examine the material. Locke wrote to Newton in March but received no reply. Deeply interested in knowing Newton's opinion of his commentary, he wrote a second letter on April 30 which he gave to his cousin Peter King to personally deliver to Newton. Reflecting upon Newton's temperament, he also gave Peter King written instructions on how to approach the esteemed author of **The Principia.** It is a rare, but possibly valid, glimpse of Isaac's personality...

> *The reason why I desire you to deliver it to him yourself is, that I would fain discover the reason of his so long silence. I have several reasons to think him truly my friend, but he is a nice [touchy] man to*

deal with, a little too apt to raise in himself suspicions where there is no ground; therefore, when you talk to him of my papers, and of his opinion of them, pray do it with all the tenderness in the world, and discover, if you can, why he kept them so long, and was so silent. But this you must do without asking why he did so, or discovering in the least that you are desirous to know... Mr. Newton is really a valuable man, not only for his wonderful skill in mathematics, but in divinity too, and his great knowledge in the Scriptures, wherein I know few his equals. And therefore pray manage the whole matter so as not only to preserve me in his good opinion, but to increase me in it; and be sure to press him to nothing but what he is forward in himself to do.[384]

Peter King did visit Newton, but because others were present he did not candidly discuss Locke's papers. Newton, however, was obviously embarrassed by the personal visit from Locke's cousin reminding him of the promise he had made. He did acknowledge that he had read many of Locke's papers, but not all. After Peter King left, Newton sent an apology to Locke with some remarks on his work on St. Paul's "Epistles...". Although Newton differed with some of Locke's interpretations he wrote, "I think your paraphrase & commentary on these two Epistles is done with very great care and judgment."[385]

On January 14, 1703, over seven months after delivering the Queen's coronation medals and shortly after taking communion in the Anglican Church, Newton was officially notified that he had retained his position as Master of the Mint. Because of his delay in writing to Locke, however, the world learned much from Locke's instructions to Peter King, which have been preserved for posterity along with Locke's revolutionary Enlightenment writings.

Later on in 1703, Locke and Newton were both dismayed when Queen Anne's Parliament passed another 'Test Act.' As you probably know, these acts were instigated in 1661 by Charles II after the death of Cromwell. They were meant to stop opposition to the Church of

England, the Anglican Church. The first acts prevented non-Anglicans from holding public office. I have already mentioned the 'Act of 1689' that prevented public worship by Catholics and Arians; however, the act of 1703 severely punished Ireland and Scotland. Not only did it require officeholders –even military officers—to be Anglicans, it declared Presbyterian ministers to be illegitimate, and all marriages, baptisms and burial rites performed by them to be illegal. Therefore, most married people were living in sin and their children were bastards. The act severely affected the "Ulster Plantation' in Ireland, where many Presbyterian Scots had fled. In fact, a migration began in 1715 when 200,000 to 400,000 Ulster Scots sailed to America within six decades.

John Locke, Isaac Newton, and the Presbyterians, must have thought that both the Queen and Parliament had gone mad.

Newton never saw John Locke again. The man, whose writings helped to provide principles for America's founding fathers, died on October 28, 1704. He was perhaps Isaac's truest soul mate. He was buried in a plain wooden coffin without a covering In accordance with one of his last wishes: "That cost will be better laid out in covering the poor."[386]

CHAPTER 36

President of The Royal Society

• • •

"MOSHE, NEWTON HAD GIVEN THE world his substance. He had provided great truths, and had brought stability and dignity to England's Mint. I have finally realized that Isaac's great passion, his religion –why he worked incessantly-- was to discover and to understand the myriad mysteries of the universe. Unlike Flamsteed, Hooke, and perhaps Leibniz, his reason for existing was to find truth –and not for the purpose of gaining fame. In fact, Isaac may have disrespected people of lesser intelligence who attempted to gain fame undeservedly. He was unlike any other mortal in unlocking nature's mysteries and finding truths.

"And when his findings were not accepted by the scientists and theologians of his day, he retreated and waited for a proper time, which in at least one case was beyond his lifetime. He had a gnawing wish to see the churches of his day return to truths that had been perverted for almost fourteen centuries, but he couldn't reveal this particular discovery for fear of losing his livelihood or even his life.

"Fortunately, after Robert Hooke died, Isaac became President of The Royal Society. As president he was bold enough to reveal some of his discoveries, especially on optics, which he had shelved for 30 years. Isaac soon published *Opticks* and more. ...

While Newton was at Oates visiting Locke and the Mashams, Lord Halifax called on Catherine Barton. One can only imagine what transpires when a man of the world calls on one of the fairest maids of London. Although he was eighteen years older and supposedly wiser, he became smitten by her. He had boasted of amorous affections with many ladies, but his ardor for Miss Barton exceeded that of past courtships, most of which were romantic failures.

Catherine, however, was a Capricorn --cautious, practical, and perhaps reservedly ambitious. Although she was mindful not to refuse all of Halifax's advances, she did not submit to his deepest desires nor would she commit to a permanent relationship, at least not without proper consideration. However, if a man truly understood Catherine, he would probably not doubt her ability to give a suitor much pleasure without selling the farm, so to speak. The desire of man seems greatest when his reach exceeds his grasp. In any event, Halifax soon began extolling Miss Barton at the Kit Kat Club, a club of Whig leaders who toasted the beautiful ladies of England and etched their names with diamonds on toasting glasses.

Early in 1703 Halifax toasted Catherine Barton. She was one of six ladies whose names were inscribed on glasses and toasted that year:

> *At Barton's feet the God of Love His Arrows and his Quiver lays, Forgets he has a throne above, and with this lovely Creature stays. Not Venus' Beauties are more bright, But each appear so like the other, That cupid has mistook the right, and takes the Nymph to be his Mother.*[387]

When Isaac returned from Oates he did not notice nor interfere with the blossoming relationship between his niece and his patron. Of course he was quite busy at the time, which is why he did not immediately respond to John Locke's commentary on Paul's *Epistles*. In addition to Isaac's concern about his investiture at the Mint, he became suddenly interested in the recent intellectual and financial decline of The Royal Society.

From 1695 to 1703 two politicians, John Somers and Newton's political patron, Charles Montague, were elected presidents of The Royal Society because of their political influence – certainly not because of their scientific knowledge. During those eight years Somers attended none of the monthly council meetings and Montague only one.[388] The Society's secretary, Hans Sloan, usually presided over the meetings. Newton's nemesis, Robert Hooke, the curator of experiments, had been ravaged by sickness for years, but still exercised considerable influence within the Society. Unfortunately, it took eight years for the society to shed its two political presidents.

But change began in March of 1703 after Robert Hooke died and Lord Somers resigned the presidency. The Society was then able to seek a president worthy of its true purpose. Ironically, Hooke's death also created a problem. The society had been occupying Hooke's chambers at Gresham College, and now the college wanted The Royal Society to vacate the premises. Fortunately, an irascible professor named John Woodward volunteered his rooms to the Society; nevertheless, the threat of eviction by the college always loomed.

Although Newton had been a member of The Royal Society Council until 1696, he hadn't attended a weekly meeting since 1686, when Hooke charged him with plagiary over the discovery of gravity. Hooke never recovered from being passed over regarding his contribution to that discovery and this snub tortured him for the rest of his life.[389] It was actually Hooke's insight on circular motion that set Newton on the track of universal gravitation. At the one meeting Isaac attended in August of 1696, he presented a new instrument he had contrived, a sextant. Robert Hooke quickly scoffed at it and said, "I had invented that type of sextant more than 30 years before."[390] Needless to say, Isaac attended no further meetings.

But after Hooke's death, Secretary Sloane had an opportunity to find a natural philosopher to be President of The Royal Society. He first approached Christopher Wren, who recommended Isaac Newton. In order to be president, however, Newton again had to be elected to the council, but despite his fame, over half of the members running for council received more votes. In fact only 22 of the 30 members present voted for him. Then when he ran for President on November 30, 1703 only 24 of an estimated three dozen members voted for him.[391] It seemed that even in death, Hooke's resentment of Newton haunted Gresham's halls. It would take two years before Newton gained the Society's confidence. After all, its members hadn't seen Newton for seven years. However, in two years Newton reformed The Royal Society as he had reformed the Mint. He was meticulous, conscientious and more than able, even if he was not popular among the members.

Isaac didn't attend the first Royal Society meeting on December 8, but on December 15 he presided and immediately commanded respect. Furthermore, he attended all council meetings. If the council met, Newton presided over it. For the next twenty years Newton would only miss three meetings.[392]

Newton also changed the content of the weekly meetings. Instead of bizarre or supernatural experiments, he emphasized Natural Philosophy, "discovering the frame and operations of Nature and reducing them to general rules or laws by observations and experiments, thus deducing the causes and effects of things."[393] He also set down five categories of natural philosophy: Mathematics and Mechanics, Astronomy and Optics, Anatomy and Physiology, Botany, and Chemistry. He furthermore urged that the society accept men who had established a reputation in one or more of these five categories.[394]

Newton started his first Royal Society meeting by introducing a new conductor of experiments by the name of Francis Hauksbee, who was called "Elder" to distinguish him from another Hauksbee. Because of some inane presentations at past meetings, Isaac needed someone to conduct credible *scientific* experiments. At Isaac's first meeting, Hauksbee demonstrated a newly invented air pump.[395] The next day, Secretary Sloane described the experiment to the venerable Christopher Wren:

> *It was a unique presentation. Elder Hauksbee first extinguished all light in the room and covered the windows with drapery. He then inverted a glass vessel and placed it on the demonstration table. After*

that, Hauksbee released mercury into the evacuated receiver of the new air pump. As the mercury spilled over the inverted glass vessel, it emitted a shower of fire descending around all sides of the glass. The room was suddenly aglow with light.

Hauksbee conducted experiments without a salary, despite Newton's appeal to the council to give him one. The council promised Hauksbee that he would be compensated "according to the proportion of his services."[396] Hauksbee continued conducting weekly experiments until he died ten years later. When he demonstrated that Newton's law of attraction worked on minute bodies in a vacuum, Newton was pleased. Isaac also enjoyed Hauksbee's experiments with static electricity, which were later expanded upon by a future society member named Benjamin Franklin. Hauksbee was never salaried nor given Hooke's title as Curator, but under Newton's administration and Hauksbee's presentations, the Society began to rejuvenate. Membership increased, finances and credibility improved, and The Royal Society began to regain its status as a great organization for enlightenment.

Despite Newton's appearance on the scene, some Society members still had an appetite for the macabre in experimentation. One demonstrator named Dr. James Douglas performed dissections in some weekly meetings. He brought in a newborn puppy without a mouth and kept it alive for ten days. After it died he brought its skull to a meeting. On another occasion a member brought in four pigs that were growing to one another in the womb of a dead sow.[397]

Newton's self-esteem improved after his election to the presidency. After urgings by John Wallis and David Gregory, he released his thirty year-old research on optics. In 1673 Hooke had denounced Isaac's findings as "hypotheses," and Isaac withdrew contributing his findings to The Royal Society, even though he considered his *Opticks* "the oddest if not the most considerable detection wch hath hitherto beene made in the operations of Nature."[398]

Opticks was published in 1704, and in its preface, Newton wrote: "To avoid being engaged in Disputes about these Matters [opticks],

I have hitherto delayed the printing and should still have delayed it, had not the importunity of Friends prevailed upon me."[399] But *Opticks* contained much more than Newton's work on light and colors. It also included two mathematical papers, a "Treatise on the Quadrature of Curves" and an "Enumeration of Lines of the Third Order." Newton also did not pass up the opportunity to inject some of his own philosophy concerning metabolism, digestion, sensation, circulation of blood, Creation, the Great Flood, moral philosophy, the inductive method and more.[400]

After thirty years, Newton had finally published some mathematical accomplishments. At long last the world could witness the genius behind his reputation as a mathematician. The impact of *Opticks* may even have exceeded the impact of **The Principia**; it was written in prose, not in geometric terms, and would reach a larger audience. In Book I and II of *Opticks*, Newton inserted "De Quadratura" because a Scot physician by the name of George Cheyne had printed "The Inverse Method of Fluxions" from material given by Newton to David Gregory, who obviously shared it. Newton not only established his priority on the subject, but also exposed Dr. Chyene's plagiarism. Needless to say, Cheyne quickly resigned from The Royal Society and changed his occupation from mathematics to medicine.[401]

At the end of Book III Newton introduced 16 Queries in place of Book IV. He added 15 more Queries in a second edition of his work in 1706. Newton's second edition of *Opticks* was his last major publication of previously unknown scientific work.[402] The first Queries concerned forces. For example, Query 1 asked, "Do not all Bodies act upon Light at a distance, and by their action bend its Rays: and is not this action strongest at the least distance?"[403]

In Newton's last Queries he expanded upon the many phenomena of nature, especially on the causes of attraction between bodies such as gravity, magnetism, electricity and more: "For Nature is very constant and conformable to herself."[404] Query 31 was considered to be the most advanced product of seventeenth century chemistry,[405] yet Newton made a disclaimer that he did not know all the causes of attraction between bodies. "Attraction was in fact any force by which Bodies tend towards one another, whatsoever be the cause. ...Whence is it that Nature does nothing in vain, and whence arises all Order and Beauty which we see in the World?"[406]

Later on, David Gregory, who had introduced Newton's philosophy to Oxford, stated "The plain truth is that he believes God to be omnipresent in the literal sense."[407] Even Newton said that "infinite space is the sensorium of God" before he revised it to "there is a Being, incorporeal, living, intelligent, omnipresent... who sees the things themselves intimately. [408]

Although Newton had previously demurred from publicizing heterodoxical philosophy, *Opticks* displayed many of his religious views. It even gained him new disciples; such as Abraham De Moivre, who guided the second edition of *Opticks* through the press; Samuel Clarke, who translated it into Latin; and perhaps John Theophilus Desaguliers, who had first learned of Newtonianism through David Gregory and John Keill at Christ Church in Oxford.

John Locke had read *Opticks* with great pleasure before he died. He had also read **The Principia**, but many parts of it had baffled him. John Machin said that *Opticks* contained more philosophy than **The Principia** --and didn't Isaac himself consider *Opticks* the greatest detection he had made in the properties of nature? Thirty years ago Isaac had hoped that his discoveries would be welcomed by The Royal Society and that *Opticks* would be recognized and unopposed by all of its members. Unfortunately that dream had become a thirty year-old nightmare.[409]

Newton's theory of colors and his discoveries of the heterogeneity of light presented to the world a lasting legacy to the science of optics. *Opticks* also gave the world an example of Newton's superior mathematical skills, a look into his concepts of the universe and a presentation of some of his religious beliefs. Newton had waited a long time to present these ideas to the world. He knew that numberless worlds were in the universe –all of them formed by the same Divine Artist and governed by the same unerring law of nature. Although Isaac did not mention Arianism by name in *Opticks*, he mentioned many of its principles –especially that there is "One Being" who is the "Architect of the Universe."

Within two years of the publication of *Opticks*," John Theophilus Desaguliers, a twenty-three year-old student of John Keill's, had digested it. In fact, Desaguliers became so influenced by Newton's treatise that it became his foundation for chemistry, electricity, magnetism, biology, geology [and moral philosophy] –in all of which he became an expert. He once said that *Opticks* contained more philosophy than **The Principia.**[410]

John Theophilus Desaguliers was one of the few people on earth whose intellect approached Isaac Newton's. Furthermore, this young genius was gifted in speech and social skills.

CHAPTER 37

John Flamsteed

• • •

"Moshe, as I had previously mentioned, Isaac's formative years instilled in him a sense of insecurity and a general distrust of human kind. His withdrawal tendency made him appear egotistical at times. To those under him at the Mint and over whom he presided in The Royal Society, he expected obedience and submission. He wanted them to support him –and this included **John Flamsteed**. To his superiors, like Lord Halifax and Queen Anne, he was kind and condescending. To his family and his peers, he was courteous and affable –unless they did not return the favor. He was courteous to John Flamsteed in their early relationships.

"By 1704 Lord Halifax had gained favor with the Court and, according to some accounts, had persuaded Prince George to provide some financial assistance for the Royal Astronomer to publish his "Catalog of the Stars." Of course, Halifax told Newton about Prince George's offer, and Isaac was more than ecstatic. With information from the catalog, especially observations of the moon, Isaac could publish a more perfect lunar theory in a second edition of **The Principia**. The drawback in getting observations in the past seemed to be a personality conflict between Newton and the Royal Astronomer. Isaac could never understand John Flamsteed's reticence in providing observations, and Flamsteed resented decisions other people made for him. ...

To be quite candid, Flamsteed had worked thirty years in the Royal Observatory and had published nothing. Some in The Royal

Society –including Newton—may have thought that Flamsteed engaged in "snuggery" or perhaps lacked the mental competence for his office.

Though Flamsteed was a member of The Royal Society, he had refused to attend society meetings during Isaac's presidency. He even remarked that the meetings "were packed with ingenious young gentlemen who were serving the interest of his enemies."[411] However on April 12, 1704, he agreed to dine with Newton at Greenwich to discuss the financial offer of Prince George. Naturally, Newton wanted to partake of any opportunity to get observations of the moon for his second edition of **The Principia**.

It wasn't the most amicable of meetings. Flamsteed had become even bolder in his later years and was willing to challenge Newton to his face, which was something Robert Hooke never did. Unlike Newton's subordinates, Flamsteed was not obedient. He had something Newton wanted, and he would hold on to that trump card as long as he could.

As the two men dined, Flamsteed, perhaps to impress Isaac, said, "When I read your fourth book of **The Principia**, I noticed a period was missing on page three. I thought it best to let you know."

Isaac did not appreciate the comment and responded, "I would thank you not to criticize my works over the dinner table. Can you hold your tongue?"

Silence ensued, and the two men resumed eating. After a long pause Flamsteed broke the silence: "I received the copy of *Opticks* you had sent to Greenwich. Thank you."

Isaac said, "I hope you approve of it."

Flamsteed jumped at another opening: "Truly I do not. You give all the fixed stars diameters of five or six seconds, and four out of five of them are not one second broad."[412]

Newton now realized that Flamsteed understood neither *Opticks* nor **The Principia**, but Isaac kept his composure and changed the subject: "John, my purpose for being here is to inquire regarding the progress on your *star* catalog, the *Historia coelestis*. Is it not true that Prince George has offered you some financial assistance to complete the work?"

"That is true, but how did you learn of it?"

"Lord Halifax has apprised me, and I would like to offer my assistance as president of The Royal Society. As you know I could use observations gathered by your superior instruments to develop a lunar theory, which I could reveal in the second edition of **The Principia**."

Flamsteed said, "Gathering and classifying all of the information has taken much time, but I am close to completion. Let me show you some of my tables and stellar maps."

The two men went into Flamsteed's library where Isaac gazed upon the vast information Flamsteed had amassed. It appeared that the Royal Astronomer was in the final stages of his catalog, so Isaac said, "As soon as everything is ready for the press, I will be glad to recommend it to the prince in hopes of gaining for you sufficient compensation."

"Please do not trouble yourself. I have much work to do before the catalog will be ready for publication."

"I would still be happy to speak to the prince on your behalf when it is ready."

"Thank you, Doctor Newton."

On that note, the two men concluded their meeting. Isaac walked Flamsteed to the door and said, "Do all the good in your power." As Newton's carriage left, Flamsteed said to himself, "Yes, 'do all the good in your power.' That has been the rule of my life since infancy, but I doubt it has been yours. I know you, Mr. Newton. You would only be my friend to the extent that I can serve your own ends."[413]

Perhaps if John Flamsteed had known about Newton's years of frustration in trying to find a correct lunar theory, he might have been more considerate. But then again, Newton had previously used Flamsteed as the scapegoat for the delay in calculating a theory of the moon. Despite the clash in personalities and the intellectual disconnect between them, hope still existed for the eventual printing the *Historia coelestis*. In fact, a month or so after Newton's visit, Prince George called on the Royal Astronomer and was so impressed with Flamsteed's observations, he offered to finance the printing and engraving of his **Star Catalog**.

On November 8, 1704 Flamsteed made an "Estimate" of what he planned to publish, including a time frame. He gave a copy or two of this estimate to his former assistant and relative, James Hodgson, who was to show it to some friends. Unfortunately, Hodgson, a Fellow in The Royal Society, took the estimate to the November 15 Society meeting to show to Flamsteed's friends; however, Secretary Hans Sloane read it to all of the members. At the next Society meeting the membership, undoubtedly prompted by Newton, voted to recommend and encourage Flamsteed's project.[414]

At the Society's annual meeting in November, Prince George, though not a natural philosopher by any means, was made a Fellow of The Royal Society. On December 7 Secretary Sloane gave the prince a copy of John Flamsteed's "prospectus" for printing, and by December 11 the Royal Astronomer officially accepted an offer of funds for his project. The Prince then authorized Newton to appoint a committee to examine Flamsteed's papers to determine which of them were ready for the press. Newton appointed himself, Roberts, Wren, Gregory and Arbuthnot. Although Flamsteed was not on the committee, he had written in his "Estimate" that the charts of the constellations (the first two parts) could be printed at once, but the third part, which contained the catalog of the fixed stars and information on the moon, had to be completed while the first two parts went through the press.[415]

Newton couldn't have been happier. The Society and the Prince had made it possible for him finally --after ten years—to receive observations on the moon from Flamsteed. On December 12, Flamsteed read the following note –or was it an order?-- from Newton:

> *Upon the orders of Prince George a committee of referees from The Royal Society has been formed to administer arrangements concerning the publication of your* **Historia coelestis**. *Please bring specimens of*

your catalog to a dinner at my home at 6:00 P.M. on December 19 in order that this committee may begin preparations.

Your very loving Friend & humble servant,

I. Newton. [416]

With only one day's notice Flamsteed obediently traveled to London and met with the referees. They were unable to complete their business and arranged for another meeting on December 27. After this second meeting, Newton visited Flamsteed on December 29 at the Royal Observatory. On this visit Isaac impressed the Royal Astronomer with his charm and solicitude, prompting Flamsteed to state in a letter to Sharp on December 30, "...he was here to visit me yesterday; stayed from 12 till near 5 o'clock; dined with me, took a new view of my books and papers, and becomes solicitor with the Prince on their behalf." But Flamsteed then added, "I shall be as cautious as I can be that he do me no injury."[417]

By January 6, 1705 Flamsteed had willingly supplied Newton with all the papers he had requested, and by January 23 the referees had submitted their findings to the Prince. From then on, however, the project became contentious. Flamsteed's first objection was that the money allowed him from the committee did not provide for funds to publish the first two parts of his catalog, which were the star catalogs from Ptolomy to his own. Flamsteed had heard that the Prince was willing to spend up to 1200 pounds, but Newton's committee offered only 863 pounds. These contentions along with the committee's selection of the publisher gave rise to many others, and soon Flamsteed began to suspect Newton's motives. Flamsteed was especially irritated with the money allotted for the publisher compared to his own remuneration. He continually brought up the 30 years he had spent compiling his unprecedented map of the heavens and was receiving less money than the publisher.

Flamsteed wanted the *Historia coelestis* printed as soon as possible; yet Newton, despite an identical objective, was the steward of the Prince's money and kept a tight rein on the purse strings. The first printing began on March 5 when Flamsteed met with Newton and his committee to inspect the first specimen sheets supplied by the publisher, Awnsham Churchill. The Royal Astronomer looked at the sheets and said, "These sheets are ill done!"[418] He then procured his own printer and printed sheets at his own expense. The committee ignored his efforts and continued with Churchill, who was correcting many Flamsteed errors.

On March 21, Francis Aston, a new member of the committee, visited Flamsteed and said, "All printing issues have been resolved except for the paper."[419] Flamsteed seemed pleased; nevertheless, due to his suspicious nature he started copying and filing every one of Isaac Newton's letters.

The bickering over money, publisher, paper, and the order of printing had put a damper on printing a star catalog, but it appeared that a contract would soon be signed and work could start. But it was not to be. In April, Newton decided to run for Parliament and would be gone for almost three months. Without Newton's presence nothing could be decided.

The underlying reason Newton had gained favor with Prince George is because Lord Halifax had again become an advisor to the throne. In the previous Parliamentary election Newton did not run because of Queen Anne's stand on religious conformity and a pamphlet by Jacobite James Drake accusing hypocrites, who pretended to be loyal members of the church, of destroying it.

But Halifax had reasoned with the Queen, who had moderated considerably, In March she decided to prorogue Parliament in order to have another election. Before Parliament adjourned, however, Halifax called on Newton to ask him to run for Parliament. Isaac held back his answer until he had visited Cambridge, which he did in the early part of March.

On March 17, Halifax called on Newton again and revealed his strategy for the upcoming election:

"Isaac, the son of Lord Godolphin will be the other Whig running with you at Cambridge. He will go to Cambridge next week. If the Queen goes to Newmarket and then to Cambridge, she has said she will do some things I have asked of her in order to help us win this election. The Tories know she wants to turn the incumbent, Mr. Annesley out. He is the Tory who defeated you in 1702."

Newton replied, "I do not share your confidence, but I will go to Cambridge and tell you my decision later."

Early in April, Newton returned from Cambridge and told Halifax, "I will stand for election."

Isaac again went to Cambridge on April 16, the same day of the Queen's visit. Halifax planned the entire day as a political rally. After sitting in a carriage in a long parade with both sides of the street packed with people, the Queen attended a banquet in the evening at Trinity's dining hall. Newton was seated on the stage with the Queen and other dignitaries. The highlight of the evening was the knighting of three persons, who had been recommended for knighthood by Lord Halifax: Isaac Newton; James Montague, brother of Lord Halifax, and John Ellis, the Vice Chancellor of Trinity. Ellis was a Tory, but wasn't running for office. Newton became a knight, not because of his mathematical and philosophical achievements nor his exemplary accomplishments at the Mint, but because Halifax needed to get him some publicity, especially with commoners.[420] Newton was already known in intellectual and scientific circles. Incidentally, Halifax, who seemed destined to reap fame and fortune, convinced the Queen to give himself an honorary doctor's degree at this banquet.

After the political affair, Newton returned to London for a week. On May 17, when he came back to Cambridge in order to campaign, he didn't like what he saw. Almost everywhere he went he encountered groups of school boys chanting, "The church is in danger! No fanatic!" It was the same hue and cry that had caused him to withdraw from the election in 1702. These youthful zealots backed the Tory party, which was the party supported by the Anglican Church. Understandably, it is hard to oppose the established church of England; yet Newton, Halifax, Locke, and others had fought against theocratic influence in government for years.

Campaigning was difficult. People screamed "occasional conformist!" at Newton because he fit the mold as someone who qualified to be a member of the Anglican Church only because he took sacraments "one time per calendar year." As a matter of fact, the Tories wanted to change these minimum requirements. If the Tories succeeded, Newton would have difficulty meeting the new requirements. His true religion might be questioned and his government position jeopardized.[421]

Isaac saw the handwriting on the wall. The climate at Cambridge was against him. In fact, Newton had written early in May to Halifax –and, ironically, also to Flamsteed: "The election appears doubtful whether I will succeed or no."[422] Flamsteed, predictably, relayed Newton's message to others. However, Halifax, who was Newton's campaign manager, sent a reply to Isaac. His letter first mentioned support for fellow Whig Francis Godolphin by the wealthy Manchesters, who were friends of the Queen. Then Halifax said:

> ... it does not look well, but I hope you still keep your Resolution of not being disturbed at the event, since there has been no fault of your's in the managemt, and there is no great matter in it[.] I could tell you some storys where the conduct [theocratic fervor] of the Court has been the same, but complaining is to no purpose and now the Die is cast, and upon the whole [we] shall have a good Parliamt. [423]

Newton responded by revealing an even more dismal assessment:

> Annesley has 26 to 28 more votes than I. If the Tory candidate Dixie Windsor were to withdraw I can pick up votes, especially if Godolphin could spare me a few. The opposition of Windsor and the vogue against me of late have discouraged my friends... and inclined different persons against me.[424]

Typically in politics, supporters expect candidates to give something for votes. Newton accordingly gave 60 pounds to Trinity and reluctantly told William Whiston he could publish Isaac's lectures on algebra.[425] Nevertheless, all of Newton's campaigning and reciprocity did not match the religious furor against him and Godolphin. He ran dead last out of the four candidates and Godolphin ran a distant third. Though he had resolved not to let failure affect him, it did. His poor opinion toward the Anglican church increased, and even his resentment increased toward John Flamsteed, who as a zealot for the church seemed to share the same religious fervor as the Cambridge youths.[426] The election wasn't a total loss, however; because of it Newton became a knight and would forever be known as "Sir Isaac Newton."

One other interesting outgrowth of the election of 1705 is that Whiston did publish Isaac's lectures in 1706 under the title "Arithmetica Universalis," but according to Isaac it had too many errors. Isaac wasn't happy with it, even though his name was omitted in the book. Sixteen years later Isaac wrote a second edition, which also had a few technical errors – after all, Newton was then almost 80 years old. The point in mentioning this fact is that "Arithmetica Universalis" became one of the most popular algebra textbooks throughout the remainder of the 18th century. However, Newton's revolutionary ground-breaking writings on calculus were only used by a few people until the 20th century, when mathematics was better understood and Newton's writings recognized as works of a genius.[427]

Upon Newton's return to London he knew that no progress had been made in printing the *Historia coelestis*; therefore, he invited Flamsteed, Gregory, Roberts and Churchill to his home for dinner in an attempt to reach an agreement. But again, due to Flamsteed's objections to the remunerations being paid to him and the publisher –among other things—nothing was agreed upon. The next day, June 12, Flamsteed wrote to John Sharp:

I prayed to God that Newton would soon see the light.[428]

A few days after that June 11 meeting, Newton and Churchill, the publisher, paid the Royal Astronomer a visit, to no avail. After the visit Flamsteed wrote in his diary:

> *Not a word of any recompense for thirty years' pains and extraordinary expense, though occasion enough offered to speak of it.*[429]

After a year of haggling, Newton began losing patience. He again wrote to Flamsteed:

> *If you stick at any thing, pray give Sir Christopher Wren and me a meeting as soon as you can conveniently, that what you stick at may be removed.*[430]

Newton was unaware that Flamsteed had been venting his spleen for months to Christopher Wren by using the "Godless" Edmund Halley as the scapegoat who had turned Newton against him. The Royal Astronomer, however, was a "Christian" and did not say anything against Newton and the referees for fear of losing his *Historia coelestis* forever.

Finally, after months of talking and disagreeing, on November 17 an agreement of sorts was reached. Churchill was to remain as publisher, but would only be paid 34 shillings per sheet, not the 114 shillings as previously proposed. Furthermore, the first 400 copies of Flamsteed's work were to be given to him, and he was given the authority to begin the remaining printing without any interference or delay. Though Flamsteed didn't like the entire agreement, he felt pressured to sign, and he did. However, he especially disliked the fact that his catalog of the fixed stars were slated to be in Volume One, not in a later volume as he had requested both in his "Estimate" and in negotiations. Quite frankly, though he knew he couldn't deliver this catalog for some time, he felt compelled to sign the agreement.

After signing the agreement, Flamsteed again wrote to his friend, John Sharp:

> *Sir Isaac Newton has at last forced me to enter into articles for printing my works with a bookseller very disadvantageous to myself.*[431]

And in his diary he wrote: *The articles were read aloud but once, and I was requested to sign them immediately, else the work was at a stand.*[432]

Unfortunately, there were more delays and the printing did not begin as planned. First of all, Flamsteed found that someone had edited four or five pages of his observation notes before they were submitted to the printer. Despite poor health, he rode to London and gave Newton and Gregory, the real culprit, a piece of his mind for an entire afternoon. He still insisted that the differences were "all the Doctor's making."[433]

As usual, the Astronomer Royal refused to admit that he had contributed to the delay. Although he had promised to deliver *first* all manuscripts for Volume One, he knew he couldn't do it. But the fact remained that he *was* the author, and though the referees had demanded the star catalog in Volume One, Flamsteed had originally asked to finish his star catalog during the printing of that volume. Furthermore, he had told Newton that the star catalog wasn't ready. Nevertheless, he was forced to sign or have the entire project cancelled.

Flamsteed considered himself a righteous individual. He tried to live up to his part of the bargain by giving a sealed copy of the uncompleted star catalog to Christopher Wren on March 8, 1706. At least he had the satisfaction of not giving it to Newton. In fact, to keep Newton from seeing the incomplete work, he instructed Wren to keep it sealed until he *alone* gave permission to open it.

At meetings with Newton and the referees on March 23 and April 19, Flamsteed again vented objections:

"It is strange that I should be so little taken notice of, who was the person mainly concerned. ...I need funds to pay my calculators."

Newton responded, "Are you aware of the delicate state of royal finances? Do you know what the war has cost us? I have already advanced 250 pounds to Churchill."

For some reason Newton didn't mention 125 pounds that the Prince had given him to pay the Astronomer Royal. Isaac wanted first to see a completed Volume One.

In September Flamsteed told Newton, "I have had to dismiss both my amanuensis and my calculators for lack of funds."

Newton did not respond.[434]

Finally a frustrated and ailing Flamsteed sent the following plea to Newton:

> *"The labor is both too hard and too much for me. For an adequate recompense I doe not expect, but I must stand on a reasonable one since God has blest my labors. ...Not to do it were not to acknowledge His goodness;and my Countries ingratitude would be attributed by Sir Isaac Newton himself to my stupidity."*[435]

The wrangling and bickering between these two men continued for six more years. And in the midst of it came another contention. The late Archdeacon of Rochester, Doctor Thomas Plume, had bequeathed 1800 pounds to Cambridge for the purpose of building an observatory and establishing a Professor of Astronomy. Richard Bentley and William Whiston, two Newton disciples who were deeply indebted to Isaac, were directed in Plume's will to choose the first Plumian Professor *only after conferring with John Flamsteed, Sir John Ellis and Isaac Newton.*

Whether it was a deliberate oversight or an unintended one, Flamsteed was never consulted regarding Whiston and Bentley's choice of John Cotes. In fact, after Cotes had been awarded the professorship, Flamsteed found out by accident that he was to have been an advisor to the nominating committee. He had been deliberately snubbed.

From that time on, the animosity between Newton and Flamsteed became so intense that objections and obstacles to printing the *Historia coelestis* accelerated for months without one page being printed. Many false accusations abounded. Newton blamed Flamsteed for incorrect observations and Flamsteed blamed the compositor for bad copy. And so it went; it was a feud for the ages. The morass ended in October of 1708 when Prince George died and no further meetings of referees were scheduled. In 1709 Newton had John Flamsteed's name stricken from membership in The Royal Society for non-payment of dues, even though other non-payers were not penalized. Flamsteed wrote to Sharp:

"Our society is ruined by his close, politic and cunning forecast."[436]

Historians have not emphasized one characteristic shared by John Flamsteed and Robert Hooke. Both men sought recognition and fame. They tried to be famous, but did not possess the intellect of Isaac Newton and other great scientists of The Enlightenment. Though Newton was concerned about his livelihood, he was primarily interested in solving the mysteries of life and the universe. He repeatedly demonstrated that he eschewed the limelight; nevertheless, he had a voracious work ethic, an insatiably curious mind, and a superhuman intelligence; all of which gave him a decided advantage over other mortals. Though he did not overtly seek glory for himself, he did take umbrage against those who he thought desired esteem undeservedly. Furthermore, although Flamsteed castigated Newton in letters to friends, Isaac carefully selected his words when writing to third parties about Flamsteed.

"The fact remains that Flamsteed never surrendered to Newton's will nor obeyed Newton's bidding. His obstinance infuriated Newton to no end. Newton destroyed all references to Flamsteed in **The Principia,** an expunging he had previously exacted on Robert Hooke. At King's School over sixty years ago, Arthur Storer learned the consequences of crossing Isaac Newton. Newton demanded loyalty and commanded respect. Few men had the courage and competence to cross the lion of Cambridge."

CHAPTER 38

1706 A.D.

• • •

"Perhaps the biggest event in 1706 was the union of England and Scotland. On April 10 Queen Anne placed Lord Halifax on the commission to negotiate the "Act of Union." Since both nations would need the same monetary system, Halifax made Newton responsible for minting in both countries. This was not an easy task. The Edinburgh Mint had coined nothing since 1701 and needed new equipment and guidance. Many of its castings were not fit for minting. Consequently, Isaac sought permission from Lord Treasurer Godolphin to appoint David Gregory, a native Scot, as Newton's representative in Edinburgh. He also sent three moneyers and a clerk to spend one year in the Scottish capital. By November of 1707, after originally suffering many technical problems, recoinage began to proceed smoothly –thanks to the extraordinary administrative ability of Isaac Newton. ...

Another event of significance in 1706 occurred two days before Halifax became a commissioner for the Act of Union. On April 8 he drew up a will naming Catherine Barton the beneficiary of 3000 pounds and all of his jewels. During that summer Newton must have accepted the relationship between his niece and Halifax because in October, Lord Halifax added a codicil to his will providing an annuity of 200 pounds per year to Catherine in Isaac's name.

1706 was also the year that Isaac Newton published his Latin edition of *Opticks*. He had been so pleased with the reception of the English version, he decided to produce *Opticks* in Latin so that the classical European scholars could savor his revolutionary work.⁴³⁷ It was at this time that Isaac had developed a close friendship with Abraham de Moivre, a young mathematician who understood *Opticks* and enjoyed discussing it at Isaac's home almost every evening. Newton had again found someone with whom to wax philosophically. Soon de Moivre became a Newton disciple and was given the opportunity of seeing Isaac's second edition of *Opticks* through the press. Another close friend and disciple, Samuel Clarke, translated the work from English into Latin. Newton was so happy with the finished product that he gave 100 pounds to each of Clarke's five children.⁴³⁸ De Moivre's and Clarke's unselfish service was a pleasant change from the relationship Isaac was currently experiencing with Flamsteed, who consistently seemed to talk about himself and what benefitted him.

But perhaps the most serious events which surfaced in 1706 were by two of Newton's disciples, who began to publicly air their religious views.

The first disciple to reveal his religious views was Fatio de Duillier of The Royal Society, who, along with his brother John, joined a group of exiled French Camisards. Protestants had been persecuted in France even before Louis XIV revoked the Edict of Nantes in 1685. But in 1702, Huguenot leaders and their followers began open warfare on the French army. The Huguenots wore a traditional smock called a *camise*, from which they got their name. Fatio de Duillier sympathized with the exiled Camisards and quickly became their secretary and spokesperson. In 1706 the exiled Camisard commander, Jean Cavalier, visited de Duillier in London and related a sad story to him:

"Monsieur de Duillier, for two years my Camisards won every battle waged against the King's troops, including a decisive victory on the Ides of March in 1704. Unfortunately, on April 17, I suffered a crippling defeat near Nimes against a large French army sent by King Louis. The entire province of Cevennes was almost destroyed. Three days later, the King's troops found our secret caves which held our food and supplies. By this time the King's great Field Marshall de Villars had taken command of the French troops and proposed terms of surrender to me. Regrettably, I was obviously a better general than a negotiator. I accepted terms which I thought included restoring freedom of thought and religion; otherwise, it would have been an unconditional surrender. Unfortunately, I misjudged the compassion of the King, who is required to approve any terms of surrender. I was under the impression that de Villars represented the King and that Louis XIV would approve the terms de Villars had agreed to.

"For more than eight days we prayed, sang hymns and listened to our preachers. Huguenots from all over the Languedoc began pouring into Calvisson, where Camisard troops were gathered. Everyone anticipated that their freedoms would be restored. But when the King's answer arrived, it was worse than any of us could have imagined. It reminded me of the response given by General Simon de Montfort to the Cathars during the Albigensian Crusade in the 13th century –which, incidentally was also in the Languedoc.

"Not only did the King deny freedom of worship, all Camisards either had to enlist in the French army or leave the country. Naturally I was devastated, as were my officers and other leaders. Fortunately, some of my lieutenants had stayed clear of the gathering at Calvisson and continued to fight. Tragically, in the next few years most Huguenot officers who didn't leave the country were assassinated, executed, imprisoned or forced to surrender. Of course my countrymen were most unhappy with me, so I fled to the Savoy with only a few of my troops.

"The last great battle of the Camisards was at Saint-Benezet in 1704, where up to 200 Camisards were killed under the leadership of one of my lieutenants. Early this year, 1706, while serving under the Duke of Savoy, I attempted an invasion into the Languedoc, but my regiment was virtually annihilated. I was severely wounded but managed to escape to England, where you now find me and many other Camisards. Unfortunately, most of them haven't forgiven me for the regrettable surrender at Calvisson."[439]

Fatio soon became passionately committed to the Camisard cause and their prophecies from the book of "Revelation," including their predictions of Judgment Day. De Duillier not only became a Camisard, he published pamphlets fashioning his own interpretations of Camisard ravings and prophecy. In 1707 the Camisards created such a stir in London that authorities arrested three of their leaders: Fatio de Duillier, Elie Marion and Jean Daude', who were convicted of spreading terror among Her Majesty's subjects. At this time Fatio had become an object of conversation throughout London. The Crown offered him a chance to leave the country, but he refused. Consequently, he and his cohorts were sentenced to standing on the scaffold of Charing Cross and The Royal Exchange on December 1 and 2. They also paid stiff fines and had to put up security for good behavior for one year.[440] In spite of the punishment, Fatio supported the Camisard cause for the rest of his life. Although Newton sympathized with the Huguenots and their sufferings, he kept his distance from the Camisards; their preachings, especially concerning judgment day, were extreme. Leibniz, though sympathetic with Fatio, wrote to a friend: "I do not understand how so excellent a man in mathematics could have embarked on such an affair."[441] Little did he know that Newton also had unorthodox views.

Incidentally, General Jean Cavalier, though ostracized by most of his followers, entered British society and was eventually appointed by the Crown to be Governor of the Isle of Jersey.

Another disciple who began to preach unorthodox views around 1706 was William Whiston, the hand-picked heir to Newton's Lucasian Chair of Mathematics and the person who published Isaac's lectures on algebra. In 1707, however, Whiston gave written evidence about his leanings when he edited a prayer in a *Collection of Sermons and Essays Upon Several Subjects* by deleting the words "Three Persons and One God." Dr. William Sacheverell, whose son had been one of Isaac Newton's students, immediately labeled Whiston's editing as an example of blasphemy and irreligion.[442]

As the end of the first decade of the 18th century approached, it was not a good idea in England to praise the Pope or oppose the Trinity of the Council of Nicaea.

CHAPTER 39

William Whiston

• • •

"Moshe, in 1706 William Whiston began to air his Arian views, which was a daring and defiant thing to do. Since the enactment of the law that forbade public worship by Catholics and non-Trinitarians, no one except an 18 year-old student in Edinburgh had been bold enough to challenge that law, and you know what happened to him. But Whiston believed he needed to reform the church, to show it the error of its ways. He wanted another reformation, one in which the church would adopt the true original Trinity, not a corrupted one that had been followed since 325 A.D.. I can imagine the conversations between Newton, Clarke, Bentley, Whiston and other Newton disciples about the Christian church existing before and after the Council of Nicaea. Whiston was probably startled by Newton in the late 17th century when he listened as Isaac privately talked about the corruption of scripture. ...

"William, I have thoroughly researched New Testament scriptures selected at the Council of Nicaea and have found that certain scriptures had been changed at that council."

"Are you certain?" asked Whiston.

"Of course,"said Isaac. "I would not reveal my research unless my conclusions are accurate. If scripture had not been changed, I would not have told you they had been."

"Which scriptures are you referring to?"

"There are many, including a scripture upon which most Christian churches are currently founded. It is the Trinitarian concept adopted by Athanasius in the 4th century"

"Which is…?"

"*The First Epistle of John*, Chapter Five, seventh verse."

"Ah yes. 'The Father, the Son and the Holy Ghost' –the Trinity."

"Correct, said Newton. However, original scripture as written by Dionysius referred to the Trinity as 'The Father, the *Word* and the *Spirit*.' Except for the change by Athanasius, John's *Epistle* makes much sense. Reason, itself, indicates that since Jesus was born eons after creation, he obviously is not equal to God, the Architect of the Universe."

"Perhaps not; however, Jesus gives a *face*, something to see, something to worship."

"Exactly! People need something they can see, something akin to themselves, and Athanasius gave it to them –a *human God*! But is that not also a violation of the first Commandment?"

"I don't think so. The three entities are merged as one."

"But that is *not* monotheism, William; that is a triumvirate. Did God not provide the other two entities? He gave his son and his spirit, but both came *from Him* –they were created by Him. Jesus spoke the *word* and was *godliness* in the flesh, as Arius agrees, but he is *not* God. Jesus died on a cross, but the *Word of God* has continued as disciples have written."

Whiston then said, "So you contend that Athanasius changed Christianity."

"Unquestionably," said Newton. "After most of the bishops at Nicaea voted for his concept of the Trinity and not for Arius's, it became blasphemous to say that our Lord was a work that came to be. People weren't allowed to say that Jesus became the Son of God at the time of his birth. According to Athanasius, Jesus was a divine Sonship from the *beginning of time*.[443]

"After Nicaea, Athanasius returned to Egypt and was one of many charismatic teachers in the vicinity of Alexandria. He wrote his 39th Festal letter, which was the first document precisely listing the 27 books of the <u>New Testament</u>. However, unlike most of the teachers and prophets in Egypt at that time, Athanasius had an imperial orthodoxy in which he was the supreme leader and messenger of Christian piety. To safeguard the changes made to the scriptures, he condemned to death anyone who advocated other concepts. Consequently, Arius became a fugitive and was forced to travel into other countries because he steadfastly maintained his belief in the original Trinity."[444]

"You have documented this?"

"Of course, but as you know, I must be careful in revealing it. If you doubt anything I have said, I implore you to study Christianity before and after the Council of Nicaea. If you are a man of reason, you will conclude that Jesus Christ had no part in creating the universe? He arrived after planets had evolved. In truth, he didn't even know most planets existed."

Although Newton revealed his beliefs to trusted disciples, he was well aware that if his words reached the wrong ears, his livelihood and his fame would be in jeopardy. In fact, Newton expected those to whom he entrusted his Arianism to conceal his name within their breasts. Assuredly, Whiston was trustworthy, as were all of the men with whom Newton shared his unorthodox religious views. At one time, Whiston spent four hours discussing the book of "Revelation" with Newton.[445] He was even privy to Newton's theological papers, which were seen by a very select few.

Whiston did study the scriptures and came to the same conclusions as his mentor. His views on Arianism became almost identical to Newton's,[446] as were Bentley's, Clarke's and others who were in a circle of free thinkers who had garnered their inspiration at Isaac's knee. However, Whiston began to profess his views on the Trinity in his Boyle Lectures. He was the only disciple who publicly proclaimed his Arian beliefs during Newton's lifetime. The other disciples opted not to risk their livelihoods.

In fact, in 1709, Whiston's friend Samuel Clarke, who also delivered some Boyle Lectures, was suspected of being an Arian. When Clarke completed his Doctorate work in Divinity, Dr. James, the Regius Professor at Cambridge, invited Clarke into his office and confronted him regarding his religious beliefs:

"Mr. Clarke, Do you believe in the Trinity?"

"Of course," said Clarke. "Why do you ask?"

"I have observed you keeping company with William Whiston."

"William can be a little outspoken with his views, I would say."

Dr. James said, "But I have heard similar views from you."

Clarke responded, "Only when I am quoting historical fact."

"I have heard you speak, Samuel, and I have read your theses. To me they embody Arianism. If you are an Arian, you are not an Anglican. Do you reject Arianism?"

"I could do that. And I could also tell you that I reject Catholicism, but Catholicism would still continue to exist. So how can my rejecting Arianism affect anything? Shouldn't we be able to discuss different religions without being accused or identified with them?"

"Are you telling me that your views regarding Arianism are strictly academic?"

"You might say so. ...Yes, you can say that if you wish. Is there anything else, Doctor?"

The doctor stammered and said, "No, Mr. Clarke. That will be all for the present."

That very evening Whiston, Clarke and Bentley dined together to celebrate Clarke's doctorate. After some jovial dinner banter, Clarke brought up his conversation with Dr. James:

"Our Regius Professor of Divinity called me into his office today. We had a most interesting conversation."

Bentley asked, "Regarding...?"

" Dr. James asked me if I rejected Arianism."

Whiston asked, "What did you tell him?"

"I think I avoided the question. I said, 'If I rejected Arianism, what good would it do? My rejecting it wouldn't make it disappear.'"

Bentley said, "So you didn't reject it. "

"You might say that."

Bentley laughed, "Well done, Samuel. I think we should write a jingle about this. . What do you think, William?"

Whiston answered, "Pray do it, Richard."

"All right," said Bentley, as he scrawled on his tablet and spoke:

The venerable Regius Professor
Wanted Clarke to be a confessor.
Sam had none of that rot,
And confess he did not.
The Professor remained still a guesser.

The three men laughed uproariously.

"Well done," said Clarke. But please translate that limerick into Latin or destroy it. There are not many in Cambridge who share those sentiments. Definitely do not use my name."

Clarke may have walked a tight rope, but Whiston defied the odds by openly admitting he was an Arian. After three years of exposing his heterodoxy, he was ordered to answer charges of violating university statutes in front of Vice-Chancellor Dr. Lany and eleven Masters from Cambridge. The hearing began in Autumn of 1710 in the Master's Hall at Trinity College. Dr. Lany sat in the center of a table with eleven Masters, all of them facing William Whiston. Lany was the first person to speak:

"Dr. Whiston, you have been charged with violating university statutes by speaking against the Trinity as established by the Church of

England, and you have denied the Trinity in your writings. Have you anything to say in your defense?"

Whiston rose and answered, "Your eminence, I have never denied the existence of the Trinity. In fact, I have defended the true definition of it. To me it is an affront to Christianity that these proceedings are even taking place."

"*We* are an affront to Christianity by holding this hearing? Have you not denied that the Trinity is God, His Son Jesus Christ and the Holy Ghost?"

"I have maintained only that these three are not equal to one another, and I think that this commission should make a likewise determination."

"So you *admit* denying the Trinity as decreed by the Holy Church."

"Dr. Lany, the Holy Church has adopted a corruption of the scriptures, and it now has an opportunity to correct this grievous error."

"What is this corruption of which you speak?"

"That Christ is equal to God."

Dr. Lany rose and exclaimed in a loud voice, "Christ **IS** God!!"

Whiston responded, "He was never considered God by Christians until 325 A.D., sir; and it is time for our church to reform as it did in 1517 when Martin Luther exposed similar church corruptions."

"Are you stating to this commission that the church is corrupt because we accept Jesus Christ as our God and Saviour?"

"I did not say the church was corrupt. But it *has* adopted corrupted scripture. We can still accept Jesus Christ as the Son of God and the greatest teacher and savior the world has known. He spoke the *word* of God and was *godliness* in the flesh –*but he is not God!* The church believed in a different Trinity before the Council of Nicaea, but *Athanasius* changed everything by equating Jesus with God. The ancient prophets and the primitive church defined the Trinity as 'The Father, the Word and the Spirit,' and that is what *we* need to do."

"In other words, Dr. Whiston, you are denying the scriptures established by the Bishops at the Council of Nicaea."

"I deny only those scriptures that have been corrupted, those which the Council of Nicaea changed. Athanasius misquoted Dionysius, who had said that homoousis –three Gods in one-- was heretical. Athanasius told the opposite to the council at Nicaea. Is it not obvious that the Catholic and Anglican Churches, along with most other sects, have adopted a concept of the Trinity that is completely false?"

Dr. Lany answered, "No, it is not obvious, Professor Whiston. What is obvious to me and the other members of this holy commission is that you are rejecting the very foundation of Trinity University *and* our Holy Church. I have heard enough. This commission will now retire in order to make a judgment regarding your actions."

Dr. Lany and the eleven members of his panel adjourned to an anteroom. Whiston took this opportunity to glance around the hearing room to check out the people in attendance. He took particular notice that his close friend, Richard Bentley, the Chancellor of Trinity, was not in the audience. Noticeably absent were other Arian friends; namely, Samuel Clarke, a fellow Boyle lecturer; Isaac Newton, Whiston's mentor and immediate past Lucasian Professor of Mathematics at Trinity; and Hopton Haynes, another Arian friend.

The panel of men returned to the hearing room in less than fifteen minutes. All sat at the table. Dr. Lany addressed William Whiston:

"Professor Whiston, you are in violation of one of Trinity University's most sacred statutes. If you do not recant your heretical concepts and accept the Trinity as adopted by your church, you will lose all preferments at Trinity University. We will convene again on October 30 in order to hear your decision."

The commission met again on October 30, 1710. Dr. Lany addressed William Whiston:

"Professor Whiston, have you a statement?"

"I have, your eminence."

"And? ...

"It would be hypocritical for me to deny the truth in order to preserve my position. And I will allow neither interest nor favor to bias my integrity. I have spoken the truth, and I implore this commission not to punish me but embrace the truth and lead the church in returning to the true Trinity."

"Is that your final word?"

"It is, your Grace."

"William Whiston, as of this date you are relieved of your Lucasian Chair and your fellowship. You are hereby banned forever from Trinity University. Please vacate the premises and turn over all keys and university property by the first day of November. May Jesus Christ reveal to you the error of your ways and have mercy upon you."

The members of the commission rose and filed out of the room behind Dr. Lany. Whiston was dumbfounded. He couldn't believe that none of the twelve theologians agreed with him. The Whiston reformation came to an abrupt defeat, but its champion never recanted nor retreated from his beliefs. He furthermore chided his Arian comrades for giving up their souls for worldly treasures, and wrote that preferment is the "utter Ruin of Virtue and Religion! Poison, sweet Poison." [447]

Whiston took his family to London, where he attempted to earn a living by lecturing and writing. He wrote mathematical, scientific and religious papers and was invited to speak on many occasions, including Royal Society gatherings. Considering himself a martyr, he continually published attacks on the church's doctrine of the Trinity. In one of his papers he defended Arianism with material he had extracted from Newton's private papers;[448] however, he never mentioned Newton's name in any of his writings.

Newton was not pleased over the Whiston episode. Whiston's attempts to immediately reform the existing church conflicted with Newton's belief that it would be centuries before any apocalypse could occur. Newton had interpreted prophecy and knew that false prophecy would continue until a true Judgment Day appeared when men would finally realize the error of their ways, when the one and *only* God would finally be accepted. But until that day, no amount of lecturing or evangelizing would succeed. The world simply had to come to truth in their own sweet time. In the meantime, Newton proceeded to privately educate one man at a time –without jeopardizing himself.

Isaac also did not want disciples removed from the high offices he had attained for them. The Church of England wielded great power, and like many organized religions, it molded the minds of its members from birth. To extricate himself from being connected in any way with Whiston, Newton severed ties with him. In fact, when Whiston later attempted to join The Royal Society, Newton threatened to resign if Whiston's name were presented for membership. Although he challenged Newton in knowledge and intelligence in many areas, no one presented Whiston's name in nomination for membership in The Royal Society, nor did Newton ever mention him.

Whiston's Arian brothers however, forever concealing their heterodoxy, elected to take the poison of preferment and avoided coming to Whiston's defense. Isaac Newton did hire Whiston's son as a domestic employee, but fired him after 3000 pounds of bank notes disappeared from Isaac's desk. The young lad soon purchased an estate –for the price of 3000 pounds. Newton refused to prosecute, perhaps out of charity or fear of ridicule.

In the meantime, Bentley, Clarke and other Newtonians did everything short of denouncing Arianism in order to preserve their preferments and their livelihoods.[449]

CHAPTER 40

Weighty Responsibilities

• • •

"As the first decade of the eighteenth century ended, Isaac was overwhelmed with numerous challenges and responsibilities. Although he was not physically involved with the Whiston inquisition, it caused him mental anguish. But Isaac didn't allow anything to interfere with an agenda that would tax a twenty-five year-old, let alone someone who was approaching seventy. ...

First of all, Isaac had undertaken the additional responsibility of overseeing England's entire tin operation during a time when tin had become unprofitable. In order to insure a monopoly on tin mining and sales, Queen Anne had agreed to buy all of the tin in order to help the tin miners. Newton had agreed to store, sell and ship the tin. Furthermore, Mint duties had increased, and Isaac had to carefully monitor the new Edinburgh Mint because its officers were quite greedy; they attempted repeatedly to take higher salaries and other benefits that were undeserved. Truly, Isaac was encountering administrative nightmares at the mints.

Furthermore in 1710, The Royal Society began to have additional problems with Dr. John Woodward, the council member who had saved the Society from eviction after the death of Robert Hooke. Shortly after the turn of the century, Woodward had ridiculed Society experiments in a newsletter called the 'Transactioneer.' In 1706 he had made impolitic remarks at Society meetings. This time the council gave him notice that if his abusive conduct continued, the 'Statute Concerning Ejection' would be taken into consideration.[450]

Woodward shaped up until March of 1710 when he began ridiculing Secretary Dr. Hans Sloane, who was presiding over a Society meeting for Isaac Newton. I won't bore you with all the details, Moshe; they don't relate to the topic of your thesis. Suffice it to say that Dr. Sloane preferred charges, and on May 3, Newton ordered the reading of the 'Statute of Ejection' as he had threatened to do in 1706. He then ordered a 'mandatory' meeting of the council on May 24, at which time 21 of 24 council members attended. Woodward and two of his friends did not attend. At this meeting the members voted that "Dr. Woodward declare he is sorry that he misunderstood Dr. Sloane and beg his pardon for the reflecting words he spake."[451]

As Newton had expected, Woodward was too proud to apologize, and the council voted to remove him. He didn't go quietly. He took legal action at the Court of the Queen's Bench to be reinstated, but his reinstatement was denied. Later, Isaac told a biographer that he had told Woodward, "We allow you to have *natural philosophy*, but turn you out for want of *moral*." [452]

Knowing that the Society was using Woodward's chambers at Gresham College for its meetings, Newton started looking for other quarters. At a special meeting of the Council on September 8, 1710, he announced that the late Dr. Edward Browne's house on Crane Court was for sale and "might be a proper place to be purchased by the Society for their meetings."[453] He then dispatched Sir Christopher Wren and Wren's son to examine the building. At the next council meeting twelve of the thirteen members present voted to purchase Dr. Browne's house for 1,450 pounds.[454] The final sale took place on October 26. Co-secretary John Harris and Walter Clavell refused to participate in the sales process. They and John Lowthorp, another Woodward backer, failed to win reelection to the council at the November 30 annual meeting, which was attended by at least 80 members. The large turnout was because Woodward had mounted a campaign to oust Newton and his supporters in the council.[455] However, the election turned out to be a mandate for the Newton faction.

As old and as busy as Newton was, he successfully mounted a campaign to rid the Council of disloyal members and to arrange the purchasing, financing and remodeling of new quarters for The Royal Society. Fortunately, the efforts by Newton and Sloane in 1706 to improve the finances of The Royal Society made the purchase at #2 Crane Court possible. In all candor, however, repairs to the Crane Court building had cost much more than estimated. Newton, therefore, contributed 120 pounds toward remodeling the premises, and persuaded many others to do likewise. Consequently, the entire mortgage and refurbishing debts were paid off in less than six years.[456]

Incidentally, during rehabilitation of the quarters on Crane Court, the Society met in the rooms of Professor Andrew Tooke at Gresham College, supposedly because Newton did not want Woodward to have an opportunity to evict The Royal Society from his premises. It turned out to be a good decision, because repairs to the new Society quarters took over ten months. Finally on August 2, 1711, Newton instructed his clerk, Henry Hunt, to take possession of the Society's new home.

As if Newton didn't have enough to do, he also changed his own residence at the end of 1709 and moved to Chelsea after living more than a decade on Jermyn Street. Yet, before the Society moved into its new quarters, Newton again changed his residence to a house on St. Martin's Street, south of Leicester Fields, which is now Leicester Square.

In the last quarter of 1709 through all of 1710, Newton was marketing tin, managing mints in England and Scotland, combating adversaries in The Royal Society, changing residences twice, working on a second edition of his **Principia** –and, of course, working on a way to get observations of the moon out of John Flamsteed. Just thinking about Flamsteed frustrated him enough to consider approaching the Queen for assistance.

Receiving a mandate from The Royal Society at its annual meeting in late 1710, Newton was given almost complete control over that distinguished body. At the first council meeting in January of 1711, Isaac instigated four new parliamentary procedures:

1. Only the President sits at the head of the table and the two secretaries toward the lower end opposite each other. A very honorable stranger may sit next to the President at his discretion.
2. If any paper is to be read, it shall be minuted and placed in the Journal to be read at the next meeting.
3. Members must address the President when speaking. Any other talk must not interrupt the business of the Society.
4. All papers must be translated into English.[457]

Newton also introduced the practice of placing the mace on the table only when the President sat in the chair. The ego of Isaac Newton had begun to expose itself.

From 1711 on, Newton molded The Royal Society to his designs, and frankly, the Society began to improve in membership, finances and experiments. By now Newton had become a world-renowned person, and many famous people from all over the world came to visit him at The Royal Society and sit at his right hand.[458]

Newton's obligations also increased at the Mint due to a special bounty for silver plate; consequently, Isaac missed the Wednesday Society meetings in the first two months of 1711. The council and the Society however, in deference to their president, voted in March to shift weekly meetings to Thursday. The Society had fallen firmly behind its President.

Now that Isaac appeared to be in control at The Royal Society, he commanded the utmost respect from Society members. If anyone opposed or contradicted him, that person might be ostracized until he changed his ways. Members of the Society had learned to be subordinate to the president, who had finally become the man his grandmother wanted him to be. Though he had always been superior in intellect, he now commanded respect as a leader. In truth, if anyone challenged Isaac Newton, he could probably expect some type of repercussion. The men of The Royal Society watched their words carefully when talking with him.

...That is all except John Flamsteed, the Astronomer Royal.

CHAPTER 41

The Incorrigible Royal Astronomer

• • •

"MOSHE, NOW THAT NEWTON HAD secured his positions at The Royal Society and the Mint, he was able to devote more time toward his second edition of **The Principia** and a more accurate theory of the moon. Unfortunately, he still needed observations from the Royal Observatory in Greenwich, and since the death of Prince George in 1708, nothing had been forthcoming from the Royal Astronomer. The power of the referees, who had been appointed to oversee publishing Flamsteed's *Historia coelestis*, had also lapsed.[459] ...

Nevertheless, at a special meeting of the council on December 24, 1710, Dr. John Arbuthnot, one of Queen Anne's physicians and a former referee, revealed a warrant he had obtained from the Queen. The Warrant specifically appointed 'Sir Isaac Newton and others as the council deemed fit to be constant visitors of the Royal Observatory.' A constant visitor has the authority to visit an institution to inspect and supervise and thus prevent or remove abuses or irregularities. The warrant required visitors to demand yearly copies of observations made by the Royal Astronomer and to direct him to make certain observations.[460] Of course, Flamsteed believed Newton was behind these royal orders and that they were unwarranted. In any event, Newton was pleased with the warrant. On March 14, 1711, Doctor Arbuthnot delivered it to Flamsteed:

> By the command of Her Majesty, the Queen of England, you are to complete the publication of the <u>Historia coelestis</u>. I also request that you

deliver any missing material that has been promised. I refer specifically to your catalog of the fixed stars.[461]

On March 25, however, Flamsteed found that printing of the catalog had already begun, and he promptly sent a letter to Arbuthnot:

> I welcome the news that publication of my catalog has already resumed. I wish to inform you that I have completed the catalogue as far as I think is necessary. Meanwhile by the good providence of God ([who] has hitherto conducted all my Labours; and I doubt not will do so to an happy conclusion), I have found some fresh discoveries that differ from existing tables relating to the placement of planets. I have begun to construct new tables, but I need help to complete them in order to make the work worthy of the queen's patronage and the memory of her consort. Will you meet with me to discuss the matter?[462]

Dr. Arbuthnot showed Flamsteed's letter to Newton, who became livid upon reading it. Newton was not pleased that it took Flamsteed three years to reveal "fresh discoveries," if, in fact, there were any. In an agitated state He composed a letter to Flamsteed. Although there is no record of Flamsteed receiving it, the letter was found in Newton's records:[463]

> By discoursing wth Sr. Arbuthnot about your book of observations wch is in the Press, Iunderstand that he has wrote to you by her Majts order for such observations as are requisite to complete the catalogue of the fixed stars & you have given an indirect & dilatory answer. You know that the Prince had appointed five gentlemen to examin[e] what was fit to be printed at his Highness expence, & to take care that the same should be printed. Their order was only to print what they judged proper for the Princes honour & you undertook under your hand & seal to supply them therewith, & thereupon your observations were put into the press. The observatory was founded to the intent that a complete

catalogue of the fixt stars should be composed by observations to be made at Greenwich & the duty of your place is to furnish the observations. But you have delivered An imperfect catalogue wthout so much as sending the observations of the stars that are wanting, & I heare that the Press now stops for want of them. You are therefore desired either to send the rest of your cataloge to Dr. Arbuthnot or... to send him the observations wch are wanting to complete it, that the press may proceed. And if instead thereof you propose any thing else or make any excuses or unnecessary delays it will be taken for an indirect refusal to comply wth her Majts order. Your speedy & direct answer to compliance is expected.[464]

On March 29, Dr. Arbuthnot and the Royal Astronomer met at Garaways coffeehouse in London. The meeting was cordial, and after the usual informal greetings and health inquiries, Flamsteed asked a question:

"Doctor, I have heard that printing is taking place, not only on my charts of the constellations, but also on my star catalog. I sincerely hope that printing is not occurring on the catalog. I have told you of fresh discoveries that require new tables in the placement of planets, and I hope that nothing is being printed regarding my star catalog. Am I correct?"

"John, I know of nothing --not a sheet. Furthermore, regarding the sheets being printed on the constellations, I will pay you ten pounds for every fault you find in the printing."

"Thank you, doctor. I was more than concerned that the sealed envelope containing my catalog, which I had given Sir Christopher Wren five years ago, had been opened without my consent. I must admit, however, that three years ago I allowed Dr. Newton to open it in order to insert some recent computations. I thought we had both agreed to reseal the envelope. It should not have been reopened without my consent. I thought I had stated as much."

Arbuthnot said, "John, if Newton said he wouldn't open it, he wouldn't."

"That is what troubles me. I don't think Newton elicited a response."

"John, you will have just, honorable, equitable and civil usage of your observations."[465]

"Thank you, Dr. Arbuthnot."

The two men parted company without further comment.

Four days after his conversation with Arbuthnot, Flamsteed received printed sheets on the constellations Aries and Taurus. He remarked to Hodgson, "The sheets are fairly printed."

Then Hodgson asked, "Did you know that Halley has been showing the contents of your sealed envelope in a coffeehouse. He is complaining about many errors?"

"What!" exclaimed the astronomer. "Dr. Arbuthnot lied to me! That envelope was to be kept sealed by Isaac Newton."

"That isn't all," said Hodgson. "The contents of your envelope are being printed by Halley after his editing."

"This entire affair is a gross deception![466] It is one of the boldest things that ever was attempted. Ever since this project started Newton could have kept me abreast of what was transpiring; yet, I have heard nothing." [467]

On May 11, Flamsteed wrote to his friend John Sharp:

Newton's conduct is a villainous outrage for which Halley is partly to blame.[468]

As Halley submitted more proofs to the printer, Flamsteed became more enraged:

For Halley to be adulterating my life's work is the worst of insults. He is spoiling my work.[469]

On April 17, Flamsteed wrote to Arbuthnot:

Do not tease me with banter, by telling me yt these alterations are made to please me when you are sensible [that] nothing can be more displeasing nor injurious, then to be told so....Would you like to have your labours surreptitiously forced out of your hands, conveyed into the hands of your declared profligate Enemys, printed w/o your consent and spoiled as mine are in impression?

Would you suffer your Enemys to make themselves judges of what they really understand not? Would you not withdraw your Copy out of their hands ...and publish your own works rather then see them spoyled and your self Laught at for his suffering. I must insist that a new copy of the star catalog must be substituted for the mutilated, incomplete manuscript in my enemys' hands. I will print it at my own expense. If this cannot be done, I will no longer cooperate with those in charge of the printing." [470]

Arbuthnot responded in four days:

I have no design to rob you of ye fruit of your labours but... I will not delay any longer but take ye same method to make out ye rest of the Catalogue yt you have done, which to employ people to Calculate from the observations what is wanting; and why we should not succeed as well in this piece of Journey work I cannot imagine. If after perusing the finished work, you do not approve of what you see, you shall be free to print your own. [471]

One month elapsed before any further communication with Flamsteed took place. Finally, on May 30, Newton broke the ice and sent an order to the Royal Astronomer signed by two other "visitors":

Please observe the upcoming solar eclipse on July 4 and send data for same to the house of the Royal Society. [472]

Late in June, Edmund Halley took his turn communicating to Flamsteed:

> *I have delivered an edited copy of the star catalog to your niece, Mrs. James Hodgson, in the hope that you will avail yourself of an opportunity to correct any mistake that you might discover. I am not so foolish as to believe that no errors exist. However, I pray that you will govern your passions, and when you see what I have done for you, you may believe that I deserve at your hands a much better treatment than you …have been pleased to bestow on Your quondam friend and not yet profligate Enemy (as you call me).*[473]

Flamsteed examined the proofs of the star catalog that Halley had submitted and promptly wrote to Newton:

> *…When I examined the star catalog as submitted by Halley, I found more faults in it, and greater than I imagined the impudent editor could, or durst have committed. As I had planned, I will print it myself—and in my own good time.*[474]

The official "visitors" printing of the star catalog went ahead despite the vehement objections of the author, and for almost four months Flamsteed had nothing to do with Newton; furthermore, he ignored Newton's order to observe and record the solar eclipse of July 4. Since nothing had been submitted on the solar eclipse, the Royal Astronomer was called before the "constant visitors" on October 26.

When Flamsteed arrived at Crane Court on that date, Halley, in an act of friendship, greeted him:

"Hello, John. May I offer you a cup of coffee? And may I also offer my assistance in your meeting today."

Flamsteed scarcely looked at Halley. Instead of shaking hands or responding to Halley's good intentions, the royal astronomer gestured to his manservant to brush Halley aside. Flamsteed then limped up the stairs to the meeting room where he found Newton, Meade and Sloane waiting for him. Newton immediately addressed the astronomer:

"Mr. Flamsteed, What instruments are at Greenwich and which are in need of repair?"

Flamsteed answered, "I make all necessary repairs myself. The instruments belong to me; they are not the property of the government."

"As good have no observatory as no instruments," said Newton.

"Why are you editing and printing my star catalog? I am being robbed of the fruits of my labors."

"You call us 'robbers of your labors'?"

"I am sorry, but you owe yourselves to be so."

"How dare you, sir! You have had ample time to correct and present your observations, but you have done nothing but prevent, delay and obstruct the observations of Her Majesty's observatory. You are an impudent puppy, a knave, a disgrace to her Majesty. You disobey her orders, not mine. You are insubordinate and disrespectful!"

"I have all admiration and respect for Her Majesty's order, for the honor of the nation and its citizens, but it is a dishonor to the nation, Her Majesty and the Society –nay, to the president himself—to use me so."[475]

Newton's face flushed as he raised his voice, "You are the one who dishonors the nation. You are hereby ordered not to remove any instruments from the observatory."

"I have already agreed that if I am turned out, I would carry only my sextant with me. Right now I only desire that you restrain your temper and your passion."

"You are a belligerent fool, John."

"Thank you, sir."

"And you are an ass!"

"Thank you, again."

"You have received 3600 pounds from the government, and what have you given in return?"

"What have you done for your 500 pounds a year salary?"

Newton was unable to compose himself. He stood up and railed at Flamsteed: "You are proud and insolent –and you have insulted me. You have even called me an 'Atheist'."

"I only know what other people say about a paragraph in your *Opticks*."

Flamsteed stood up and limped toward the door as he spoke, "I bid you good day, Sir."

Dr. Sloane, who had remained silent during the shouting match, rose to help the royal astronomer down the stairs. Flamsteed thanked him, and at the bottom of the stairs encountered Halley who, as Flamsteed reported in his diary, "doubtless had heard Sir Isaac Newton show his best."[476] The astronomer again brushed by Halley as he left.

One historian has claimed that the outburst by Newton was fueled by his serious problems in 1711. Isaac's relationship with his warden Craven Peyton at the Mint was deteriorating, and Gottfried Leibniz had sent a letter to The Royal Society in the spring asserting his claim as the inventor of the calculus. Coupled with working on a second edition of **The Principia**, Newton had to have been beside himself over Flamsteed's disrespect.[477]

Halley's one volume edition of Flamsteed's *Historia coelestis* was printed in the spring of 1712 with the star catalog in the beginning against the author's wishes. Halley's preface listed a number of Flamsteed's 'obstructions' which the Astronomer Royal labeled a tissue of "lies and false suggestions." Flamsteed wrote in his diary that Halley "offered to burn his copy of my catalogue, if I would print my own."[478]

Flamsteed turned down Halley's offer, which was probably a Newton strategy to either sidetrack the royal astronomer or get additional information out of him. Because of Flamsteed's insubordination, Newton deleted his name in fifteen places of the second edition of **The Principia,** which went to press in 1712. Newton did allow Flamsteed to be mentioned in the section devoted to the comet of 1680-81.[479]

On December 5, 1712, about seven months after Halley printed what Flamsteed called a "mutilated" volume of the star catalog, The Royal Astronomer printed his "correct" enlarged edition. He then began working on observations obtained with aid of the great mural arc, only part of which had been included in his catalog.

"Moshe, let me digress a moment to mention the romantic relationship of Catherine Barton and Lord Halifax, which seemed to have reached a high point during the Flamsteed-Newton controversy. As you may have surmised, Lord Halifax had limited his arduous affections to Catherine Barton, who at this time was living with her uncle. But in 1713 she was living in Halifax's home.[480] Most historians believe she had moved in with him at this time because in February of 1713, Halifax again changed his will. He added a codicil granting an annuity of 100 pounds to Isaac Newton. But to Catherine Barton he bequeathed 5000 pounds, the rangership and lodge of Bushy Park, and the manor of Apscourt in Surrey; a total bequest of over 25000 pounds –a fortune in 18th century England. [481]

"Undoubtedly, something more than friendship was taking place, Moshe, and Newton appeared to consent to it. Although couples today openly live together out of wedlock, such a relationship was unheard of in 18th century England. I don't know if Halifax, Newton and Catherine Barton were ahead of their time, or if some other circumstance existed. So I'm going to tell you what I think, Moshe, and you have every right to disagree with me. In my humble opinion Lord Halifax was head-over-heels in love with Isaac's niece, and she appears to have requited his advances. As I have mentioned previously, she enjoyed life to the fullest, and enjoyed the opposite sex. She was undoubtedly a sensuous person.

"Catherine was fortunate to have captured the affections of a wealthy and powerful government official. History is filled with such a pattern. She obviously had no qualms about being wooed and perhaps even seduced by her uncle's best friend. She would not have spared her charms in pleasing him. But what is particularly singular to me is the fact that all three of them –Newton, Halifax and Catherine Barton-- defied the customs, mores and scandal- mongering of their day. In 1713 Catherine Barton undoubtedly moved in with Lord Halifax as if it were the twenty-first century –without a formal wedding ceremony by church or state-- and Newton did not intervene. In fact, he kept a portrait of Halifax in his chamber for the rest of his life.

"But, let me return to the Flamsteed controversy….

On August 1, 1714, Queen Anne died, and George I of Hanover succeeded her to the throne. In less than one year, in May of 1715, Lord Halifax died from an attack of pleurisy, and Newton's influence at court all but disappeared. After Halifax's death, Flamsteed wrote to Doctor Sharp: "I [now] have my own prime officers at court that will not suffer me to be used as I have been formerly." One of these officers was Charles Paulet, the Duke of Bolton, who held the office of Lord Chamberlain. Flamsteed convinced Bolton that by virtue of a contract signed with the referees, all copies of the *Historia coelestis* were legally Flamsteed's. On November 25, 1715, Bolton issued a warrant to Isaac Newton to turn in all copies of Halley's "mutilated" *Historia coelestis*. Newton and Halley complied, and in March of 1716, Flamsteed burned all of Halley's printed copies of the catalog in a "sacrifice to heavenly truth –a ritualistic bonfire of victory and revenge."[482] Halley was devastated to see the fruits of many years of his labor go up in smoke.

Flamsteed was the only person who not only openly defied Newton to his face and survived, he bested the lion of Cambridge and defied a warrant from the Queen of England. With continuing references that his efforts were supported by God, Flamsteed never winced nor bowed his head to the enormous pressures that had been heaped upon him by the most powerful people in England. He would spend the last three years of his life writing his magnum opus, his legitimate *Historia coelestis*. But even after Flamsteed's death, Newton, Halley and most members of the Royal Society remained convinced that Flamsteed had subverted their efforts to bring more light into the world.

CHAPTER 42

The Priority Dispute

• • •

"MOSHE, ALTHOUGH NEWTON DID NOT succeed with Flamsteed, the priority dispute with Gottfried Leibniz was another matter. But before I delve into the Leibniz affair, let me again report on the progress of John Theophilus Desaguliers, who, as you know, had been smuggled out of France in 1683 and educated in England by his father. Leibniz, Newton's greatest rival, and Desaguliers, perhaps his most intelligent disciple, made strong appearances upon the Newton stage around 1713. ...

After his father's death in 1699, Desagaliers entered a school in Warwickshire, where he developed a friendship with the son of John Wilkins, a member of Parliament. In 1705 he enrolled in Christ Church in Oxford and began studying under John Keill, a strong advocate of Newton philosophy. In 1709 at age twenty-six, Desaguliers received his Bachelor of Arts degree and began giving the Hart Hall lectures, replacing Keill, who had resigned. Emulating his predecessor, Desaguliers lectured on Newtonian natural philosophy.[483] At this time he also developed a friendship with Thomas Payne, the younger brother of George Payne, a businessman in London.

Before John Keill resigned his position at Christ Church in 1708, he became a member of The Royal Society and a loyal disciple of Newton's. He also became the principle defender of Newton in the calculus dispute with Leibniz. It was none other than John Keill who refuted an article in Europe's scientific publication, *Acta Eruditorium*, which had backed

Leibniz's claim as the sole inventor of the doctrine of fluxions. Keill published a time-line in *Philosophical Transactions* that was most unfavorable to Leibniz. The article implied that the German philosopher had formed calculus from letters sent by Newton to John Collins, who in turn had forwarded the letters to Leibniz.

Leibniz filed a complaint to The Royal Society in 1711 stating that Keill had accused him of being disreputable and dishonest. In his complaint, Leibniz asked Newton to be a witness to his integrity and that Keill should publicly disavow the conclusions implied in his time-line rebuttal. Newton gave Leibniz's request to The Royal Society, which appointed a committee to look into the matter and the documents involved. The committee concluded:

> Sir I. Newton had invented his method before the year 1669, and of consequence 15 years before Mr. Leibniz had given anything on the subject...[484]

The committee also stated that Keill was justified in his implications.[485]

After receiving the committee's conclusions, Leibniz stopped communicating with Newton and The Royal Society. But the controversy wasn't over because Leibniz continued to proclaim to the community of European scientists his priority in creating calculus and his philosophical differences with Newton. In the past, Leibniz had failed to stump Newton on the mathematical questions he had surreptitiously posed to him through Bernouilli and others, but on some philosophical differences, Leibniz felt he had an upper hand.

For example, Leibniz took issue with some of Newton's early philosophical statements; such as space being "a sensorium of God, who had to wind up His watch from time to time" in order to keep the universe operating. Leibniz also took exception to Newton's concept of space being a vacuum and of "an electric spirit which lies hid in the pores of bodies and is exceedingly subtle & easily permeates solid bodies."[486]

By the end of 1714 the great controversy with Leibniz had manifested itself for four years. During that time –and for two more years—Newton and Leibniz exchanged some very candid and accusatory letters through intermediaries. One letter from Newton concluded with "... he [Leibniz] is the aggressor & it lies upon him to prove his charge."[487] Newton gave this letter to Abbe Conti, an Italian cleric of noble birth, who was a Leibniz supporter. Conti kept it for a month before sending it to Leibniz.

Conti had come to England with some French scientists in April of 1714 to observe the solar eclipse, but decided to stay. He had heard the worst about Newton, so he exhibited his best charm and respect to the Society President and discovered Newton not only tolerable but likeable. The feeling was mutual --Newton liked Conti. In a letter to a friend Conti said:

> *I go to Newton's home three times a week... You have no idea how learned he is in ancient history and how reasonable and accurate are the reflections he makes on the facts. He has read much and meditated a great deal on the Holy Scriptures, and he speaks about them with great wisdom and good sense.*[488]

On one of Conti's visits Newton told him, "I was myself when young a Cartesian, but the light soon dawned on me that Cartesian metaphysics ultimately prove to be nothing more than a tissue of hypotheses." [489] Conti remained the messenger for letters between Newton and Leibniz until Leibniz's death in November of 1716. Interestingly, in his letters to the German mathematician, Newton was never drawn into philosophical discussions with him. Newton's philosophy was experimental, and he termed Leibniz's, hypothetical. After all, Leibniz was a Cartesian.

Throughout 1714, Conti's grand design was to heal the notorious rift between Leibniz and Newton. Unfortunately, his dream collapsed in December of 1715 when Conti received a letter from Leibniz with a postscript strongly asserting that Newton had not been master of "the Essence and the Algorithm of the infinitesimal method before me."[490] Unfortunately, Leibniz also revealed the name of Johann Bernouilli, who had taken part in the conspiracy to embarrass Newton and would soon bear witness to Leibniz's priority. Leibniz's last letter was the end of any type of reconciliation, especially when Newton found that Bernouilli was a co-conspirator against him.

After the death of Queen Anne and the coronation of King George I in 1714, Princess Caroline of Ansbach moved to the Court of England as the daughter-in-law of the new king. She had married his son, the future George II, in Germany in 1705. While Caroline was in the Court of Hanover prior to 1714, she was tutored by Gottfried Leibniz. By letter, Leibniz introduced Caroline to Abbe' Antonio Conti, whom she met when she went to England. However, before she left for England, Leibniz warned her, "Take care lest your uncomplicated faith be compromised by the irreligious English. Be particularly wary when confronting …the materialism of Newton, whose *Principia* seemingly reduces the Creator of the universe to the role of a master mechanic."[491]

Almost all of Caroline's tutelage was in German, the language of the first Hanoverian Kings of England. In fact, her father-in-law spoke German and French, but not English.

Shortly after George I's ascension to the throne of England, Newton wrote a one-sided document on the calculus controversy: "An Account of the Book entitled *Commercium Epistolicum*" by John Wallis. Newton's document justified John Keill's indictments of Leibniz. It extracted every scrap of evidence that was damaging to Leibniz and favorable to himself. It filled all but three pages in *Philosophical Transactions* for January and February of 1715. Naturally, Newton did not affix his name to this "Account." It concluded with a defense of his philosophy of nature, which Leibniz had attacked in the *Acta Eruditorium*.

But Leibniz wasn't much better in his writings. At the request of Bernoulli, Leibniz published a *Commercium Literarium* to counteract the evidence of Keill and Wallis. Bernouilli is quoted as advising Leibniz:

> *For as the English try to prove everything by letters and narratives of events ... you should disclose yours... left out by Newton's toadies or craftily suppressed.*[492]

In January of 1715, Bernoulli urged Leibniz to issue a third mathematical challenge to Newton, since the first two did not accomplish their purpose:
"You would do well to publicize some [problem] where Newton would, as you know, find himself in difficulties."[493]

Leibniz did as suggested, however he had been careless in his statement of the problem and allowed that if any phase of it were deciphered, it could be considered solved. Almost every Newton disciple was able to solve a phase of it. It is interesting to note that at age 73 Newton didn't do as well as a few of his followers; nevertheless, it was his solution that appeared anonymously in ...*Transactions.*[494] Newton undoubtedly was grateful that Leibniz never knew who wrote the solution that appeared in print.

The bantering and vilification between Leibniz and Newton continued with no man giving any quarter. Princess Caroline wrote to Leibniz, "Great men are like women, who never give up their lovers except with the utmost chagrin and mortal anger --and that, gentlemen, is where your opinions have got you."[495]

In England, Princess Caroline soon came to enjoy Conti's incisive wit and became an enthusiastic supporter of his efforts to heal the wounds between Leibniz and Newton. At Leibniz's suggestion, Caroline called on the Bishop of Lincoln to help her translate Leibniz's *Theodicy*, but the bishop referred her to Reverend Samuel Clarke, stating that "There is no one capable of doing it except Dr. Clarke."[496] Caroline relayed this information to Leibniz and sent him some of Dr. Clarke's books. She also told Leibniz that Clarke "was a close friend of Chevalier Newton."[497] When Caroline first called on Reverend Clarke she showed him part of a letter that Leibniz had written to her:

> *Sir Isaac Newton says that space is an organ, which God makes use of to perceive things by. ...Sir Isaac Newton and his followers have also a very odd opinion concerning the work of God. According to their doctrine, God Almighty wants to wind up his watch from time to time; otherwise it would cease to move. He* [God] *had not sufficient foresight to make it a perpetual motion.*[498]

If there were anything positive that came from the Newton-Leibniz dispute, it was the transformation of Princess Caroline and the subsequent influence she had on her husband. Although Princess Caroline was a pupil, friend and follower of Leibniz, after September of 1715 her letters to Leibniz displayed an erosion of her allegiance. When the German-speaking Caroline asked Dr. Clarke to translate Leibniz's *Theodicy*, he refused. Caroline wrote to Leibniz on November 28, 1715:

"Dr. Clarke is too opposed to your opinions; ... he is too much of Sir Isaac Newton's opinion and I am myself engaged in a dispute with him."[499]

Each week Reverend Samuel Clarke would call on Princess Caroline, and each week Caroline moved closer to his views, which he had gleaned first-hand from Isaac Newton. In 1704 Newton had selected him to deliver the Boyle Lectures, and in 1705 to translate *Opticks* into Latin; he was definitely a loyal disciple and communicated with Newton regularly. Caroline and Leibniz also wrote often, and Leibniz's letters contained words like the following:

"Natural religion itself seems to decay [in England] very much. Many will have human souls to be material; others make God himself a corporeal being.

"...Newton says that space is an organ, which God makes use of to perceive things by.

"Since Newton and his followers argue that God Almighty wants to wind up his watch from time to time ... [it seems].. odd that a supposedly perfect God should construct a machine of such imperfect design that he is obliged to clean it now and then... and even to mend it, as a clockmaker mends his work."[500]

Since Caroline was still working with Conti in attempts to reconcile Newton and Leibniz –at least to get them communicating— she turned Leibniz's letter over to Dr. Clarke. Clarke sent a formal reply to Leibniz, and Leibniz responded. The two philosophers exchanged letters four more times –ten letters in all-- on topics such as God, nature, time and space. A year later their give and take ended with Leibniz claiming that space being a vacuum was philosophically and scientifically absurd. Clarke responded by citing Guericke's experiments with the air pump and Torricelli's work with mercury barometers.[501] The letters between Leibniz and Clarke are considered to be among the most celebrated of the famous eighteenth-century philosophical debates.[502] After several months of her weekly meetings with Dr. Clarke, Princess Caroline wrote to Leibniz on April 24, 1716 about her current state of mind:,

"Mr. Clarke's knowledge and his clear way of reasoning have almost converted me to believing in the vacuum."

Three weeks later, after seeing experiments on colors and vacuums by Desaguliers, Caroline again wrote Leibniz, who was becoming discouraged –especially with a body racked with gout. She told him about seeing the experiments:

"They [have] almost converted me. It is for you to lead me back into the right way, and I await the answer which you make to Mr. Clarke. ...None of Clarke's replies were written without Newton's advice." [503]

Leibniz would have continued his correspondence with Clarke, but his health failed. In late October of 1716 he had an acute attack of arthritis and died on November 4 at seventy years of age. Learning of Leibniz's poor health, Conti sailed to Germany in order to meet Leibniz, but he was too late. From Hanover on November 29 he wrote to Newton:

"M. Leibniz is dead; the dispute is finished." [504]

Despite Leibniz's death, Newton never let the debate die, and neither did Leibniz's co-conspirator, Bernoulli. These two men continued the dispute for another six years. As far as priority is concerned, Leibniz and Newton developed calculus independently at different times; however, Newton is generally acknowledged as the first inventor.

PART 4

The Proliferation of Newtonianism

• • •

CHAPTER 43

The Lectures of John Theophilus Desaguliers

• • •

"Moshe, when Desaguliers received his Master's degree in 1713, he moved to Channel Row in Westchester, married Joanna Pudsey and began lecturing on Newtonian philosophy for a livelihood. Other than Isaac Newton's lecturing as the chair of mathematics in Cambridge, the first lectures on experimental philosophy began at Trinity College by Roger Cotes and William Whiston. These courses ended abruptly when Cotes died and Whiston was banished from Cambridge. However, similar lectures soon started at Oxford by John Keill, who learned experimental philosophy from David Gregory, a Scotsman who had studied the writings of Isaac Newton. By this time "new knowledge" had not only reached Oxford, but London as well. It flourished in the last years of Queen Anne's reign, when open discussion on religious and political matters was permitted with little restriction. ...

Coffee houses, sometimes called "penny universities" sprang up and became centers for learning and the dissemination of news. Over a cup of coffee people would converse with friends and strangers and learn about natural and experimental philosophy from lecturers.

By 1713 it had become popular to know new sciences. Until the eighteenth century, natural phenomena had received little attention. But after 1700 some conventional beliefs had become controversial, partly because of the discoveries by Newton and other natural philosophers. Whatever the reason, teaching "new knowledge" became a noble occupation.

The first London courses in natural philosophy were taught by Francis Hauksbee and James Hodgson, who demonstrated Robert Boyle's vacuum pump and Isaac Newton's optics in Marine Coffee House. Hauksbee also manufactured scientific instruments and other mechanical devices. In 1703 Newton appointed Hauksbee the Curator of Experiments for the Royal Society, a responsibility which he performed conscientiously with meager compensation.

In January of 1713, Desaguliers also brought his expertise in lecturing and experimentation to London. His first course on "Mechanical and Experimental Philosophy" was conducted on January 7, 1713 outside Temple Bar at the Black Swan and Bible bookstore of Mrs. Jonas Brown. Desaguliers was practically unknown in London and this first course was not well-attended. The course was advertised in London's *Evening Post* and consisted of four parts: Mechanics, Hydrostatics, Pneumatics and Opticks.[505] People could sign up for the course in five locations, including George Payne's leather office, Mrs. Brown's bookstore, and Desaguliers' French school in Islington, which is believed to have been run by Desaguliers' mother.

When Francis Hauksbee died in 1713, Desaguliers began lecturing at widow Hauksbee's home at Hind Court on Fleet Street. At this time his name and reputation had been established and his lectures were well-attended. Desaguliers also demonstrated a compassionate nature. He rented space from Mrs. Hauksbee and purchased many of her late husband's instruments. He quickly caught the attention of The Royal Society, especially since many people of prominence took his courses. He developed a following with his striking lectures and experiments on Newtonian philosophy. As a result, his college mentor, John Keill, spoke to Isaac Newton about his former protégé. ...

"Sir Isaac, Do you know the man who is lecturing at widow Hauksbee's home?"

"Not really. I have heard there is a Frenchman with a difficult name to pronounce."

"Isaac, John Theophilus Desaguliers is the best student I have ever taught. Although he has a Master of Arts and has taken Deacon's orders, his leanings are in natural philosophy and things scientific. He has read your "Opticks" and **The Principia.** He thoroughly understands them and explains them in his courses on experimental philosophy."

"Has he done experiments on the properties of light?"

"Most definitely!"

"On what else does he conduct experiments?"

"Mechanics, hydrostatics, pneumatics, astronomy and much more. His courses are well attended."

"You say he was your former student. What do you know of him?"

"He is the son of a Huguenot minister who fled France in 1682 before King Louis revoked the Edict of Nantes. His mother smuggled him out of France in 1683. She joined her husband on the Isle of Guernsey. From my conversations with John Desaguliers, he is also a strong advocate for religious and political tolerance."

"Would you contact this 'Master Desag... --how do you pronounce it?"

"De–sag–you–lee–ay --John, Thee-off-ill-us, De-sag-you-lee-ay."

"...Yes. Would you contact him and request that he conduct an experiment for The Royal Society at next Thursday's meeting?"

"Yes, sir."

Desaguliers acquiesced to Keill's request. His first experiment was an overwhelming success especially after he had demonstrated a thermometer that measured great heat, measuring molten lead at over 400 degrees Fahrenheit. By December, he was retained as the curator of experiments for The Royal Society. His pay was to be commensurate to the worth of his experiments. Six months later, on June 24, 1714, at Newton's personal request, Desaguliers presented a flawless demonstration on optics. The Fellows of The Royal Society absorbed every part of it. Of course, Desaguliers' lectures did not demand a knowledge of adavanced mathematics, which was necessary when Newton lectured, causing some students to feel intimidated.

Desaguliers was the consummate lecturer. He seemed to know his audiences and how to communicate with them. Yet, just to make sure his lectures were known and understood by all members of The Royal Society, especially foreign and distant members, Desaguliers began publishing a summary of his lectures in "Philosophical Transactions." In fact, in his summary of *Opticks* he referred to the unsuccessful experiment at Liege, France 30 years ago. A copy of his optics lecture in French was mailed to members of the Academie of Sciences in Europe and was singularly responsible for the conversion of European scientists to Newton's findings. Desaguliers was doing a prodigious amount of work and was relieved when The Royal Society took its summer break in 1714.

In October of 1714, Desaguliers was named a Fellow of The Royal Society as was the Prince of the Romano-Russian Empire. Desaguliers' dues were remitted by the Society as a partial payment for curator work.. For the remainder of the year Desaguliers continued his meticulous and exhaustive presentations on Newtonian subjects such as magnetism, motion, gravity and centrifugal force. He also supplied intricate machinery for every demonstration.

On March 24, 1715, Desaguliers performed experiments for some foreign gentlemen, including W. Jakob 'sGravesand, a representative from Holland who was attending the ascension to the throne of King George I. 'SGravesand was a friend of Keill and Desaguliers and became a Fellow of The Royal Society in June. Around this time Desaguliers received a manuscript from Cotton Mather, a Puritan from New England and the first American to become a Fellow in The Royal Society. In Mather's manuscript, *The Christian Philosopher*, he writes: "Philosophy is no enemy but a mighty and wondrous incentive to religion." Before the summer break in 1715, Desaguliers was translating letters to The Royal

Society from France and doing experiments on chimneys and the heating and ventilation of buildings.

An occurrence in 1715 worth noting is that Desaguliers took Stephen Gray, John Flamsteed's assistant, into his home to live with him. Newton took no offense with his curator for providing lodging for Gray; however, Gray was not admitted into The Royal Society for 18 more years despite his expertise in electricity and astronomy. In 1716, Gray began assisting Desaguliers with his experiments at Royal Society meetings.

Newton liked Desaguliers for many reasons besides his knowledge and his lecturing skills. Desaguliers was very personable, and Newton found that he shared many of Newton's theological and philosophical views. Desaguliers, unlike Locke, was also a master of things mathematic and scientific.

It wasn't long after Desaguliers had been elected to The Royal Society that he and Newton discussed philosophy, and during one discussion Newton asked:

"John, aren't you a Huguenot at heart?"

Desaguliers replied, "I am an ordained Anglican priest, Dr. Newton."

"I am aware of that, John, but I am sure that your father taught you some Huguenot history. I would think that you would be sympathetic toward the Huguenots. Is it not so?"

"Yes; that is true, Sir Isaac. I do prefer the Huguenot faith over the state religion of France. I sympathize with the Huguenots and their sufferings."

"You are referring to the revocation of the Edict of Nantes, I presume."

"It is not solely the revocation, Dr. Newton. I also prefer the Geneva Bible and a person's right to worship God as he wishes. I was happy to see the Bible translated into English so that everyone could read it. I feel that religions should be more tolerant; I do not care for bigotry or tyranny by governments or religions."

"What are your thoughts concerning the status of Jesus Christ?"

"He spoke the word of God. He gave people hope."

"But as an Anglican priest at Whitchurch, have you not taken Holy Orders to worship Jesus as God?"[506]

"Yes, I have taken Holy Orders, but I still maintain my own religion, which I do not usually divulge. I find much truth in the **Bible**, but I find additional truth through experiments and study. To me, understanding nature and nature's laws helps me understand God. Frankly, Dr. Newton, I abide by the two greatest Commandments and the teachings of Noah, Moses *and* Jesus Christ. True, I may be an ordained Anglican, but when I find a truth from research and experiments, that truth supersedes anything else. Above all, God is truth and love to me."

Newton leaned back in his chair, smiled and said, "I find nothing wrong with that, John. Frankly, in one part of the world today there is great animosity toward the Christian religion as defined by the Council of Nicaea, especially after the Crusades. Over five centuries before the Crusades, both Muslims and Jews were united in warfare against polytheists in the Mid-East. In fact, John, in the first three centuries after Jesus' time, Christianity and Judaism were both monotheistic. After the Crusades, however, the Muslims developed an even greater hatred for the 'Franks,' whose Christian armies worshipped Jesus Christ as God. Is it any wonder that as Islamic fighters beheaded the crusaders when their Christian army was annihilated at the Horns of Hattin, the Muslims shouted, 'There is no God but Allah!' I fear that in the future, the world will again find itself in conflict with religions which zealously oppose other religions.

"But let me return to the former religion of your father. Did you know that my home in Leicester Square adjoins the Huguenot Chapel where Thomas Payne preaches and where your father preached in 1695. I provided the ground floor of my home near there as a home for Huguenot refugees. Some of them were scientists, and a few of them have been elected Fellows in The Royal Society."

Before Desaguliers moved to London, he had developed a friendship at Oxford with Thomas Payne. In fact, Thomas introduced Desaguliers to his brother, George Payne, who was a member of the Rummer and Grapes Masonic Lodge in London. Ever seeking to better himself, Desaguliers petitioned for membership in George Payne's lodge around the year 1715. For some reason, cathedral construction had waned after the Reformation, and men began joining Masonic lodges for social and charitable reasons. Even Robert Moray, the first president of The Royal Society, joined a Masonic Lodge in 1641 for similar reasons; however, he also sought architectural knowledge that masons used in building the great cathedrals of Europe. After James II fled the throne in 1688, Masonic lodges and other free-thinking societies began to spring up in England.

After Desaguliers became a Mason, he was invited into Newton's office at The Royal Society, where Newton inquired of him:

"John, I hear that you have joined a Freemason's Lodge. May I ask why?"

Desaguliers responded, "I enjoy socializing with like minds intent on improving the world we live in; however, in time I hope to expand upon what the lodges inculcate. In addition to architectural knowledge, they impart some moral principles, which I agree with."

"What specifically do you plan to expand upon?" asked Newton.

"I hope to provide the members with philosophies that you and I have found to be true. Your *Opticks*, your **Principia**, and your studies of the Scriptures have revealed information that mankind needs to know. I want to use the Masonic fraternity to launch important truths."

Newton said, "An ambitious and noble enterprise indeed, but you had best be careful not to go afoul of the law —especially the law regarding blasphemy and profaneness. Whatever you do, if you wish to preserve your fraternity do not openly dispute the Trinity. In fact, you might be wise not to discuss any type of sectarianism. The greatest conflicts on earth have occurred because of religious differences."

"Dr. Newton, I want to impart light. I wish to reveal incontrovertible truths from Scripture, research and nature –including the cosmos. I will not denounce or condemn. I will disseminate truth –nothing less and nothing more. My weekly lectures have proven this fact."

"John, all I can say is Godspeed. I think that you and I may be of a similar mind. Perhaps you will be able to reveal light in a way that men may understand. I regret that most people have not fully understood much that I have written. Complex mathematics confuses most people. However, I wish you success in your endeavors, and I hope you will keep me abreast of your progress from time to time."

"Thank you, sir. May I now take the opportunity to tell you that I have found your conclusions and discoveries to be most accurate. I think that **The Principia** is the epitome of scientific expression. You have provided me and many others with the structure of our universe, not solely because of the effects of gravity, but also celestial mechanics, dynamics, magnetic force and inertia. You have revealed truths to us and have proven them to be accurate. I don't think anyone will ever surpass your efforts."

The experimental courses and lectures presented by John Theophilus Desaguliers began to attract and amaze scientists, nobility and Royalty. Perhaps due to the cost of tuition, wealthy persons composed the majority of his classes. From 1714 through 1719 he conducted courses for large numbers of auditors. Included among the subscribers to his courses were no less than the King of England, the Prince of Wales and Princess Caroline, who in 1717 received private lectures at Hampton Court. Desaguliers was given private lodging in one of the pavilions at that time, but during the day he presented philosophical experiments for the royal family. Fortunately, the language at Court was French, which was Desaguliers' first language; the King spoke no English and his son did not fare much better.

When the Prince of Wales and his wife, Caroline, returned to their apartment after Desaguliers' first lecture, the Prince asked his wife:

"Caroline, what are your thoughts about Desaguliers' lectures?"

Caroline replied, "I thought they were excellent. I have now become a convert to Newtonian philosophy."

"What did you think of Desaguliers himself?"

"I thought I was looking at a wizard. He certainly looked the part of a priest, especially in those black clerical vestments extending from his chin to his shoes …and a liturgical collar too! I had trouble watching the demonstrations at first."

"And what did you think about the demonstrations?"

"I really liked them. I learned much. And those instruments…? How did he transport all of those heavy instruments to Hampton Court?"

"He brought them by barge down the Thames. Which demonstration did you like the most?"

"I thought his demonstration of the cosmos was the best. All of those globes. I was awed by our planetary system. He gave us a good model of our solar system and the orbiting of the planets. What did he have… ten, twelve globes? I now understand our universe and our seasons."

"I too liked that demonstration –along with his demonstrations of gravity. What a genius he is."

CHAPTER 44

Indisputable Discoveries and Decisions

• • •

"As I have mentioned, Moshe, at the time Newton was wrangling with Leibniz and Flamsteed, he found another follower in the person of John Theophilus Desaguliers. At this time, however, the Leibniz dispute occupied much time and distracted Isaac from research and his duties at the Mint and The Royal Society. He also had personal obligations, including the welfare of his niece, especially after the death of Lord Halifax. ...

It seems that Halifax's nephew was also a beneficiary of Halifax's estate, and he decided to contest his uncle's will –especially the codicil bequeathing property to an unrelated single female. The nephew met with some success due to the male dominated world of 18th century England. Nevertheless, with some help from Newton, Catherine Barton inherited the lion's portion of Halifax's gifts to her. After the final settlement was decided in late 1716, Catherine wrote to her uncle from the Halifax residence:

> *I desire to know whether you would have me wait here. . . or come home.*
>
> *Your Obedient Neece*
> *And Humble servt*
> *C. Barton ...*

Newton of course welcomed Catherine to his Leicester House with open arms. Immediately after she arrived, the two of them walked to Isaac's room and respectfully contemplated the portrait of Lord Halifax hanging over the fireplace. As if fate were watching over Catherine, within months after she moved in, her uncle invited Captain John Conduitt to the house in order to discuss a remarkable discovery that Conduitt had made.

John Conduitt hailed from a wealthy Hampshire family. He had attended Trinity College in 1705 as a Westminster scholar but left school without a degree to travel on the continent. He joined the British Army in 1711 and became secretary to a general during the War of the Spanish Succession. In 1713 he became the commissary for the British Army at Gibraltar, and while in Spain discovered the ruins of the ancient city of Carteia, an ancient Roman Colony built in 171 B.C.. In 409 A.D. Carteia was sacked by the Visigoths and gradually deteriorated under Byzantine rule until the 9th century when it was relegated to ruin.

In December of 1716 and in March of 1717, Conduitt had written to The Royal Society about his discovery. And when he returned to England, he was invited to speak to The Royal Society about Carteia. After hearing his speech on June 20, 1717, Isaac invited him to his Leicester home. Isaac was working on a "Chronology of Ancient Kingdoms" and wanted to learn more from Conduitt about ancient Mediterranean cities.

Needless to say, when twenty-nine year-old Conduitt arrived at Newton's home he was immediately smitten by the beautiful Catherine Barton. Even though she was thirty-eight years of age, it was love at first sight. After a whirlwind romance they were married on August 26, 1717, only two months after they had met. Without question, Catherine Barton soon became a respected member of British society, and Isaac Newton again appeared to have been the catalyst that brought his niece and a lover together.

During the first year of their married life, John and Catherine Conduit lived periodically at Leicester House with "Uncle Isaac," and they stayed with him on occasion even after that. Their main residence, however, would be at Cranburg Park, the ancestral home of the Conduitts.

"Now, Moshe, let me give you some examples to show how correct Isaac's decisions and discoveries were. As you know, Europe was not convinced with Isaac's findings about the composition and behavior of light. But after Halifax's death in 1715 a group of French savants visited Greenwich to see another solar eclipse. As President of The Royal Society, Isaac also invited them to see demonstrations on optics by John Theophilus Desaguliers. After these demonstrations were published in 'Philosophical Transactions,' the Frenchmen returned to the continent and announced the truth about optics that for thirty years had not been accepted. Newton's discoveries about the composition and behavior of light were correct and the Academie of Sciences in France accepted them primarily because of Desaguliers' expertise in communicating and conducting experiments. ...

Within the next three years Newton published Desaguliers' optical experiments on the continent in Latin. Isaac was now receiving high praise from the French, who had finally disassociated themselves from the theories of Descartes, Huygens and Hooke. One honorary member of the *Academie Royale* by the name of Sebastien Truchet' successfully performed Desaguliers' optical experiments and wrote to Newton, "Were I not a Carmelite Brother and confined to a monastery, I would enjoy meeting and conversing with the wisest of men."[507] Soon the French scientist Varignon wrote to Newton echoing Truchet's sentiments.

It was the precise, easily understood presentation of Newton's optical experiments by John Theophilus Desaguliers that had convinced the European continent of the truth and wisdom of Isaac Newton. It became abundantly clear that whenever Newton published something, it was correct. His intelligence was unmatched, and his conclusions indisputable.

Isaac's genius also manifested itself in his work at the Mint. England already knew how he meticulously handled the counterfeit epidemic, but

Isaac was also quite adept with other problems inherent with his Mint responsibilities. For example, as early as 1713 the Lord Treasurer held a meeting with Mint officers and copper merchants about coining copper. Many suppliers attended, eager to increase their copper sales. In order to speak with authority on all matters related to copper, Newton studied and mastered the technical details necessary for minting copper coins. Therefore when a question came up about assaying the purity of copper, Newton insisted that the Mint would test all copper to guarantee the purity needed for it to be hammered into red-hot sheets that would not crack. In fact, Newton's method of assaying copper was the first standard for selecting pure copper.[508]

These first attempts to begin coining copper died at the death of Queen Anne, but it revived in 1717 under George I due to a pressing need for small coins. The Treasury then advertised for bids from copper suppliers. All bids were submitted by July, and on August 14 Newton was authorized to select the best bid and proceed with refining copper in order to get the purity needed to coin it. Newton's integrity, his obsession with perfection and his superior intellect were never better exhibited than when he developed copper coining.

First of all, his self-taught knowledge of copper and copper production enabled him to select a grade of copper that was suitable for coining. Second, after twenty years at the Mint, he also had adopted procedures that produced the best possible coinage. To round out these qualifications, Newton had a righteous character that made him a good steward of the Crown and the people. He correctly and honestly earned his salary and commission. He did his own cost-accounting to arrive at the proper cost of a finished copper coin. After he had received all bids, Newton then selected an offer from Hines-Appleby that met Newton's price, which was 18 pence per pound of copper.[509]

After awarding the bid to Hines-Appleby, Newton received a warrant from the Treasury to begin coining in September of 1717. Unfortunately, Newton had to delay coining because cracks were appearing in the stamped coins. Newton was forced to change the entire refining process. The delay resulted in complaints from all corners: the public, the suppliers and the Lords of the Treasury. Newton was obliged to send the Treasury a letter.

The first thing Isaac addressed in his letter was the fact that he had never really wanted to coin copper in the first place, but since he was Master of the Mint, the "lot" fell upon him. But then Newton became quite candid and offered the Lords a choice:

> ....*things are upon such a foot that I can get nothing but discredit by coyning the Money ill...*
> *I am willing to lend the Copper room in the Mint to any body* [else] *to take care of this coinage & content my self wth the coinage of ye gold & silver; but if it be your Lords' pleasure that I go on with it, I will take the best care I can do to have it well performed.* [510]

As expected, the Lords chose to let Newton continue with the coining at his own pace. In about four months he developed a grade of copper that met his requirements, and by April of 1718 the Mint produced six tons of flawless half pennies.[511]

Throughout the bidding and coining problems, however, Newton had to deal with many unscrupulous attempts by copper merchants to get the Crown's business. Even a poor grade of copper had been smuggled into the Mint and stamped without Isaac's knowledge. The coins that were poorly produced were then presented to the Lords of the Treasury as samples of the coins produced by the Mint under Newton's watch. At the same time, the merchants submitted perfect copper coins as examples of coins produced by them.[512] The commotion caused by unsuccessful bidders was enough to cause the Treasury to summon Newton and instruct him to accept five tons of copper from each of two unsuccessful bidders, but even this act didn't placate other copper merchants who wanted a share of the Mint's business.[513]

The Lion of Cambridge, however, would not compromise. He studied copiously, and his conclusions were correct. And when he made a decision, King, Prince, Pope or Parliament could not get him to yield. Newton defied the Treasury by disqualifying merchants who could not prove they were supplying English copper. But Newton didn't stop at disqualifying suppliers; he assayed copper from other bidders. After his tests, the other bidders voluntarily withdrew from contention.

Newton also had to deal with sales agents who represented people in high places. William Derham, a long-time council member of The Royal Society, told of an incident related to him by Newton. Derham said that one agent offered Isaac £6000.

Isaac told the agent, "That is a bribe."

The agent replied, "There is no dishonesty in accepting an offer. You do not understand your own interest."

"I know well enough my duty, and no bribes can corrupt me."

"I come from a great Duchess. She is a person of impeccable character and considerable influence."

Newton responded, "I desire you to tell your ladyship that if she were here and made such an offer, I would have asked that she leave my house, as I desire you, or you shall be turned out."[514]

Derham said that Newton found the identity of the duchess, but kept it to himself in deference to her position.[515]

Through November of 1719 disappointed copper merchants continued to harass Newton, but to no avail. Newton stuck to his convictions and eventually Hines & Appleby still proved to be the best choice of copper suppliers. Nevertheless, criticism by merchants convinced the Pyx to place Newton on trial. At the trial six half pennies were submitted by the critics and were tested against the coins provided from the Mint. All of the critics' coins shattered when hammered red hot, but all of Newton's coins stood the test.[516]

Newton's indisputable findings also held true for his scriptural research, and in the near future, John Theophilus Desaguliers would reveal Newton's principles in ways that mankind could understand. But Desaguliers would present only incontrovertible truths, tenets, and discoveries from his own and Isaac Newton's experiments and research.

CHAPTER 45

Desaguliers and Freemasonry

• • •

"Moshe, I must digress from talking about Isaac Newton in order to tell you about Desaguliers and his work in Masonry. [517] As you have obviously discerned, Desaguliers was more devoted to natural philosophy and freedom of conscience than to his duties as an Anglican priest. For centuries inquiring minds had been suppressed by disciplines imposed by church and state. The Desaguliers' family, for example, were victims of religious intolerance. However, around the year 1715, a Mason named George Payne recommended Desaguliers for membership in the Rummer and Grapes Masonic Lodge. In that lodge Desaguliers found a respite from political and sectarian constraints. By the year 1716, he became a strong devotee to the fraternity and soon became the driving force behind its growth and success. ...

The institution of Masonry claims to have descended from the guilds of stonemasons who built the great cathedrals and castles of the middle ages. Journeymen stonemasons also may have built the massive fortresses of the Crusades. The first operative masons met in temporary buildings next to the structures they were working on. When cathedral building waned, these skilled craftsmen continued to meet in order to help one another and hone their craft. They kept some secrets of their trade from the uninitiated, and passwords were used to enter lodge rooms. These operative masons used rituals and conferred degrees on members in order to differentiate levels of their craftsmanship.

However, in the middle of the seventeenth century, operative lodges began admitting men who wanted to be a part of an ancient brotherhood and glean knowledge that the lodges imparted. Also, since lodges held 'members only' meetings, they were not vulnerable to outside interference or mischief. As I have mentioned, Moshe, in 1641 Robert Moray joined a Scottish Lodge for reasons other than learning a trade, and in 1646 Elias Ashmole joined a British lodge for similar reasons. By 1670 as the Enlightenment took root, operative lodges were admitting learned men who wanted to be in a brotherhood of men, learn ancient wisdom, and garner some architectural knowledge --all of which were useful in discussing the new philosophies and scientific knowledge that were emerging at this period of time.

When James II abandoned the throne in 1688, England became more tolerant of religious and political dissent. Many groups sprang up with unorthodox beliefs. However as tolerance increased, these groups began to dwindle. The Freemasons in London may have survived because they offered a universal ideology and had members from a wide spectrum of social classes. Commoners and tradesmen were able to exchange views with noblemen, scientists and clergymen, but more probably the Masonic lodges survived because they merged into a Grand Lodge through the efforts of John Theophilus Desaguliers and others. The Masonic movement began to grow rapidly and extensively due to the efforts and reputation of John Theophilus Desaguliers, who had become renowned as a lecturer, a Fellow of the Royal Society, and a Grand Master of the Grand Lodge of London. Desaguliers had conferred degrees on nobles and royalty. He had given private lectures for George I, the Prince of Wales and his wife, Caroline.

Most Masonic lodges took their names from the taverns or locations where they met. Desaguliers had joined the Rummer and

Grapes Tavern in Channel Row, and in 1716 he addressed his lodge about forming a Grand Lodge. Although no records exist of the exact words spoken, he undoubtedly must have given a speech similar to the following:

"Brethren, there are three other Masonic lodges in our fair town, and all of them espouse similar rituals and teachings. Other groups also gather in coffee houses and taverns to profess their philosophies and beliefs, but we have advantages over them. First of all, we profess a trust in God, and we have regulations and rituals that have survived the test of time. Other societies have little in common with each other; but our lodges have much in common.

"I think it would behoove our lodges to unite into one Grand Lodge. We can hold joint meetings on regular occasions, and we could combine our efforts in conferring degrees and raising funds for charitable causes. The attention created by such a lodge might help to increase our membership."

After convincing the brothers of the Rummer and Grapes to consider forming a Grand Lodge, Desaguliers personally visited London's three other Masonic lodges to recommend the alliance he had proposed to his own lodge.

Finally, on June 24, 1717, Saint John the Baptist Day, the Masons from the Crown Alehouse near Drury Lane, the Apple Tree Tavern at Covent Garden, and the Rummer and Grapes Tavern in Westminster met with members of the Goose and Gridiron Alehouse at St. Paul's churchyard to form the Grand Lodge of London. Anthony Sayers, the longest tenured Mason, was elected to be the first Grand Master. Under him, George Payne and John Desaguliers were elected Senior and Junior Grand Wardens, respectively. Next year at Grand Lodge, George Payne became the Grand Master. His brother, Thomas Payne, had introduced Desaguliers to George in 1715. In 1719, Desaguliers became the third

Grand Master. He also received an honorary Doctorate in Civil Law from Christ Church that year.

George Payne was re-elected Grand Master in 1720. At that time he and Desaguliers asked Masonic lodges to turn in all information in their possession relative to Masonic history – especially information regarding regulations, rituals, ancient charges and landmarks. In 1721 the Grand Lodge commissioned Reverend James Anderson of the Swallow Street Presbyterian Church to write one document from all the collected information. That document would become the first constitution for all Freemasons. Incidentally, Desaguliers' father once preached at Anderson's Swallow Street Church when it was a Huguenot chapel.

During and after Desaguliers' year as Grand Master, an increase in membership occurred in Masonic lodges. Men of higher status, including noblemen, royalty and Fellows of the Royal Society joined the Masonic fraternity. The lodges attributed the increase to Desaguliers, who, along with his prolific lecturing, initiated many men into Masonry. Because of Desagulier's efforts in forming Grand Lodge and initiating members, he would one day be called "The Father of Modern Speculative Masonry."

But there is another reason why Desaguliers inherited this title. From 1717 on, he wrote rituals, charges and lectures for the new Grand Lodge. Much of his material came from the *Bible* and the Masonic documents that London's lodges had provided, but a larger portion came from the discoveries and knowledge of the men of the Enlightenment – especially Isaac Newton and John Locke.

"Moshe, I think you should know that I have also received the three basic Masonic degrees, and I can tell you without a doubt that they are filled with Newtonianism and the reasoning of the Enlightenment. More importantly, the degrees instill in Masons the importance of brotherly love, morality, truth and charity.

"Let me give you an example. In one of the Masonic degrees, *Geometry* is described as 'the first and noblest of sciences.' Of course geometry was used by the cathedral builders in the Middle Ages, but Euclidian geometry was the main vehicle used by Isaac Newton in **The Principia.** Desaguliers accordingly wrote the following words about Newton's emphasis on Geometry in a Fellow Craft Degree lecture:

> *By Geometry we may curiously trace nature through her various windings to her most concealed recesses. By it we discover the power, the wisdom and the goodness of the Grand Artificer of the Universe, and view with delight the proportions which connect this vast machine. By it we discover how the various planets move in their different orbits and demonstrate their various revolutions. By it we account for the return of the seasons and the variety of scenes each season displays to the discerning eye.*

"As you can see, Moshe, Desaguliers didn't use complex mathematics to impart the Newtonian philosophy. He used language that everyone understood. Today discoveries of the Enlightenment are recited in Masonic lodges all over the world. Desaguliers appears to have taken the knowledge of Newton and other men of the Enlightenment *and placed it in Masonic rituals!* And they remain unaltered to this day. ...

Finally in 1723, the *Constitutions of the Freemasons* was published by James Anderson. The *Frontispiece* of this historic document shows the *Constitutions* being passed from the current Grand Master, the Duke of Montague, to his successor, the Duke of Wharton. Behind these two Grand Masters are Desaguliers, Wharton's Deputy Grand Master, and Grand Wardens, Josua Timson and William Hawkins. Between the Dukes is a geometric sculpture depicting the 47th problem of Euclid, the Pythagorean Theory, to emphasize the fact that Geometry is the foundation of Masonry. It is significant that Desaguliers became a Deputy Grand Master three times; therefore, he bore many responsibilities of the fledgling Grand Lodge, including the publication of the *Constitutions.* Although Desaguliers and George Payne provided much of the material to be used in the *Constitutions,* James Anderson took sole responsibility for the material in the largest section, the historical legends of Masonry.

Unfortunately, most of Anderson's historic legends could not be authenticated and were stricken from later editions of the *Constitutions.* In the year the document was first published, six years after the creation of Grand Lodge, the number of lodges had increased from four to twenty. The Rummer and Grapes Lodge had risen to a membership of 73 and was now meeting at the Horn Tavern in Westminster.[518]

After Grand Lodge had formed, Desaguliers wrote the lion's share of the Masonic rituals. In the "Charge" of the Fellow Craft Degree he wrote:

> *The study of the liberal arts, that valuable branch of education which tends so effectually to polish and adorn the mind, is earnestly recommended to your consideration, especially the science of Geometry, which is established as the basis of our art. Geometry, …being of a divine and moral nature, is enriched with the most useful knowledge; while it proves the wonderful properties of nature, it demonstrates the more important truths of morality.*

But perhaps the most important words that Desaguliers wrote are meant to instill virtues such as honor, truth and fidelity into the character of a Freemason. Some of these words eventually found their way into the Master Mason Degree, which Desaguliers wrote after Newton's death:

> *Universal benevolence you are always to inculcate, and by the regularity of your own behavior, afford the best example for the conduct of others less informed. Your virtue, honor and reputation are concerned in supporting the dignity of the character you now bear. Let no motive therefore make you swerve from your duty, violate your vows or betray your trust; but be true and faithful…*

Even in the first degree, the Entered Apprentice Degree, Desaguliers engages in character building. In the 'Charge' of that degree he urges Masons to inculcate three duties; *To God, your neighbor, and yourself.* A Mason is to treat his neighbor:

> *...by acting upon the square and doing unto him as you wish he should do unto you.*

In the same degree, Desaguliers wrote:

> *Let not interest, favor or prejudice bias your integrity or influence you to be guilty of a dishonorable action.*[519]

"Yes, Moshe, Desaguliers wrote thousands of words which inculcate principles that he thought people should live by. The way people act toward one another is really the basis for a happy society. Desaguliers wrote practical applications of the Golden Rule. The way we treat one another is more valuable than the worthless gold doled out by governments. After all is said and done, we will all leave this precious planet as penniless as when we entered it. Between birth and death, everything we think, say and do with everyone in whom we come in contact will contribute toward making a heaven on this earth, which is a consummation we should all devoutly desire.

"Desaguliers said that the cement of a Masonic Lodge is 'Love and Friendship,' and he gave the first Grand Lodge of Masonry its foundations. He may be the 'Father of Modern Masonry,' but he was also the product of John Locke, Isaac Newton and the Enlightenment. His family had been a victim of intolerance, and he wanted nations to be lodges of virtue. John Theophilus Desaguliers exemplified the virtues that he wrote about in his Masonic degrees. He believed in freedom of conscience and the brotherhood of man. He believed in highlighting injustice, righting wrongs and stemming the tide of indifference where compassion is needed.[520] He taught these virtues to the greatest men of his generation. His words and actions provide reasonable standards for us to live by, and his influence continues to this day. I believe it is a sad commentary that such a gentle and peaceful society, which advocates only the highest of thoughts and deeds, has been banned by many religious sects and even some nations. In one state, membership in Freemasonry was once punishable by death.

CHAPTER 46

Newtonianism

• • •

"MOSHE, WORLD THINKING BEGAN TO change before the eighteenth century. As I have said, these years are described as the era of the *European Crisis of Conscience,* Following that era, and primarily because of John Theophilus Desaguliers, the Masonic lodges started a metamorphosis from operative masons' guilds to an intellectual and moral society spurred by the scientific, political and religious revolution that arose about that time.[521] Modern Speculative Masonry was born during the Enlightenment and continues to be a testimony to it. Desaguliers embraced the monotheism of Noah, Moses and King Solomon – and the philosophy of Isaac Newton and John Locke.

"By the efforts of Desaguliers and others, the modern Masonic lodge began to assimilate concepts of morality and personal character. Membership also increased, and more men learned truths that superseded long-standing myths. A new world order was in the making. New truths were learned and morality and virtue were taught as well. A positive voice was heard that made sense and presented an alternative to some long-standing misconceptions.

"Some of these new truths and beliefs were shrouded in Newtonianism, which finally had found an outlet. And the catalyst for the proliferation of Newtonianism was John Theophilus Desaguliers, who through his lectures and Masonic rituals personally began to spread the 'new science.' What is astonishing is that Desaguliers' rituals still exist in substantially their original form. They have outlasted nations, governments, political parties and religious sects, almost all of which have undergone changes of some kind. What is even more astonishing is that his rituals and instructions eschewed violence and did not criticize nation or church. They had one primary requisite: a trust in God, *a benevolent God;* yet, the fraternity did not allow religious or political discussion during open lodge.

"Although Newton and Desaguliers didn't discuss the Nicene Trinity, they concurred that God alone is supreme and that every person and everything is subordinate to Him. To be honest with you, Moshe, I think these two giants of science may have recognized that a great many people need a God they can visualize. It is not easy to worship something that can't be seen. The followers of Moses are a testimony to this tendency. Even today people worship statues, cows, and deified human beings. Japan's emperor was once worshipped as a God as were kings of many countries. People idolize movie stars, music stars and political leaders. Newton, Locke and many Arians attended churches where Christ was worshipped as a God, but privately they did not equate him with God. Newton, a Biblical scholar, knew very well the first commandment: *Thou shalt have no other Gods before thee.* ...

By 1720 Desaguliers had become a household word among the educated and wealthy. He became well-known among the nobility and the scientific and royal families of Great Britain and Europe. He also had become well-known in Masonic circles as a lecturer and a leader. "New" science and Masonry seemed to embrace each other and had become fashionable. With support from the House of Hanover, both Newton and Desaguliers saw Newtonianism proliferate. Enlightenment was spreading throughout the world, and *Let there be light* became a slogan for the Freemasons. Desaguliers was quite busy giving scientific courses, conducting experiments, giving Masonic lectures and initiating men into Masonry. His work with The Royal Society and with the Freemasons undoubtedly were discussed with Isaac Newton. I have thought deeply about these discussions, and I am confident that one took place in the 1720's when Newton followed up with Desaguliers about his progress with the Masons:

"John, have you accomplished what you set out to do with your Masonic rituals?"

"I believe I have made some progress, Doctor Newton. I have been doing much writing and editing, but I still have much to do."

"Have you broached any religious issues?

"I've inserted some religious principles, if you can call them that; I have placed an emphasis on brotherly love, charity and truth."

"I see no fault with those principles, John."

"I hope not. I personally think that the tenets I have adopted for Masons are universal."

"Do you mention Jesus Christ?"

"Not specifically by name. I mention that the wise men of the East were guided by a star to the place of our Savior's nativity."

"I find no fault with that either, John. You have spoken truthfully. In my research I have also found that Jesus changed the lives of many people. In fact, he changed the world. He may have been the greatest teacher to occupy earth. But let me ask, did you refer to him as God in your Masonic writings?"

"No. I have written ritual that includes his teachings and teachings of the prophets, and I mention the God they worshipped. In truth I think Jesus was perhaps the greatest prophet, but as you know, he worshipped the Creator of the universe as did other prophets."

"John, have you broken any Anglican laws –or laws of any church for that matter?"

"I have offended no one, Dr. Newton, unless it is someone who doesn't trust in God."

"Fair enough, John. Let's lay religion aside for a moment. You have told me that you are trying to inculcate morality in your rituals. Would you mind elaborating?"

"Certainly. First I must say that Masons pay dues to hear our lectures, but since your teachings are part of these lectures, I consider you exempt from this obligation.

"I charge every initiate with duties to God, his neighbor and himself. His duties to God are simply those things that all good men exemplify –mainly, that God is the chief good and we should apply to Him for strength and wisdom, imploring His aid before our laudable undertakings. I also admonish members not to use His name in vain. As far as duties to ourselves are concerned, I have copied your example and charge all Masons to avoid irregularity and intemperance."

Newton responded, "I do my level best, but I didn't realize that you would use my temperance as an example for others, John."

"Well, I also expound upon geometry and your discoveries in the universe, which I do in my public lectures."

"John, I appreciate the fact that you have not included my criticism of certain church scripture; I can ill afford to have some of my discoveries in scripture revealed."

Desaguliers said, "Have no fear, sir, salt will not cure a gaping wound anyway. I avoid mentioning matters that could be controversial. Discretion is the key. People can believe in stones if they wish. I just don't want them throwing those stones at me or anyone else. If there are flaws anywhere in scripture, I don't mention them. I center on what is universally acceptable and important."

"John, you may be addressing a way to bring the world together. Wouldn't it be wonderful if everyone could agree on some fundamental truths, and leave the rest for study and debate? Do you realize that almost every war in the history of the world has been about religion?"

"Dr. Newton, Your writings have always been an inspiration for me. And now you, yourself, have indicated why we do not discuss religion or politics in Royal Society meetings. ...But now may I now ask you a personal question?"

"Of course, but I reserve the privilege not to answer if I so desire."

"Sir Isaac, my first question concerns a statement made by your niece and her husband. They have publicly stated that you are the greatest Christian they have ever known. How do you accept such praise in view of the fact that you do not worship Jesus Christ?"

"An excellent question, Mr. Desaguliers, a very good question –and I will answer it. There are many religions in this world, and all of them demand obedience to some creed or philosophy. If you don't believe in that philosophy, you are described as one who is outside of the faith and are labeled a heretic or an infidel.

"I am a heretic, John. And you are correct in thinking that I do not accept Jesus as a God, but as a savior who speaks God's words. What I accept are his ways, his teachings and his truths. He has shown the way to salvation; but to me, salvation is not achieved by simply loving *him*. I love what he has done and what he imparts. The greatest thing he has taught me is to love God, whom he called *his Father* and *my Father*.

"I have scrutinized scripture to find over twenty-two passages where Jesus refers to God as his superior. Therefore, to answer your question, I ask you in return, how can one call himself a Christian who does not practice Christ's teachings, and, in fact, accepts a contradiction of the second commandment handed down from Moses, Solomon, *and Jesus*. One is a Christian by living a Christian life, not by believing in something that is false. I ask you, John, who is more Christian? One who professes to love Jesus and disobeys his teachings, or one who practices his teachings and loves God. Who is more Christian? One who says 'I believe in Jesus' and practices few virtues, or one who searches for truth and lives the moral life that scripture teaches and Jesus exemplifies?

"John Locke wrote that reason is the candle of the Lord, and that faith should not override it. I have spent my entire life finding truth. I have revealed many truths, and I have come to the realization that it is more 'Christian' to follow Christ's religion than to simply believe he is a God and worship him as a God. To me, heretics are those who believe in the trinity of Athanasius and commit idolatry by worshipping someone other than God.

"Have I answered your question sufficiently, John?"

Desaguliers hesitated before speaking. He sat quietly in his chair as Newton awaited his reply. Finally, Desaguliers spoke:

"Dr. Newton, you are in conflict with the bedrock of Christian churches everywhere."

"Yes, John, I am. But I don't consider myself in opposition with Jesus Christ. In fact I think that Christian churches today are concerned to a great extent with building earthly empires for themselves, not for making a heaven on earth. They have stagnated thought and reason and insist on blind faith. Those of different bent, regardless of its reasonableness, meet with antagonism. Is this 'Christian?' I predict endless strife in this world because of religious conceit. Religions will attempt to destroy other religions because they are different, regardless of the fact that all of them are supposed to believe in charity and peace. Ironic, isn't it? You only need to look at LaRochelle, Montsegur, and Medina, where murder was committed in the name of God. This is absurd! It is insane! I am still haunted by the death of that young lad who was hanged in Cambridge for being an Arian.

"My closest friend, John Locke, warned against the manipulation of men's minds and the perils of blind faith. Like him, I maintain that reason is a gift from God, and faith comes from finding truth. As you have found in your experiments, faith is lost in sight. When the truth is learned, ignorance and myth disappear. I have faith in what is true in the **Bible** and elsewhere.

"The current Trinity came into being in 325 A.D. when Jesus was made a God by the bishops of the church. But I have studied to find that the evidence supporting that world-altering decision was flawed. After thoroughly researching the Trinity, I have returned to monotheism. I trust in one God, 'The Architect of the Universe.' If Jesus were the God who created the universe, why did he not know or speak of the innumerable planets in our solar system?"

Desaguliers spoke, "I now see why you have not openly professed your beliefs, and desire that I not attack church or state. The zealots and guardians of church dogma are many and powerful. I assure you, Doctor Newton, that you can trust me. In all of my writings I will not reveal any corruptions you have discovered, nor will I write anything offensive. I will continue to write of things true and beautiful. Perhaps, men *may* have changed scripture, but I will write what is everlasting and true from natural philosophy and scripture. I have no desire to arouse enmity among men. I, too, wish we could all love creation and one another."

Newton nodded in agreement and said, "John, when Jesus was asked, 'What are the greatest commandments?' He answered, 'To love God and your neighbor as yourself.' This was the religion of the sons of Noah established by Moses, Solomon and Christ and still in force.[522] Jesus said that we should also repent of our sins.

"Prophecy has written that it will be hundreds of years before churches will have an epiphany. Anything we say at this time regarding changing church doctrine will only cast seeds on barren rock. From *Revelation* I have calculated that any second coming of a Messiah will not occur until at least the year 2060, but it could be later."[523]

Newton then reached into his desk, removed a large scroll of paper, and said: "John, please accept this detailed floor plan of King Solomon's Temple that I have drawn. It took much time and research, but I think you will find it to be accurate. I am currently working on a chronology of ancient kingdoms, and I thought you would like to have the dimensions and layout of what I believe is the first temple built to honor God, the architect of our universe. Perhaps you can use this drawing in your Masonic rituals."

Desaguliers responded, "Thank you, Dr. Newton. I may use it and the era of King Solomon in my Masonic writings."

CHAPTER 47

Newton's "Bucket List"

• • •

"Moshe, as Newton entered the last decade of his life. He decided to perfect and republish *Opticks* and **The Principia**. However, his major objective was to complete and publish a final treatise, *The Chronology of Ancient Kingdoms*. You might say that Isaac had a 'bucket list'. Unfortunately, though Leibniz had died, Isaac's priorities were being interrupted by the calculus dispute. In late 1718, the French mathematician Re'mond de Monmart responded to a statement by Brook Taylor of the Royal Society that 'no one but Isaac Newton had contributed to the invention and improvement of calculus.' Monmart did not dispute the fact that Newton had invented calculus, but the Frenchman claimed that Leibniz and Bernoulli were its true and almost sole promoters. ...

> *It is they and they alone who taught us the rules of differentiation and integration; the way to use the calculus to find tangents to curves, their points of inflection and reversal, their extrema, evolutes, caustiques by reflection and refraction; the quadratures of curves, centers of gravity, of oscillation and of percussion, problems of the inverse method of tangents... which excited so much admiration by Huygens in 1693. It is they who first expressed mechanical curves by equations... and who finally, by many and beautiful <u>applications</u> of the calculus to the most difficult problems of mechanics... have set us and our descendants on the path of the most profound discoveries.* [524]

Newton did not respond to Monmart's letter, which Taylor had shown him. He had invented calculus and that is all that mattered to him. However, Newton did cultivate a friendship with Pierre Varignon, a member of the French Academie of Science, in an attempt to curry favor with the Academie. Newton had proposed Varignon for membership in The Royal Society in 1714, and since becoming a fellow in that society, he had supplied Newton with copies of the Academie's *Memoires*. Newton reciprocated with copies of the second edition of *Opticks*. Varignon gave one of his copies to Bernoulli as "a gift from Isaac Newton." Bernoulli responded with a thank you letter to Isaac, praising him as "a man of divine genius of whom our age has no equal."[525] However, Bernoulli also stated that Newton "had been told many lies and inventions about me. ...Whatever has been published anonymously in this way is falsely imputed to me." [526]

Newton took Bernoulli's letter for what it was, a flagrant fabrication. Nevertheless, he sent a carefully worded reply: "Now that I am old, I take very little pleasure in mathematical studies."[527] Newton overlooked a patent lie rather than continue the Leibniz dispute. Despite Newton's wishes, the dispute continued because Newton was not able to thwart the publication of the Newton-Leibniz letters by Pierre Des Maizeaux, who had received them from Conti. In fact, Bernoulli asked Newton to stop this publication, which also contained some of Keill's attacks. Unfortunately, Bernoulli had the audacity in his request to mention that he had some letters with a 'different story.'[528] Newton did not take kindly to Bernoulli's threat, and the dispute again reared its ugly head.

Although Newton had restrained Keill for two years, he now took the Oxford scholar off his leash and let him attack Bernoulli with a fury that Keill had been harnessing for some time. Newton also withdrew his objection to Des Maizeaux about publishing the Newton-Leibniz letters. [529] Varignon tried in vain to be a peacemaker, but he died in 1722. Bernoulli continued to exhort Newton to take a stand against publications that were averse to him –even publications that didn't mention

Bernoulli's name, but used terms such as "anonymous mathematician," "pretended mathematician," "novice," etc. Ironically, though Bernoulli denied being the person these terms referred to, he still took offense.

In February of 1723, Bernoulli wrote to Newton about a book by Nicholas Hartsoeker which accused Newton of plagiary in *Opticks*. But Bernoulli had also found words in the book that were critical of himself, and that some of the words appeared to be penned by Newton. Consequently, in his letter Bernoulli said, "I would gladly learn from your own pen what you decide to do in order to defend your innocence."[530]

Newton's innocence didn't need defending and he did not respond to Bernoulli. He treated Bernoulli's request with the contempt it deserved. Finally, in Newton's last four years of life, the priority dispute died with a whimper. He had been ignoring it anyway. He was working arduously on the three priorities he needed to complete before the end of his life.

Opticks was the easiest project. After Desaguliers successfully demonstrated Newton's optical experiments, the French finally accepted *Opticks* and published a French translation of it. Varignon took over a second edition in 1721 and completed it in August of 1722.[531] After one more minor criticism of the work and a subsequent masterful experiment by Desaguliers, *Opticks* vaulted into perpetuity as the supreme authority on light and colors.

A third edition of **The Principia** was a more arduous undertaking. After Isaac recovered from a serious illness in 1722, he urgently took on this edition in 1723. Henry Pemberton, a young member of The Royal Society, was selected as the editor. Pemberton had read **The Principia** in medical school in Leyden, and it had a profound impact on him. In an attempt to gain favor with Newton, Pemberton then wrote a critical essay on Leibniz's measure of force, which also contained some laudatory words about Isaac Newton. Dr. Mead showed the essay to Newton, who promptly placed it in *Philosophical Transactions*. A second essay, published in 1723, extolled Newtonian science and demonstrated Pemberton's competence in mathematics. To say that Newton was favorably impressed would be an understatement; he sent a letter to Pemberton giving him full responsibility for the third edition of **The Principia**.

This edition did not involve major changes. Though Pemberton wrote suggestions to Newton at least thirty-one times, Newton brushed off most of them. Perhaps his age prevented him from undergoing major changes. Nevertheless, there were changes, one of which was Desaguliers' results in the scholium that treated the experimental investigation of resistance. Newton also added some new observations of the shape of Jupiter and its satellites. From Halley's observations he also treated the orbit of the comet of 1680 as an ellipse, not as a parabola.[532]

Perhaps the most notable change in the third edition of **The Principia** was the addition of 'Rule IV' at the beginning of Book III. This rule emphasized the differences in philosophy between Newton and Leibniz. Isaac insisted on inserting it:

> *Rule IV. In experimental philosophy we are to look upon propositions inferred by general induction from phenomena as accurately or very nearly true, notwithstanding any contrary hypotheses that may be imagined, till such time as other phenomena occur, by which they may either be made more accurate, or liable to exceptions. This rule we must follow, that the argument of induction may not be evaded by hypotheses.* [533]

Throughout 1724 and 1725, Pemberton worked zealously and meticulously to prepare **The Principia** for publication. He was staking his future on it[534] and undoubtedly was seeking some recognition for his efforts. Although Newton forgot to mention Pemberton when he first drafted his preface to **The Principia**, he remembered his oversight in time to insert his regards for "Henry Pemberton, M.D., a man of the greatest skill in these matters ..." [535] The third edition of **The Principia** was copyrighted on 25 March, 1726 and contained a royal privilege to the publishers for fourteen years.[536] The publishers, William and John

Innys, printed 1,250 copies. Fifty copies were printed on superfine paper, which Newton presented to some of his friends and certain societies. Six copies were given to the Paris Academie of Sciences.[537]

An addition worth noting in the 1726 **Principia** is an experiment with gravity conducted on April 27, 1719 by John Theophilus Desaguliers at St. Paul's Cathedral. Desaguliers enlisted King George to pull a lever which released a piece of paper, a guinea and a feather from atop the cathedral to dramatize the effects of gravity. Newton did not forget to credit Desaguliers in this last edition of **The Principia** as the conductor of this experiment.

CHAPTER 48

The Chronology of Ancient Kingdoms

• • •

"As previously stated, Moshe, Newton's last years were devoted primarily to theology. But Newton had not turned to religion simply because he was facing mortality. Religion had been his major interest throughout his life, and he had never abandoned it. It may have been preempted at times by mathematical and scientific work, but it was always a priority with him. ...

Between 1705 and 1710, though Newton was revising editions of *Opticks* and **The Principia,** he never neglected theology. In the last years of his life he was in fact preoccupied with religion, and his discoveries in theology were as unorthodox and unprecedented as those in experimental philosophy. Yet, even as death loomed, Isaac found it difficult to publicly reveal his heretical views. He had concealed them ever since his professorial days over fifty years ago.

Newton had been interpreting the prophecies and other Biblical works for at least ten years before Abbe Conti appeared on the scene during the Leibniz dispute. At that time Newton had already written "Origines," which would gradually evolve into the *Chronology of Ancient Kingdoms.* In *Chronology...* Newton shocked other chronologists by cutting almost five centuries out of long-accepted Greek history,[538] but he did not change Hebrew kingdom chronology by even one year. Newton appears to have intended to justify Israeli kingdoms as sacrosanct along with the theology of these kingdoms, which was the original primitive Christianity that Newton believed in.

After Conti arrived and cultivated a close friendship with Newton, one of their favorite topics of conversation was the chronology of ancient kingdoms. Of course, Conti also engaged in conversations with Princess Caroline, and one can easily imagine what took place in these conversations, especially one that undoubtedly occurred in 1716 when Caroline was talking with Conti about Isaac Newton:

"Antonio, I have learned much about Isaac Newton from you and from Reverends Clark and Desaguliers. Sir Isaac has redefined science and dispelled much ignorance and myth."

Conti said, "I have also learned much from him, Princess Caroline, especially concerning religion. Have you ever discussed religion with Sir Isaac?"

"Not really; however, he has mentioned God's presence in nature and the universe."

"I have found Dr. Newton to have some interesting views regarding theology. In fact he has written a large treatise which appears to refute the chronology of the ancient kingdoms as presented by Greek historians."

"I would love to see such a treatise. I did not know he had written such history."

The Princess of Wales wasted no time in summoning Isaac Newton to court, where she asked him for a copy of his *Chronology of Ancient Kingdoms*. Newton was taken off guard, but he knew he could not refuse a request from a member of the royal family. Frankly, in its present form *The Chronology* contained information that was heretical enough to get him discharged from the Mint. Newton decided to stall for time and answered the princess:

"Your grace, *The Chronology* is currently in an imperfect and confused state, but I will form an abstract that will be acceptable for your perusal."[539]

Although Newton was reluctant to relinquish any of his compositions, especially one that contained some theological views, in a few days he drew up a shorter chronology and delivered it to the princess. Conti, upon hearing that the princess had received a copy, requested one for himself. Newton, of course, refused the abbot's wishes. Conti then appealed to the princess to request a copy for him, which she did. Newton had no recourse but to comply. However, when Conti arrived to pick up the "Abstract," Newton made him take an oath not to give the document to anyone.[540]

Newton wanted to keep the abstract of his *Chronology* from public view even though there was little in it that was heretical. It had been sanitized to eliminate the controversial information found in "Origines," which emphasized the original Christianity of the ancient Israelis. By cloaking his radical theology into a chronology and then excising it in his "Abstract," Newton made it safe for the scrutiny of royalty. Nevertheless, Newton continued to revise his larger *Chronology* up to his final days on earth.

Regrettably, Abbe Conti did not abide by the oath he had given Newton. After he returned to Paris in late 1716, he began telling people in learned circles of his close association with the great Isaac Newton and freely showed them Newton's abstract. In 1720 an expert on chronology, Father Etienne Souciet, asked Conti which method Newton used to shorten historically accepted dates. His inquiry went all the way to Newton, who gave an oral response to John Keill. On behalf of Newton, Keill relayed the response to Souciet: "The manuscript held by Conti is an abstract of a longer work in which I relied on astronomical calculations...."[541]

Not being an astronomer, Souciet dropped the matter, though there seemed to be a hint of heresy in the treatise. However, another scholar, Nicholas Fréret, pursued the inquiry. He translated the "Abstract" into French and then composed a refutation of it. He then gave both the "Abstract" and his refutation to a Paris publisher, Guillaume Cevelier, who wrote to Newton asking him to make corrections to the translation before he published both documents. Newton ignored Cevelier's request, but received two more from him, the last one on

March 20, 1725, which threatened publication "as is" with Fréret's criticisms.[542] Newton responded within two days stating that he had written a chronological index for a friend on the condition that it not be communicated to anyone.[543] Newton explained that he could not give consent to publish the "Abstract," known in France as "Abrege'de la Chronologie."

Newton continued, "I do not know if the manuscript held by you is the chronological index that I gave to a friend, nor will I meddle with what has been given to you under my name -- nor will I give you consent to publish it." Cevelier published the documents anyway claiming that he didn't receive Newton's response in time. Newton received a copy of the "Abrege" and Fréret's criticism on November 11, 1725 and took umbrage. He promptly wrote "Remarks upon the Observations Made upon a Chronological Index of Sir Isaac Newton." Newton wrote seven drafts before publishing it in the July and August 1726 issues of *Philosophical Transactions*.[544] Newton may have been 82 years of age, but he still did not let criticism of his work go unanswered.

In his "Remarks..." Newton castigated Cevelier and the unnamed person who criticized his abridged chronology. He described the anonymous Fréret as someone who "attempted to translate and confute a work that he didn't understand in order to get a little credit."[545] Cevelier in turn was depicted as one without enough basic intelligence to refrain from printing an unseen translation of papers written by an unidentified person –and with a refutation attached to it.[546] But Newton saved his best barbs for Abbe Conti, who had violated a solemn trust. He accused Conti of pretending to be a friend while assisting Leibniz "in engaging me in disputes." Newton even said that Conti had "stirred up criticism" on the continent of his and Desaguliers' optical experiments.[547]

By this time Newton was suffering severely from the infirmities of old age. In 1722 he had become seriously ill, and in 1724 he had passed a kidney stone the size of a pea. From that day on, Newton suffered incontinence. In 1725 Martin Folkes began assuming Isaac's duties at the Royal Society, and John Conduitt, his duties at the Mint. In January of

1725 Newton contracted a severe cough and inflammation of the lungs. He didn't recover for weeks. Because of his lung problems, Isaac moved to Kensington in order to escape the severe smoke and air pollution of London.

But nothing interfered with Isaac's dominate passion, *religion*. He was now focusing on the *Revelation of St. John* and the *Book of Daniel*. In these books Newton found prophecy that was abundantly true.[548] Consequently, he persisted to write his "theological" **Principia**, the *Irenicum* –an *ecclesiastical polity tending to peace*. It was actually his *Chronology*, the abstract of which he had given to Princess Caroline and Abbe Conti.

In the *Irenicum* Newton emphasized that all nations were originally given one religion based on the precepts of Noah's sons. This religion continued through the great Hebrew patriarchs until Moses brought it to Israel. Newton then found that Pythagoras had passed it on to the Greeks, who in turn gave it to Egypt, Syria and Babylonia. Newton's fundamental premise was that this ancient religion contained the two greatest commandments, which were also taught by Jesus Christ: to love God and your neighbor as yourself. In this thesis Newton viewed the Jews and their patriarchs as the progenitors of the only true and everlasting church.

Newton, however, added a third commandment which was foretold in prophecy and preached by Jesus Christ and his disciples: "Repent and be free of sin." Newton wrote, "This is the religion of the sons of Noah established by Moses, preached by Christ and is still in force."[549] Newton's contention was that if all nations returned to the world's first religion, peace could again be achieved on earth.

In *Irenicum* Newton reiterated his heresy: everything needed for salvation was present in the primitive church --that Christ was subservient to God, different from Him in substance and nature.[550] The *Irenicum* was not sanitized. Isaac firmly believed that Christianity could be traced to the earliest days of Judaism when all nations were of one religion. According to Newton, the doctrine of the Trinity written by Athanasius had been created hundreds of years after the age of prophecy; therefore, it is void of any divine authority. Newton went on to chastise St. Jerome for inserting a 'heretical Trinity' into the vulgate in the 4th century, when Jerome was translating the scriptures from Greek into Latin.

Newton's subtitle for the *Irenicum*, the *ecclesiastical polity tending to peace*, inherently exhibited his rejection of the Church of Rome --and any church that had adopted Athanasius's Trinity. Nevertheless, Newton's friend William Stukeley said, "Sir Isaac was an intire Christian, upon fundamental principles." [551] Newton's closest confidants knew the 'fundamental principles' Stukeley referred to.

Newton kept writing and editing his *Irenicum* at a frenetic pace in the last days and weeks of his existence on earth. Zachary Pearce, Rector of St. Martins-in-the-Fields, observed Newton a few days before he died and wrote the following:

> *I found him writing over his Chronology of Ancient Kingdoms, without the help of spectacles, at the greatest distance of the room from the windows, and with a parcel of books on the table casting a shade upon the paper.... He read to me two or three sheets of what he had written which had been mentioned in our conversation. I believe that he continued reading to me, and talking about what he had read, for near an hour, before dinner was brought up.*[552]

Regrettably, Newton's *Chronology of Ancient Kingdoms* is not a 'correct and indisputable' treatise, as are his other publications and research. In 1728 all 87,000 words of it were posthumously published by John Conduitt –after urgings by William Whiston, who was champing at the bit to refute it. Others besides Whiston found flaws in the document, and minor criticisms continued for fifty years. But for the most part, the *Chronology* remained viable, perhaps due to Isaac Newton's reputation and the lack of evidence available to historians and astronomers in the 18th century.

However, in the 20th century, after archeological discoveries and newly observed astronomical data, Newton's work has received justifiable criticism, first from a 1963 book by Frank Manuel entitled **Isaac Newton, Historian,** and then a 2012 book by Jed Buchwald and Mordechai Feingold, **Newton and the Origin of Civilization.** Buchwald and Feingold provide a preponderance of evidence that proves that Newton was 'off course' with his evidence (and consequently, his conclusions), especially regarding the astronomy.[553]

In Newton's defense, he had to rely on information that was available in the 18th century. After all, he was a genius; literate in Latin, Greek and some Hebrew, in addition to his command of the English language. He also had access to the astronomical information provided by the Royal Astronomer, his friend, Edmund Halley.

The greatest mistake Newton made was starting with a hypothesis. In his entire life, he had criticized people who relied on hypotheses instead of facts. He was critical of Leibniz and Descartes' for this reason. Yet, to his discredit, Newton believed that Solomon was the first God-worshiping king in the world, and he selected evidence to support this assumption and threw out evidence to the contrary. Newton's hypothesis was that all ancient civilizations derived from the Israelites. Newton took the date of the flood during Noah's time at face value and then proceeded to set the duration of large kingdoms long enough to allow the spread of 'primitive Christianity' through many generations by the eight people who survived the flood.

In deference to Newton, any 18th century scholar attempting to find correct dates prior to 600 or 700 BC had little, if any, factual information. Most of the information and dates were fictitious and were written by those who wanted to demonstrate the superiority or precedence of their own sect or nation. Factual history was simply not available. Newton took fictional information, which he thought was true, and added to it. For example, he assumed that certain names in history were mythological figures: Noah was Saturn; Shem, Jupiter; the Egyptian pharaoh Sesostris was Osiris; and the Biblical figure Sesak was Dionysis.[554]

Newton attempted to justify his theory regarding the precedence of the Israelite kingdom by using astronomy as a means of calculating dates. Without going into his detailed calculations of equinoxes and solstices, Newton found a difference between the solar year and the calendar year; consequently, he concluded that less time had elapsed than the length of time recorded in Greek chronology. Newton knew that equinoxes change one degree every 72 years, and using this information, he calculated the Argonaut expedition at 936 B.C., which is about 44 years after the death of King Solomon. Newton used this difference to connect the Egyptian calendar to the Chaldean one. He shortened the duration of a kingdom to between eighteen and twenty years, thus taking out almost five centuries, or four-sevenths of the time line used by Greek chronologists, who calculated that three kingdoms lasted 100 years.[555] To Newton this proved that the date of the Hebrew kingdom preceded all others; therefore, his belief in primitive Christianity was not just correct, it had precedence over all other religions.

Unfortunately, Newton uses subjective information in his research and chooses information that helps to make his case. Isaac misidentifies Pharoahs, reverses calendar inheritance and misplaces the beginning of the year at Equinox. Though his theory is original and innovative, evidence available to him was limited at best.[556] Newton presumes to have facts; however, he has only unclear observations in a poorly known system of signs, constellations, and limited archeological knowledge. For example, information on the Pyramids was entirely textual and was limited to a few undated monuments.[557] Newton's claim that Pharaonic Egypt was not a kingdom of major significance until after the time of King Solomon is now contradicted by the archeological evidence available today.

Although modern evidence does not support Newton's *Chronology* – especially regarding the precession of the reign of King Solomon and primitive Christianity— his *Chronology* has been resurrected by fundamental Christians who find the document in agreement with Biblical accounts, not to mention that it is written by a man who has been described by many as one of the great geniuses to have inhabited earth. [558]

There is one chapter in *Chronology*, however, that provides accurate information. In Chapter V, 'A Description of the Temple of Solomon,' one will find meticulous detail concerning King Solomon's Temple, its construction, dimensions, classes of workmen, sources of building materials and much more. In fact, John Desaguliers makes the reign of King Solomon and the construction of his temple an example which he used to write a large portion of Masonic degrees and rituals. Let me read a part of the first paragraph of Newton's Chapter in *Chronology* entitled 'A Description of the Temple of Solomon':

> *The Temple looked eastward and stood in a square area called the 'Separate Place,' and before it stood the Altar, in the center of another square area called the 'Inner Court' or 'Court of the Priests, and these two square areas, being parted only by a marble rail, made an area 200 cubits long from west to east, and 100 cubits broad. This area was compassed on the west with a wall, and on the other three sides with a pavement fifty cubits broad, upon which stood the buildings for the Priests with cloysters under them; and the pavement was faced on the inside with a marble rail before the cloysters. The whole made an area 250 long from west to east and 200 broad and was compassed with an outward Court called the 'Great Court' of the People,' which was an hundred cubits broad on every side, for there were but two Courts built by Solomon, and made a square area 500 cubits long and 500 broad...* [559]

Newton goes into even more detail as he describes sanctuaries, chambers, gates, steps, porches, pathways, columns, doors and so on. To say that Newton goes into meticulous detail is an understatement. In his final work on Earth, Newton did what he could to promote Arianism without mentioning it. He intended to make *Chronology* compatible with the course of nature, astronomy, historical books of the *Old Testament*, Herodotus' *History*, and with itself. In truth, Newton accomplished the last three of these.[560] Until Newton's *Origines'* manuscripts were released in the 20th century, few people had suspected that *Chronology* conflicted with currently accepted Christian theology.

In the twenty-first century, the *Chronology of Ancient Kingdoms* is considered a dull document without much purpose, but Newton's information and exact descriptions of King Solomon's Temple in that document remain correct and indisputable.

CHAPTER 49

Final Days

• • •

"Moshe, although Newton's demeanor in his last days exhibited a cheerful and outgoing old soul, as Conduitt and Stukeley attested, their written evidence also reveals a man disappointed with lesser mortals[561] and religious hierarchies which perpetuated a false doctrine despite historical evidence to prove otherwise. In fact, Newton isolated himself in his last years as he once did at Trinity and at Grantham. By this time he had become internationally famous and was even the object of pilgrimages. Nevertheless, men like Benjamin Franklin and Voltaire could not obtain an audience with the famous and esteemed genius.[562] William Stukeley, however, who also hailed from Newton's Lincolnshire, was a regular visitor at Newton's home ever since he was admitted into the Royal Society in 1718.

"In 1725 Stukeley reported that he saw Newton adding a sheet of figures 'without the aid of spectacles, pen, or ink.' It was about this time that Newton had become incontinent, and had told Stukeley that his breakfasts consist of 'boiled orange peel, sweetened tea, and a little bread and butter.'[563] Conduitt added that although Isaac 'had no specific [eating] regimen, he was very temperate in his diet. He ate no flesh and lived chiefly on broth, vegetables and fruit.'[564] Though Newton had to give up carriage rides because of kidney stones and bladder problems, he traveled in a sedan chair, still with both arms dangling out from the sides. His silver hair remained thick and full.[565] He always had 'the bloom and colour of a young man, and never wore spectacles, nor lost more than one tooth to the day of his death.'[566] Stukeley said that Newton's 'natural disposition was of a cheerful turn. When he was not engaged in thought, he could be very agreeable and even sometimes talkative.'[567]

"As I have previously mentioned, Moshe, in 1724 Newton had relinquished most of his duties at the Mint and the Royal Society to others. Yet when he was asked by Lord Townshend whether a counterfeiter named Edmund Metcalf should be hanged as scheduled, Newton replied that it is 'better to let him suffer than to venture his going on [in counterfeiting] until he can be convicted again.'[568]

"Before Isaac became too infirm to socialize, there was an occasion in 1721 that might interest you, Moshe. A gathering that year was held at the Ship's Tavern at Temple Bar in London for natives of the county of Lincolnshire, the boyhood home of Newton and Stukeley. Knowing of Newton's introvert nature, Stukeley went alone to the gathering which took place during the evening in an upstairs dining room. While talking with other Lincolnshire countrymen, Stukeley was interrupted by someone proclaiming, 'There is an old gentleman downstairs, who appears to be Sir Isaac Newton!'...

Stukeley remarked, "I seriously doubt it," but proceeded downstairs to see for himself. Before he and another friend had reached the bottom of the stairs, he saw Isaac Newton sitting alone. He approached Isaac and struck up a conversation as his friend turned and scurried upstairs to report that indeed the venerable Isaac Newton was in the tavern. Soon another diner came downstairs and asked Stukeley and Newton to join the party on the upper level.

Stukeley answered, "The chief room is where Isaac Newton is."

Hardly a minute had elapsed before almost all reunion attendees descended downstairs to join Stukeley and Newton. Throughout the evening Newton was jovial and accommodating. He answered questions from everyone. Eventually the subject of opera came up and Newton was asked, "What is your opinion of this musical art form?"

Being fond of music, Newton replied, "Opera is too much of a good thing. I went to the last opera. The first act gave me the greatest pleasure. The second quite tired me. At the third I ran away." [569]

When another admirer asked Isaac, "What is your opinion of poetry?" Newton said, "I'll tell you that of Barrow, who said that 'poetry is a kind of ingenious nonsense.'"[570]

Perhaps Newton's opinion was similar to Barrow's because noticeably absent from Isaac's extensive library were any works by Chaucer, Shakespeare, Spenser, Milton or John Dryden, who was a Newton contemporary. The evening continued as a fascinated audience asked questions and listened to Newton's answers for a considerable length of time. When the unusual affair finally ended, Newton paid for everyone's drinks.[571]

"Moshe, Newton was also a generous person. He was a patron to many young scientists, and printed many of their manuscripts. He once gave money to one of them in order for him to return home from Venice so that Newton could recommend him for a professorship. Newton once gave £100 to support astronomer James Pound, for whom he also purchased Huygen's great lens –at a considerable price. Newton also opened his doors to host many French visitors. One French astronomer, Joseph Nicolas Delisle, wrote enthusiastically about his reception by Newton in 1724.[572] ...

Newton continuously studied and wrote in his last years, but in the background of these years were many acts of charity to relatives and non-relatives. When a family member was in need, Isaac, the most prosperous member of the clan, reached out to help. When his half sister, Mary Smith Pilkington, was widowed, Newton supported her and her five children for several years.[573]. Newton also loaned money to or became a surety for family members. He was generally present at family weddings, giving £100 to the brides and setting up the grooms in a trade or business.[574] Newton made provisions for his half-sister Hannah

Barton and her three minor children after her husband died, and when Catherine's brother, Robert, came of age, Newton helped cultivate his career in the military. When Robert was killed in the assault on Quebec in 1711, Newton helped Robert's wife obtain a government bounty and a yearly pension. Before Newton died he purchased an estate at Boyden for Robert's three children. He purchased a £4000 estate in Kensington for Kitty Conduitt, daughter of John and Catherine. There was a continuous stream of destitute relatives coming to Newton for help, and he helped all of them.

When Isaac reached age 82 and realized he would never return to good health, he began to dispose much of his estate. To his godson, Isaac Warner, the son of Margaret Barton Warner, he gave £100 for four years of rent payments. He also purchased a farm for his second cousin Robert Newton and gave land worth £30 per year to John Newton, the great-grandson of Isaac's uncle Robert. When Newton died intestate, the son of John Newton [John Jr.] inherited Isaac's estate at Woolsthorpe. Before Newton died, he gave £100 to an Ayscough and £500 to the black sheep of the family, Benjamin Smith.

Isaac also extended alms to many non-relatives. Some of them shared his surname, but were related in name only. Even if they didn't share his name, they came to him for help. I can give you names of many who received aid, such as John Corker in 1717, Elizabeth Johnson (at least three different times), Mary or Ann Davies in 1723, and eight others whose names were found on the backs of Isaac's scratch paper. There were dozens more, but Isaac destroyed the papers containing their names. As John Conduit was known to say, 'Isaac's charity had no limits.' Newton was also quoted as saying, 'They who gave away nothing until they died never gave.' Conduitt seemed to sum it all up by saying that no one in Newton's circumstances ever gave away so much in alms in the encouragement of learning and in the support of relatives [and other people in need].[575] His charity to unfortunates and his lasting friendships help to soften the images he evoked in quarrels with Flamsteed, Leibniz, and

Hooke. The record clearly shows that Newton became a significant dispenser of charity in his last years.[576]

As expected, Newton's primary beneficiaries were family members, but they were surprised that he had no will. Most of them had surmised that Catherine Barton Conduitt would receive the lion's share of Newton's fortune; however, his half-nieces and half-nephews shared his estate equally. Even Benjamin Smith, whom Newton considered a reprobate, received an equal share. In fact, Newton had sent him chastising letters in the plainest and severest terms possible. Fortunately the letters were destroyed by Reverend William Sheepshanks, sparing embarrassment for England's most shining genius.[577]

In his last years Newton reminisced at times with John Conduitt about things which he had accomplished during his life, but he was careful to avoid theological subjects.[578] In one of these talks, Isaac mentioned that the great comet of 1680 would eventually fall into the sun, increasing the sun's temperatures so much that life on earth would be extinguished. Newton said, "Mankind is of recent date and there are marks of ruin on the earth which suggest a similar cataclysm may have occurred in earth's distant past."

Conduit then asked, "How did the earth get repopulated if life had been destroyed?"

"That requires a Creator, John."

"Why don't you publish these theories, uncle?"

Isaac said "I do not deal in conjectures." He then picked up **The Principia** to show Conduitt the places in which he had alluded to cataclysmic phenomena.

Conduitt asked, "Why didn't you just come out and say what you believed?"

Newton laughed and said, "I have published enough for people to know what I mean."[579]

Before he died, Newton made a statement to Andrew Michael Ramsey, a Scot scholar visiting from France, which explains in one sentence Newton's opinion about his life:

I don't know what I may seem to the world, but, as to myself, I seem to have been only like a boy playing on the sea shore, and diverting myself in now and then finding a smoother pebble or a prettier shell than ordinary, whilst the great ocean of truth lay all undiscovered before me.[580]

"In the last few years of his life, Newton's health deteriorated. After voiding a kidney stone and suffering from incontinence in 1724, he moved to Kensington to escape the air pollution of London. From then until his death, Isaac missed more Society meetings than he attended. ...

In 1724 Conduitt admonished Newton, "Do not walk to church." Newton replied, "Use legs and have legs."[581]

Conduitt and Stukeley also tried to discourage Newton from leaving the country air by traveling to London, but Newton ignored them and continued to go there, though infrequently. It was on one of these trips that Isaac burned several boxes of papers, the contents of which have both baffled and plagued scholars to this day. Some have lost sleep over it.

In April of 1726 Stukeley notified Newton that he was returning to live in Grantham.

Newton said, "I applaud such a move, William. I've often thought of spending my last days in the town where I attended grammar school. When you get there, would you inquire whether the Vincent house just east of the church is for sale? If it is and the price is right, you have my authority to purchase it on my behalf."[582]

Stukeley said, "I will inquire about the house, Isaac. Perhaps we will both spend our last days in Grantham."

"Thank you, William."

Nothing materialized regarding Newton's request, but by simply making it, Newton exhibited some nostalgia for his boyhood years.

When Newton reached 82 years of age, he realized that he would never return to good health. It was at this time that he had begun disposing of his estate.

In February of 1727, though susceptible to serious coughs, Newton decided to attend the March meeting of The Royal Society. It was an important meeting in which a letter from the Academy of Science at St. Petersburg was to be read. The letter was the formal announcement of the founding of that Russian academy with their request to instigate regular communications with The Royal Society.

Newton arrived in London on February 27 and presided at the March 2 meeting. He stayed that night at the residence of his niece and her husband. The next morning John Conduitt said he hadn't seen Isaac better in years. Unfortunately, by the time Newton returned to Kensington on March 4, the stress, socializing and rigors of travel, not to mention London's air, had triggered a resurgence of Newton's chronic cough. Isaac began to deteriorate rapidly, and in a few days his abdominal "old complaint" had returned in a violent form. About the seventh of March upon hearing of Isaac's condition, Conduitt called on Dr. Richard Mead and Dr. William Cheselden, who traveled by carriage to Isaac's home. The prognosis couldn't have been worse. Newton had a bladder stone and there was no hope of recovery. [583]

The Conduitts, the doctors, the servants and William Stukeley immediately began a vigil at Newton's bedchamber. Their observations candidly reveal Newton's suffering. They describe long periods of excruciating pain rarely interrupted by brief respites. John Conduitt wrote: "Though the drops of sweat ran down his face, he never complained or cried out, or shewed the least signs of peevishness or impatience, and during the short intervals from that violent torture, would smile and talk with his usual cheerfulness."[584]

Stukeley was even more candid: "The pain rose to such a height that the bed under him, and the very room, shook with his agonys to the wonder of those that were present. Such a struggle had his great soul to quit its earthly tabernacle!"[585] It was also obvious to those near to him that Isaac was most concerned about his soul. In fact, during one of his respites Reverend Zachary Pearce, rector of Newton's home parish, visited Isaac and asked if he wished to receive the last rites of the Church of England. Throughout Newton's life he had revealed his true religion to only a select few, whom he swore to secrecy. He had never revealed it to an official of the church. But now on his death bed and alone with Reverend Pearce, *Isaac Newton refused the last rites of the church.* The stunned clergyman was visibly shaken and walked out of the bed chamber without saying a word.

Newton had planned to refuse the sacraments. It was to be his most significant act before dying.[586] Yet people would not have known about this last gesture if Newton hadn't informed his niece and her husband about it. In his last hours Newton planned to make a belief statement that he had refused to make for over fifty years.[587] In fact, Newton had stricken objectionable segments from the theological works to be published after his death.[588] However, he definitely wanted people to know about this final gesture; otherwise, he would not have told Catherine and John Conduitt about it. In order not to jeopardize Isaac's memory, however, the Conduitts were cautious about releasing Newton's defiant and heretical action. Not even Stukeley was privy to it.

On Wednesday, March 15, Newton appeared to revive, and his bedside attendants began to wonder if Newton might astound the experts and recover. In fact, on Saturday morning Isaac read the papers and talked for a considerable time with Dr. Mead. But suddenly at six o'clock Saturday evening Isaac slipped into a coma that lasted through Sunday. He died between one and two A.M. on Monday morning the 20th of March, 1727, the exact hour of his birth over 84 years ago.[589]

The Royal Society had lost its greatest president, the man who was responsible for its resurgence and its fame, credibility and success. On the 23rd of March a note appeared on the Society's door:

> *The Chair being Vacant by the Death of Sir Isaac Newton, there was no Meeting this Day.*[590]

Announcements of Newton's death appeared in gazettes throughout England. In one gazette were three pages of encomiums, one of which contained the following description:

"…the greatest of Philosophers, and the Glory of the British Nation."[591]

John Thomson's "Poem Sacred to the Memory of Sir Isaac Newton" was into its fifth edition of printing before the end of 1727.

CHAPTER 50

The Estate and the Manuscripts

• • •

"Most of Newton's heirs did not mourn his death, Moshe. Only Catherine Barton Conduitt and her husband expressed concern over preserving Isaac's memory. From the date of Isaac's death until his funeral on April 4, bickering and suspicion prevailed over the administration of Isaac's estate. The estate, though not enormous, was sizeable. It consisted of Isaac's manor at Woolsthorpe, £32,000 in liquid assets and his library. There were also innumerable manuscripts, which were virtually impossible to appraise. ...

Distributing Newton's liquid assets was not a problem. They could be divided equally among eight half-nieces and half-nephews: three Smiths, including Benjamin; three Bartons, including Catherine Conduitt; and three Pilkingtons, children of Mary Smith Pilkington. Disposition of the real estate in Woolsthorpe was also handled expeditiously when John Newton, the great-grandson of Isaac's uncle Robert, presented himself as Isaac's nearest patrimonial heir. Reverend Thomas Mason of Colsterworth described John Newton as "a poor representative of so great a man."[592] Stukeley also knew John Newton and had the same opinion as Reverend Mason. The description proved to be true. John Newton borrowed money against the property until he lost it by gambling and drinking. He died intoxicated, falling down the stairs of a pub with a pipe in his mouth. The pipe broke and the stem lodged in his throat.[593]

Except for Catherine Conduitt and her husband John, all of Newton's heirs were more concerned about Isaac's money than his memory or his achievements. To them he was only "Rich Uncle Isaac," and they began haggling over his estate.[594] John Conduitt was handllng the administration of the estate, but the other heirs were overly suspicious and demanded that three of them administer it. Within a month Conduitt would acquiesce to their demands. The heirs also requested that all of Isaac Newton's manuscripts be sealed until the rest of the estate had been settled. As previously indicated, the 'rest of the estate' was distributed with little, if any snags. The stocks were easily appraised and the value of the library was determined by accepting an offer above its appraised value from John Huggins, the warden of Fleet Prison. [595]

However, deciding how to distribute the value of Isaac's manuscripts became a contentious issue. To be candid, it was impossible to place a monetary value on them. Seven heirs believed that anything with Isaac Newton's name on it could be sold at a high price, and they were eager to immediately put every manuscript on the market.[596] The Conduitt's, however, valued the manuscripts as the writings of a great man which needed to be preserved along with his memory. Regarding Newton's theological manuscripts, Catherine Conduitt wrote that her husband wanted to insure that "the labour and sincere search of so good a X-[Chris]tian and so great a genius may not be lost to the world."[597]

Isaac Newton's funeral took place on April 4, 1727 when the haggling of his heirs was at its peak. Newton's remains had lain in state in the Jerusalem Chamber of Westminster Abbey since March 28, but on April 4 Newton received a send-off fit for royalty. The pall-bearers were all members of the Royal Society: The Lord High Chancellor, two Dukes and three Earls. The procession was led by the Honorable Sir Michael Newton, a Knight of the Bath, followed by many mourners, including relatives and public figures. The service was conducted by the Bishop of Rochester, assisted by church officials and a choir. After the conclusion of the service when all mourners had departed, Newton's body was lowered into its crypt. His resting place was in the nave of Westminster Abbey, a location that had previously been denied to many noblemen.[598]

After the funeral the heirs resumed their squabbling, however they had a new problem. It appears that the net income earned from coinage at the Mint now belonged to the Crown. Newton had always managed for the Mint to return a profit, and the amount owed to the Crown was calculated at £34,330. John Conduitt, the spouse of Newton's niece, was the only person in a position to pay it. Having assumed Isaac's duties at the Mint for over two years, he knew its people, and used his connections and his wealth to great advantage.

A disagreement also arose concerning Newton's manuscripts. Because of the contentions among the heirs, a court order had been issued on April 3 to adjudicate the disputes between them. The order was legally confirmed on April 27 when seven of the eight heirs appeared in court.

The court order stipulated that Conduitt would step down as estate administrator and be replaced by Benjamin Smith, Thomas Pilkington and Catherine Conduitt. All of the heirs were to peruse Isaac's papers. After reading them they would be collected and given to Thomas Pellet from The Royal Society. Pellet would examine all manuscripts and select those worthy of publication. These would be printed and sold "to the best advantage." Catherine was placed in charge of the manuscripts until they were given to Pellet. Money was also set aside for a monument, funeral rings, one year of servants' wages, and the poor of Colsterworth.[599]

In the meantime, John Conduit was to get a release from the Mint of the debt owed to the Crown. He was also to oversee the trial of the Pyx at the Mint, which settled and closed the accounts managed by Isaac Newton. In return for his efforts, Conduitt was to maintain all of the Newton documents that were not approved by Pellet for publication. Conduitt was also required to post a bond of £2000 to back up his accountability to the heirs "should he publish or make any advantage" of the manuscripts entrusted to him.

On May 17, Conduitt presented to the administrators a receipt of payment to the Crown of the balance owed from the Mint. The estate was now absolved from any claim by the Crown. On the next day, May 18, the heirs dined at the Doctors Common to celebrate the resolution of Isaac Newton's estate. In two more days the administrators distributed all of the liquid assets and called in Dr. Pellet to evaluate and select those manuscripts worthy of publication.

Dr. Pellet spent three days judging Newton's manuscripts. The heirs were undoubtedly disappointed to see him stamp "Not Fit to Be Printed" on every manuscript but one: Newton's *Chronology of Ancient Kingdoms*. Two booksellers immediately purchased the rights to the *Chronology* for £350. Dr. Pellet may have been correct; *Chronology* was probably Newton's most suitable work for the general public's consumption. The heirs, however, asked Pellet if he would reconsider Newton's other documents. Pellet responded by naming four other papers to be placed on the market, but only two of them were purchased and printed: the original draft of the final book of **The Principia** and Newton's *Observations upon the Prophecies*.[600] Upon Pellet's completion of the selection process, Conduitt posted a bond of £2000 to become the de facto owner of the rest of Newton's manuscripts.

Conduitt was also fortunate to procure the Mastership of the Mint, which was probably the biggest monetary plum obtained from Newton's demise. Since 1725, Newton had been easing Conduitt into the mastership. Though a rumor had spread that the position was first offered to Samuel Clark, Conduitt's warrant as Master of the Mint was dated March 31, 1727, less than two weeks after Isaac's death and three days before the funeral.

John Conduitt died in 1737; his beautiful wife, Catherine, died two years later. Their daughter, Catherine (Kitty), married the Honorable John Wallop in 1740. The Wallops' son became the Second Earl of Portsmouth, and it was he who inherited Isaac's manuscripts, later known as "the Portsmouth Papers." Thanks to the foresight of John

Conduitt, Newton's papers remained preserved for almost 175 years before they were purchased and scrutinized by universities and scholars.

John Theophilus Desaguliers also obtained a copy the *Chronology of Ancient Kingdoms* after Newton's death. From the *Chronology*, Desaguliers gleaned information about the realm of King Solomon, which he inserted into Masonic rituals and lectures. 'The Temple of Solomon' was the most accurate chapter in Newton's *Chronology of Ancient Kingdoms*.

Thanks to John Conduitt, the world is privileged to examine Isaac Newton's manuscripts, some of which have only recently been publicized.

CHAPTER 51

Newton's Legacy

• • •

"MOSHE, IN MARCH OF 2003 the British Broadcasting Company produced a documentary entitled *Newton, the Dark Heretic*. One man interviewed for that documentary produced a manuscript in which Newton prophesied the end of the world in the year 2060. Although scholars had known about this prophesy, this was the first public announcement of it. Newton predicted this date fairly late in life and he vigorously upheld its authenticity. He had taken 1260 years from *Revelation 12:6* as the duration of the corruption of the Church. To the 1260 he added 800 years, 800 A.D. being the year Charlemagne was crowned emperor of Rome and the Holy Roman Empire. Quite simply, 800 A.D. plus 1260 added up to the year 2060.

"Newton's prophesy quickly reached the front pages of newspapers throughout the world, and suddenly the world realized that Newton was much more than a scientist; he was also a theologian and a prophet. He exemplified the fact that religion and science were compatible.

"As you know, Moshe, Newton's theological and alchemical papers were sold by the Portsmouth family in 1936 at Sotheby's in London. Most of these papers were purchased by the Jewish scholar Abraham Yahuda, who willed them to the State of Israel upon his death in 1951. Unfortunately, the will was contested and the papers were not delivered to Israel until 1969. They are in this very library in which you and I are talking. Although these papers have only recently been publicized, much of Newton's religion and philosophy had been disclosed since the early 18th century in Masonic rituals and lectures written by John Theophilus Desaguliers, Newton's curator of experiments for the Royal Society.

"Let me give you some examples. First of all, Newton described Geometry as 'the first and noblest of sciences.' Geometry, in fact, is the basis upon which Newton's **Principia** was written. In Newton's time, geometry and masonry were synonymous terms. Secondly, the first landmark of the seven landmarks of Masonry is monotheism, which is the main emphasis of Newton's religion –the religion of Noah, Moses, Solomon and even Jesus Christ. Third, the first Newton book published after his death was the *Chronology of Ancient Kingdoms*, in which Newton placed great emphasis on the kingdom and religion of King Solomon. Without a doubt, Desaguliers took this information about King Solomon and his temple from Newton's *Chronology* and incorporated it into many Masonic lectures, rituals and dramas. He divulged information about the practices, beliefs, organization and life surrounding King Solomon's era, and he had obtained this information from the writings of Isaac Newton.

"I don't mind telling you, Moshe, Desaguliers not only lectured on Newtonian mathematics and sciences, but he also incorporated Newton's religion into the Masonic fraternity. It is even possible that Desaguliers gleaned some of John Locke's philosophies from Isaac Newton –especially regarding the church and state. To this date political and religious discussion are not permitted in open Masonic lodges. Desaguliers actually showed more loyalty to the Masonic fraternity than he did to the Anglican Church, which he neglected on many occasions."

Moshe asked, "Why would Desaguliers neglect his duties as an Anglican clergyman?"

"I can't say with complete surety, Moshe. Perhaps Desaguliers' Huguenot roots had something to do with it. I'm sure that he held an aversion toward state religions. After escaping from France as a child, Desaguliers only returned to his native country to visit Masonic lodges. Perhaps Desaguliers didn't like the fact that the Anglican Church was 'the Church of England,' a moniker that denotes a religious state with religious restrictions. Religious tyranny had already reared its head in England by punishing those who believed in certain other religions. Locke and Desaguliers both advocated the right of a person to select his own religion and not have it forced upon him. In parts of the world today, Moshe, the consequences of theocratic rule are hardship, suppression, and even death.

"But let me continue with the proliferation of Newton's beliefs before the publication of his papers in the twenty-first century. Many of Newton's philosophies are contained in Masonic writings. I have previously mentioned his strong stand against idolatry, which Newton called false worship. In his *Origines* Newton declared that God prefers to be worshiped, not for the necessary aspects of His being, but for what He has done: 'Ye wisest of beings requires of us to be celebrated not so much for his essence as for his actions. ...the wisdome, power, goodness & justice wch He always exerts in His actions are his glory... .'[601] I have already told you that in the 'Middle Chamber Lecture' of the Fellow Craft Degree of Freemasonry you will find the words, 'power, wisdom, and goodness' just as if Newton had written them. Desaguliers explicitly states that "By it [geometry] we discover the power, the wisdom, and the goodness of the Grand Artificer of the Universe... ."[602]

Moshe asked, "Did Newton ever become a Mason?"

"No, Moshe. Newton was quite old when Masonic lodges changed from operative to speculative Masonry. Furthermore, Newton was not the most sociable of creatures; he was usually buried in research and study. Nevertheless, he was more than supportive of Desaguliers' efforts to insert Newtonianism into Masonry, especially Newton's primitive religion 'to love God and one's neighbors.' Desaguliers added a third duty, however, which appears in the Entered Apprentice' Charge' and stems from Newton's puritanical roots: "to avoid all irregularity and intemperance that might impair your faculties or debase the dignity of your profession."[603]

"The fact is, Moshe, Desaguliers inserted a lot of Newtonianism in his Masonic writings. I could provide you with numerous examples. Of primary importance, however, is that Newton and Desaguliers desired that every nation, religion, person and enterprise abide by three simple, fundamental rules:

1. To respect the Power which created our universe and the gifts it has given us, especially those gifts which we are unable to create ourselves.
2. To respect and love one another. To do to others as you wish they would do to you, and to respect the laws which safeguard us from those who cannot abide by this rule.
3. To sincerely admit and regret our human frailties, to atone for our faults and strive not to repeat them. This last rule was the topic of Desaguliers' sermon to King George I: 'Repent and Be Saved;' and as I have told you, it is the only sermon of Desaguliers for which there is a written record.

"To me, Moshe, these few rules apply to people of every country, state or opinion. They are the legacy of the great men of the Enlightenment, spearheaded by Isaac Newton, John Locke, John Theophilus Desaguliers, Robert Boyle, Edmund Halley and others. The truths uncovered by the men of the Enlightenment contain principles upon which civilized nations of the world have been founded. These men only searched for truth. As Newton wrote in his Wastebook in 1663:

Plato is my friend. Aristotle is my friend, but truth is my greater friend.

"Write your thesis, Moshe. Newton's religion may be what the world needs now more than ever. The world needs to worship the deeds, examples, and discoveries of great human beings --not simply worship their names."

Moshe said, "Professor, I don't know how to thank you. I think that you have reaffirmed some things that many of us have forgotten or misplaced. But, sir, I don't even know your name."

"My name is unimportant, Moshe. What is important is love, morality, truth, virtue and a reverence for creation."

The professor rose from the table, pushed in his chair and walked out of the library.

Epilogue

Isaac Newton discovered that a founding tenet of Christianity had been changed in 325 AD. Although he believed that the new tenet was tantamount to idol-worshiping, he couldn't reveal the truth due to civil and religious laws. Newton found that since 325 AD, people, nations and religions had adopted a "new" Trinity but appeared to have forgotten the most important religious truths:

1. To respect creation and its architect.
2. To do unto others as we would wish done to ourselves.

Regrettably, almost every war on Earth has been a religious one. Perhaps the first wars to have a worldly impact were the Muslim Holy Wars which began in 639 AD against the Roman Church that had adopted a new Trinity and was worshiping a triune God. In 1095 AD The Christians of Western Europe attempted to stem Muslim advances and started a Crusade. The annihilation of the Cathars at Montsegur, France occurred in 1244. In 1572, 100,000 French Huguenots were slaughtered during the Saint Bartholomew's Day massacre. Fifty-five years later 25,000 Huguenots died in the siege of La Rochelle. In the 20th century, millions of Jews along with many others were exterminated by Nazi Germany. Since the 7th century, 270 million deaths have been attributed to Islamic jihads.

All of this carnage occurred because the "most important religious truths" were forsaken for selfish reasons. The greatest and best of people have abided by these truths. Isaac Newton believed that *true* Christianity was based on them. Newton believed in a *Primitive Christianity* that started with Noah but was corrupted at the Council of Nicaea. Three centuries after that council, Muslims were chanting "There is no God but Allah." Wars and rumors of wars have continued. Thankfully, civility has triumphed over tyranny in most countries of the world.

The majority of people in our world seem to agree that education is vital for a free and civilized society. In the United States, teaching religious sects is prohibited in public schools –as it should be. However, the moral principles of our founding fathers need to be inculcated, especially a respect for what has been created for us. John Locke wrote that believing in nothing will destroy a nation. Nations must strive to respect life, liberty, and the pursuit of happiness, regardless of one's race, color, creed, nationality, gender or sexual orientation. People do not choose how they are created. Public schools can be a vital link in instilling the love of life, the love of one another, and an appreciation of creation.

Today's Masonic Lodges attempt to inculcate principles of some of America's greatest founding fathers and the great men of The Enlightenment. George Washington, a Master of a Masonic Lodge, once said that he wanted America to be a land of virtues. America has come a long way toward being virtuous, but it has a way to go.

James E. McNabney

ENDNOTES

1. Christianson, Gale "In the Presence of the Creator," MacMillan, Inc. New York, NY p. 33

2. Gleick, James "Isaac Newton" Pantheon Press, New York, NY. p. 18-19.

3. Keynes Manuscript Collection 136, pp.4-5, Kings College Library, Cambridge, England.

4. Op. Cit. Christianson, p. 21.

5. Bauer, Alain. "Isaac Newton's Freemasonry," Inner Traditions Rochester, VT. pp.41-45. 2007

6. Ibid. p. 49.

7. Op. Cit. Christianson, p. 45.

8. Ibid, p. 46

9. Ibid, p.17.

10. Conduitt, John. "Newton's Life at Cambridge," Keynes MS 130.4 pp 1-2. King's College Library, Cambridge, UK.

11. Ibid. p. 3.

12. Op. Cit. Christianson, p. 29.

13. Ibid. p. 35.

14. Ibid. p. 37.

15. Whiteside, D.T. "Sources and Strengths of Newton's Early Mathematical Thought." <u>The Annus Mirabilis of Sir Isaac Newton</u>, ed. R.Palter, M.I.T. Press, Cambridge, MA. 1930. P. 72.

16. Ibid. pp. 74-75.

17. Ibid. p. 75.

18. Op. Cit. Christianson, p. 59.

19. Op. Cit. Keynes, MS 130 (10), f.2v.

20. Op. Cit. Christianson, p.65.

21. "The Correspondence of Isaac Newton" Ed. by H.W. Turnbull, J.F. Scott, A.R. Hall and Laura Tilling. Cambridge, England,1957-77. Vol. III p. 393.

22. Hervival, John. "The Background to Newton's "Principia." Oxford, 1965. pp. 35-41.

23. Cambridge University Library "Additional MS" p.4004, f.10v, Cambridge, England.

24. Op. Cit. Cambridge University Library. F.11. Cambridge, England.

25. Isaac Newton's "Wastebook", May 20, 1665.

26. Op.Cit. Whiteside. p. 72.

27. Op.Cit Christianson. p. 68.

28. Ibid. p 71.

29. University Library of Cambridge Manuscript Addition 4000, 15r; Addition 4004, 57r/57v.

30. Ibid. Add 3955.2, 30r/30v.

31. Ibid. Add 4004, 50v/50r, Nov. 8, 1665.

32. Op.Cit. Whiteside, D.T. p. 82.

33. Op. Cit. Christianson, p. 88.

34. Ibid.

35. Ibid. p. 100.

36. Ibid. p. 107.

37. Ibid. p. 110

38. Op. Cit. Gleick. p. 11.

39. Op. Cit. I.N. "Correspondence" 1:13

40. Op. Cit. Christianson, p. 122.

41. Ibid. p. 123.

42. Ibid. p. 124.

43. Westfall, Richard S. "Never At Rest," Cambridge University Press, New York, N.Y. 1980 p. 185.

44. Ibid. p. 188

45. Ibid. p. 184.

46. Ibid. p. 190.

47. Op. Cit. Christianson, p. 119.

48. Op. Cit. Westfall p.214.

49. Ibid. p. 217.

50. Stukeley, William. "Memories of Sir Isaac Newton's Life" ed. A. Hastings White. London 1936.

51. Op. Cit. "Correspondence" I, p. 16-20.

52. Op. Cit. Westfall, p. 222
Ibid. P. 224.

53. Op. Cit. "Correspondence" I, 27.

54. Op. Cit. Westfall. P. 225. 226.

55. Op. Cit. "Correspondence" I, 36. Collins to Newton, July 19, 1670.

56. Ibid. I, 43-44.

57. Whiteside, D.T. "The Mathematical Papers of Isaac Newton." (8 Vols.), Cambridge, UK 1969 -80.

58. Op. Cit. Westfall, p. 227.

59. Ibid. p. 232.

60. Op. Cit. Christianson, p. 141.

61. Op. Cit Westfall, p. 234.

62. Op. Cit. Correspondence. 1, p. 73.

63. Op.Cit. Westfall. p. 236.

64. Op. Cit. Correspondence. 1, p. 80.

65. Ibid. 1, p. 82.

66. Op. Cit. Christianson, p. 147.

67. Ibid. p. 150.

68. Op. Cit. I.N. "Correspondence," 1:102.

69. Ibid. 1:108-9.

70. Ibid.

71. Op. Cit. Gleick, p. 85.

72. Op. Cit. Christianson, p. 156.

73. Ibid. p. 160

74. Op. Cit. Westfall, p. 244.

75. Ibid. Westfall, p. 241.

76. Op. Cit. Gleick, p. 84.

77. Op. Cit. Christianson, p. 164.

78. Op. Cit. "Correspondence…" 1:144.

79. Isaac Newton's Papers &Letters on Natural Philosophy, ed. J. Bernard Cohen, Cambridge, MA. 1978. p. 106.

80. Ibid. p. 109

81. Op. Cit. "Correspondence," 1:171-172.

82. Ibid.

83. Ibid.

84. Ibid.

85. Op. Cit. "Correspondence" 1:173.

86. Op. Cit. Christianson, p. 170.

87. Ibid. p. 171.

88. Op. Cit. Christianson, p. 179.

89. Ibid.

90. Op. Cit. IN Corres. 1:262

91. Op. Cit. Corres. 1:282

92. Op. Cit. Westfall. P. 251

93. Op. Cit. Christianson, p. 181

94. Op. Cit. Christianson, p. 181

95. Op. Cit. "Correspondence" (Newton to Oldenburg) 1. 294-297, June 23, 1673.

96. Op. Cit. "Correspondence" (Newton to Collins) 1 -309. June 20, 1674.

97. Op. Cit. Westfall. p. 282.

98. Op. Cit. Westfall. P.222.

99. Op. Cit. Westfall. P. 21

100. Op. Cit Westfall. p. 290-292

101. Op. Cit. Christianson. p.58

102. Holmyard, Eric J. "Alchemy" London, 1957.

103. Op. Cit. Christianson.

104. Op. Cit. Westfall. p. 311

105. Op.Cit. Christenson. P. 215.

106. Op. Cit. Keynes. MS 2, f X 1.

107. Op. Cit. Yahuda MS, 14f.83v

108. Op Cit. Westfall. p. 314.

109. Op, Cit Bauer. P. 63

110. Op .Cit. Westfall. pp. 312-313.

111. Ibid. p. 313

112. Op. Cit. Keynes, MS 3, p. 14.

113. Op. Cit. Christianson. P. 257

114. Op. Cit. Yahuda MS, 41, ff 6-7.

115. Op. Cit. Westfall. P 356.

116. Op. Cit. "Correspondence…" (Newton to Oldenburg) 1:328-329.

117. Op. Cit Westfall. P. 332.

118. Op. Cit. Christianson. p. 185.

119. Op. Cit. "Correspondence," 1:358.

120. Ibid, pp. 1:356-357.

121. Ibid, p. 1:359.

122. Op. Cit. Christianson. p. 190.

123. Ibid. p. 195.

124. Op. Cit. "Correspondence" 1, 412-13.

125. Ibid. p. 416.

126.

127. "Correspondence" Newton to Oldenburg, Jan. 10, 1676.

128. Op. Cit. Westfall. p. 275.

129. Ibid.

130. "Correspondence 2, 182-3" Newton to Oldenburg, 18 Nov. 1676.

131. Op. Cit. Westfall. p. 277.

132. "The Diary of Abraham de la Pryme," ed. Charles Jackson, Durham, Andrews & Co., 1870, p. 23.

133. Op. Cit. Westfall. p. 278.

134. *Corres* 2, 254-60, 262-3.

135. Op. Cit Westfall. p. 280.

136. Op. Cit. Christianson. p. 154.

137. Correspondence of H. Oldenburg. Ed. By Rupert and Marie Boas Hall, Madison, WI. 1965. Vol. IX:566.

138. *Correspondence*. Isaac Newton, 11:39.

139. Op. Cit. Christianson. p. 156.

140. Ibid. II:134, 153, fn25.

141. Op.Cit. Christianson. p. 158.

142. Isaac Newton Correspondence to Collins II:179

143. Op. Cit. Westfall, p. 343.

144. Op. Cit. Westfall, p. 343.

145. Op. Cit. Christianson. p. 286.

146. Op. Cit. Westfall. p. 152.

147. Op. Cit. p. 382.

148. Op. Cit. p. 382.

149. Op. Cit.. p. 383.

150. Op. Cit. p. 383.

151. Op. Cit. p. 385.

152. *Correspondence* Hooke to Newton. 9 December 1679.

153. Op. Cit. Westfall. p. 388.

154. *Correspondence 2, 313*. Hooke to Newton, 17 January, 1680.

155. Op. Cit. Herivel, John. pp. 247-253.

156. Op. Cit. Westfall, p. 388.

157. Op. Cit. Westfall, p. 395.

158. Boyer, Carl B. "Cartesian & Newtonian Algebra in the Mid-Eighteenth Century," Warsaw, 1968, 3, pp.195-202.

159. Op. Cit. Westfall, p. 398.

160. Joseph Halle Schaffner Collection, University of Chicago Library, MS 1075-7, 1977.

161. Op. Cit. Westfall. p. 403.

162. Op. Cit. Hervivel, pp. 277-89. Westfall. p. 404.

163. Op. Cit. Keynes. MS 135.

164. Ibid.

165. *Correspondence.* Newton to Flamsteed. 2, 407.

166. Op. Cit. 2, 419-420.

167. Op. Cit. Herivel p. 302, (original Latin p. 291.)

168. Op. Cit. Christenson. p. 423.

169. Ibid. p. 424.

170. *Prin*cipia. Add. MS 3965.3, f. 11, Cf. p. 190.

171. *Correspondence* 1, 445. Newton to Halley. 14 July 1686.

172. Op. Cit. Christenson. p. 312.

173. Mine.

174. Op. Cit. Christenson. P. 406.

175. World Book Encyclopaedia. 1974.

176. Op. Cit. Westfall. p. 414.

177. Op. Cit. Herivel. p. 311.

178. Op. Cit. Westfall. p. 417.

179. Op. Cit. Westfall. p. 437.

180. Op. Cit. Westfall. p. 437.

181. "Principia," pp. 202-3.

182. Op. Cit. Westfall, p. 441.

183. Newton to Halley, June 20, 1686, *Corres.* 2, p.437.

184. *Correspondence 2* Halley to Newton, *p.* 431.

185. Ibid. p. 433-4.

186. Ibid. p. 434-5.

187. Op. Cit. Westfall, p. 447.

188. Ibid. 448.

189. Ibid.

190. Ibid.

191. Ibid. p. 449.

192. Op. Cit. *Corres 2*, 441-3.

193. Op. Cit. Westfall. p. 450.

194. Op. Cit. *Corres 2*, 444-5.

195. Op Cit. Westfall. p. 451.

196. Op. Cit. *Corres 2*. P. 446-7

197. Op. Cit. Westfall. P. 452.

198. Op. Cit. Isaac Newton *Correspondence* II. P. 419.

199. "Principia," P. 498.

200. Op. Cit. Christenson, P. 309.

201. Halley to Newton *Correspondence II:* 464.

202. Op. Cit. "Principia" P. 415.

203. Op. Cit. Isaac Newton *Correspondence*. P. 233.

204. Op. Cit Christenson. P. 318.

205. Op. Cit. Christenson. P. 319

206. Op. Cit. Keynes MS 130.5 Sheets 2-3.

207. Op. Cit. "Correspondence II,"

208. Op. Cit. Westfall. P. 475. (Endnote 24)

209. Ibid. P. 476.

210. Ibid. P. 476.

211. Burnet, Gilbert. "History of His Own Times" Oxford. Vol.3, P. 143. 1823.

212. Ibid. P. 144.

213. Op. Cit. Westfall. P. 477.

214. Op. Cit. Christenson. P.323

215. Ibid. P. 324.

216. Cooper, Charles Henry, "Annals of Cambridge, III:621

217. Ibid. P. 626.

218. Ibid. P. 626.

219. Op. Cit. Westfall. P. 479

220. Ibid. P. 480

221. Op. Cit. Christenson. P. 327.

222. Op. Cit. Christenson. P. 329.

223. Various and sundry authors.

224. Op. Cit. Christenson.

225. Op. Cit. Westfall. P. 484.

226. Ibid.

227. Ibid. P 481.

228. Ibid. P. 493.

229. Ibid. P. 485.

230. Ibid.

231. Ibid.

232. Ibid. P. 486.

233. Ibid. P. 487.

234. Op. Cit. Christenson. P. 330

235. Op. Cit Westfall. P. 488.

236. Thomson, Garrett. "On Locke," Wadsworth/Thomson Learning. Belmont CA, 2001. PP65,66.

237. Ibid. P. 491.

238. Ibid. P. 490.

239. Op. Cit. Westfall. P. 489.

240. Mine.

241. Newton to Locke. *Corres. 3*, P. 79. 28 Oct. 1690. Ibid. 3, P. 82, 83-122.

242. Ibid 3, P. 138.

243. Ibid. 3, P. 108.

244. Op. Cit. Westfall. P. 491.

244. Ibid. P. 493.

245. "John Locke's "Letter Concerning Toleration" London. 1689

246. Ibid. P. 5.

247. Ibid.

248. Op. Cit. Christenson, P. 337.

249. Op. Cit. Christenson, P. 341

250. Ibid.

251. Op. Cit. Westfall, P. 493

252. Ibid. P. 344.

253. Ibid.

254. Ibid.

255. Ibid. P. 345.

256. Ibid.

257. Ibid.

258. Mine.

259. Op. Cit. Christianson, P. 345.

260. *Corres.* 3, 390-1. Fatio to Newton, 29 February, 1690.

261. Op. Cit. Westfall, P. 496.

262. Ibid. P. 497.

263. Ibid. P. 498.

264. Ibid. P. 497.

265. Ibid.

266. Isaac Newton Correspondence VII: 392.

267. Op. Cit. Christianson, P. 346.

268. Ibid.

269. Isaac Newton Correspondence III, 242-245.

270. 2Op.Cit. Christianson, P. 351.

271. Ibid.

272. Ibid., P. 352

273. Ibid.

274. Ibid.

275. Isaac Newton *Correspondence* III, 235-236.

276. Keynes MSS on Isaac Newton, 130.6 Book 2; 130.7, Sheet 1.

277. Op. Cit. Westfall. P. 500.

278. Ibid. P. 500-501.

279. Ibid. P. 501.

280. Op. cit. Christianson, P. 356

281. Ibid. P. 357.

282. Ibid. P 356.

283. Op. Cit. Westfall. PP. 502

284. Op. Cit. Westfall, P. 513.

285. Ibid. P. 514.

286. "The Mathematical Papers of Isaac Newton," ed. D.T. Whiteside, Vol 7, PP. 56-72. Cambridge, MA 1967– 80.

287. Op. Cit. Westfall, P. 515.

288. Gregory's memorandum of May 5-7, 1694, *Correspondence* 3, 338.

289. Op. Cit Christianson, P. 503.

290. Ibid.

291. *Correspondence of Henry Oldenburg.* Ed. A Rupert Hall and Marie Boas Hall. Madison WI, 1965-73.

292. Op. Cit. Christianson, P. 504.

293. Ibid.

294. Ibid. P. 505.

295. Ibid. II:39.

296. Op. Cit. Christianson, P. 507.

297. Hofmann, Joseph H. "Leibniz in Paris," Ch. 20. Cambridge Univ. Press, 2008.

298. Op. Cit. Christianson, P. 507.

299. Ibid. P. 508.

300. Ibid. P. 509.

301. Op. Cit. Isaac Newton *Correspondence* II: 219, 234.

302. Op. Cit. Christianson. P. 510.

303. Ibid.

304. Op. Cit. *I.N. Correspondence II:* 235,110.

305. Westfall, Richard S. "The Life of Isaac Newton". Cambridge University Press, 1993. P. 206-207.

306. Op. Cit. Westfall, "The Life of Isaac Newton." P. 208

307. Op. Cit. Westfall, "Never At Rest."P. 537.

308. Op. Cit. Westfall, "The Life of Isaac Newton." P. 218.

309. Op. Cit. I.N. *Correspondence IV,* 72. 18 January 1695.

310. Op. Cit. Westfall, P. 542.

311. Ibid. P. 543.

312. Op. Cit. Christianson, P. 367.

313. Ibid.

314. Op. Cit. *I. N.* Correspondence *IV:* 54-55, 58.

315. Ibid. IV: 62

316. Ibid. *IV:* 87, 16.

317. Ibid. IV: 135

318. Ibid.

319. Op. Cit. Westfall, "Never At Rest." P. 545.

320. Ibid.

321. Op. Cit. I.N. Correspondence IV: 143.

322. Ibid. IV:143.

323. Ibid.

324. Op Cit. Westfall, "Never At Rest." P. 547.

325. Op. Cit. Westfall, "the Life of Isaac Newton." P 203

326. Ibid. P. 550.

327. Op. Cit. Christianson. P 374.

328. Ibid. P. 377.

329. Ibid. P. 378.

330. Ibid. P. 380.

331. Op. Cit. Westfall. "Never At Rest." P. 555.

332. Op. Cit. Christianson. P. 384.

333. Ibid. P. 385.

334. Ibid. P. 390.

335. Op. Cit. Westfall, P. 559-560.

336. Ibid. P. 561.

337. Ibid.

338. Ibid. P. 563.

339. Ibid.

340. Ibid. P. 564.

341. Op. Cit. *Correspondence* IV, 207-8.

342. Op. Cit. Westfall, P. 566.

343. "Mint Papers in the Public Record Office" Parliament, London, England.

344. Op. Cit. Westfall, P. 567.

345. Ibid.

346. Op. Cit. *Correspondence IV,* 209-210.

347. Op. Cit. Westfall, P. 568.

348. Op. Cit. Keynes, 130.7, Sheet 2.

349. Op. Cit. Westfall, P. 369.

350. Op. Cit. Christianson, P. 405.

351. Ibid. P. 405.

352. Op. Cit. Westfall, P. 570.

353. Ibid. P. 566.

354. Westfall, Richard S. "The Life of Isaac Newton." Cambridge Univ. Press, New York, NY, 1993. P.229-230.

355. Chaloner, William, "Guzman Redivivus," P. 12.

356. Op. Cit. Christianson, P. 413.

357. Ibid.

358. Op. Cit. Christianson, P 415.

359. Op. Cit. Isaac Newton's *Correspondence*, IV:225.

360. Op. Cit. Christianson, P. 415.

361. Keynes MSS, 130 (5), f.1;130(6), Book 1. King's Colldge Library, Cambridge, England.

362. Whiteside, D.T. "The Mathematical Papers of Isaac Newton," Cambridge England. 1967-80.VIII:9.

363. Op. Cit. Westfall. "The Life of Isaac Newton," P. 233.

364. Gordon, Thomas. "A Cordial for Low Spirits," 3rd Ed. London, 1763.

365. Hazard, Paul. "The European Mind," tr Jay Lewis May, World Publishing Company, Cleveland, Ohio. 1963.

366. Ibid.

367. Op. Cit. Westfall. "The Life of Isaac Newton." P. 584

368. Ibid. P. 585.

369. Baily, Francis. "An Account of the Reverend John Flamsteed…" London, 1835-7. PP. 166-8.

370. Op. Cit. Westfall. "The Life of Isaac Newton," P. 586.

371. Ibid.

372. Ibid.

373. Ibid.

374. Op. Cit. Christianson. P. 421.

375. Op. Cit. Westfall. "The Life of Isaac Newton," P. 589.

376. Keynes MS. 130 (6), Book 1.

377. Kerr, Philip. "Dark Matter." Three Rivers Press, New York, N.Y. pp. 215-221. Note: Catherine Barton's relationship with Ellis is portrayed in Kerr's novel. Portrayals of her personality are the author's.

378. Swift, Jonathan, "Journal to Stella" ed. By Williams. I:31, 230

379. Ibid. II:383.

380. Op. Cit. Westfall, "Never At Rest" Pp. 623-624.

381. Op. Cit. Christianson. P. 433.

382. "Galatians" 4.6-7.

383. Lord Peter King. "The Life and Letters of John Locke, New ed. London, 1858. P. 263

384. Op. Cit. "Correspondence" IV: 406.

385. Cranston, Maurice. "John Locke: A Biography," London and New York, 1957, P. 480.

386. Op. Cit. Westfall, "Never At Rest, P. 595.

387. Ibid. PP. 628, 630.

388. Op. Cit. "Westfall, "Never at Rest. P. 451.

389. "Journal Book of the Royal society. 10:145, 1696.

390. Op. Cit. Westfall, "Never at Rest" P. 629.

391. Ibid.

392. Ibid.

392. Ibid.

393. Op. Cit. Westfall, "Never At Rest." P. 632.

394. Ibid.

395. Ibid. P. 634.

396. Op. Cit. "Correspondence" 1, 82.

397. *Opticks*, P. cxxi.

398. Op. Cit. Christianson, P. 445.

399. Op. Cit. Westfall, "Never At Rest" P.639.

400. Ibid. P. 641.

401. Op. Cit. *Opticks* PP. 3390

402. Ibid. PP 375-6.

403. Op. Cit. Westfall "Never At Rest" P. 644.

404. Op. cit. *Opticks*, P. 376.

405. Op. Cit. Westfall, "Never At Rest" P. 647

406. Ibid.

407. Op. Cit. Christianson, P. 447.

408. DeSaguliers, John Theophilus "Course of Experimental Philosophy" 3rd Ed. I:VIII, London, 1763.

409. Ibid. P. 45.

410. Op. Cit. Westfall "Never At Rest" P. 657.

411. Op. Cit. Christianson, P. 452.

412. Ibid. P. 453

413. Op. Cit. Westfall, "Never At Rest" P.654.

414. Op. Cit. Christianson, P. 453

415. Op. Cit. Baily, Francis.

416. Op. Cit. Christianson, P. 455.

417. Ibid.

418. Op. Cit. Westfall "Never At Rest." P. 625

419. Ibid. P.626

420. Ibid. P. 625

421. Op. Cit. "Correspondence" 4, 445.

422. Op. Cit. Westfall "Never At Rest" P. 625.

423. Op. Cit "Correspondence" 7, 437.

424. Mine.

425. Op. Cit. Christianson, P. 468

426. Ibid, P. 455.

427. Ibid. P. 456.

428. Op. Cit. I.N."Correspondence" IV:447.

429. Op.Cit. Christianson. P. 456.

430. Ibid.

431. Op. Cit. Baily. PP. 257,259.

432. Op. Cit. Christianson. P. 457.

433. Ibid. P. 458.

434. Ibid.

435. Ibid. P. 465.

436. Ibid.

437. Joutard, Philippe "Les Camisards" Virtual Museum of French Protestantism, PP. 1 & 2, France, 1934.

438. Op. Cit. Christianson. P. 469.

439. Manuel, Frank. "A Portrait of Isaac Newton" Cambridge, MA. 1968. P. 210.

440. Op. Cit. Westfall. "Never At Rest." P. 651.

441. Brakke, David. "Canon Formation &Social Conflict in 4th Century" Harvard Theol. Rev. Vol. 87. #4. Oct. 27, ... 1994, PP. 395-419.

443. Ibid.

444. Ibid.

445. Op. Cit. Westfall. "Never At Rest." P. 650.

446. Ibid.

447. Whiston, William."Collections of Authentick Records …the Old and New Testament" London, 1928 P. 156.

448. Op. Cit. Christianson, P 471.

449. Ibid. P 483.

450. Ibid. P 474.

451. Ibid.

452. Stukeley, William. "Memoirs of Sir Isaac Newton's Life." Ed. By A. Hastings White. London. 1736.

453. Op. Cit. Christianson. P. 477.

454. Ibid.

455. Op. Cit. Westfall. P. 679.

456. Op. Cit. Christianson. P. 479.

457. Op. Cit. Westfall. P. 681.

458. Ibid. P. 684

459. Op. Cit. Westfall, P. 688.

460. Ibid. P. 688.

461. Op Cit. Baily. P. 280.

462. Ibid. P. 280-1.

463. Op. Cit. *I.N.Correspondence* V:102.

464. Ibid.

465. Op. Cit. Christianson. P 487.

466. Op. Cit. Baily. PP 94-95.

467. Op. Cit. Christianson. P 487.

468. Ibid.

469. Ibid.

470. Ibid. P. 488

471. Ibid.

472. Ibid. PP. 488-489.

473. Ibid. P. 489

474. Op. Cit. "I.N. Correspondence." V:165-66.

475. Op. Cit. Christianson. P. 489-490.

476. Op. Cit. Baily. PP. 228-229, 97.

477. Op. Cit. Westfall. P 698.

478. Op. Cit. Christianson. P. 491.

479. Ibid.

480. Op. Cit. Westfall. P. 599.

481. Ibid. PP. 599, 600.

482. Op. Cit. Christianson, P. 492.

483. Hall, A Rupert. "Desaguliers, J. T. Complete Dictionary of Scientific Biography,"Scribner & Sons, P.1, 2008.

484. *Philosophical Transactions* "Commericum Epistolicumde Analysi Promota" #924, 1712.

485. www.significantscotselectricscotland.com, P.3, June 9,2013.

486. Additional MS in the Cambridge University Library (the Portsmouth Papers) 3965.12, f.361v.

487. *Correspondence 6*, P. 285-8.

488. Leibniz, Wilhelm Gottfried. "Die Philosophischen Striften," ed. By C.J.Gerharct. Berlin, 1875-90, III:655.

489. Op. Cit. Christianson. P 545.

490. Ibid.

491. Ibid.

492. Op. Cit. Christianson. P. 546.

493. Ibid.

494. Ibid.

495. *Die Werke von Leibniz.* Ed. by Onno Klopp (Hanover, 1888) XI:115,90.

496. Ibid. P. 549.

497. Ibid.

498. Op. Cit. Westfall. P. 777-778.

499. Alexander, H.G., "The Leibniz-Clarke Correspondence. New York, 1956, P. 190.

500. Ibid. PP 11,12.

501. Op. Cit. Christianson. P. 550.

502. Ibid.

503. Ibid.

504. Op. Cit. "I.N. Correspondence" VII:289.

505. Ibid.

506. "Desaguliers, John Theophilus. Complete Dictionary of Scientific Biography. 2008 [www.encyclopedia.com]

507. Op. Cit. Christianson. P. 559.

508. Op. Cit. Westfall. P. 842.

509. Ibid.

510. Ibid. P. 844.

511. *Calendar of Treasury Papers.* 1718. 32(2), 37. London.

512. *Calendar of Treasury Papers.* 1714 -1719. P. 360 (Newton to Lord's Commissioners, ca July 1718.)

513. *Calendar of Treasury Books.* 32(2), 17. *Correspondence.* 6, 434.

514. Keynes MS 133, PP 12-13.

515. Op. Cit. Westfall. P. 845.

516. Ibid.

517. Carpenter, Audrey T. "John Theophilus Desaguliers" Bloomsburg Publishing, London 2011. Most of the information from this chapter is from the author's own knowledge, as well as Carpenter's book.

518. Ibid.

519. Most Worshipful Grand Lodge of Free and Accepted Masons, State of Indiana "Indiana Monitor." 1946.

520. Rees, Julian, "John Theophilus Desaguliers" Internet website, May 17, 2012.

521. Bauer, Alain. "Isaac Newton's Freemasonry" afterward by Roger Dachez. P 83. Inner Traditions, 2007.

522. Keynes Collection of Newton manuscripts in Kings College, Cambridge. MS 3, pp. 5 – 7.

523. Op. Cit. Westfall. P. 816.

524. *Correspondence 7, 21-22,* Monmont to Taylor, Dec. 18, 1718.

525. Op. Cit. Westfall, P. 787.

526. Ibid.

527. *Correspondence 7, 70.* Newton to Bernoulli, September 29, 1719.

528. Op. Cit. Westfall, P 788.

529. Ibid. P. 788.

530. Ibid. P. 789.

531. Ibid. P. 795-796.

532. Ibid. P. 800.

533. Newton, Isaac, *Mathematical Principles of Natural Philosophy*, P. 400. London (UCLA, Berkley, 1934)

534. Op. Cit. Westfall, P. 801.

535. Op. Cit. *Mathematical Principals*, P. XXXV.

536. Op. Cit. Westfall, P. 802.

537. Ibid. P. 803.

538. Op. Cit. Christianson, P. 805.

539. Op. Cit. Westfall. P. 805.

540. Ibid. P. 807.

541. Ibid. P. 808.

542. Ibid. P. 809.

543. *Correspondence 7*, P. 322.

544. Op. Cit. Christianson. P. 563.

545. Ibid. P. 565.

546. Ibid.

547. Ibid.

548. Ibid. P. 566.

549. Op. Cit. Keynes MS 3, PP 1-27

550. Op. Cit. Christianson, P. 567.

551. Ibid.

552. Ibid. P. 565.

553. Davis, Ernest. *How Did Newton Go ... Off Course?* Soc. for Indus. & Applied Math. Philadelpia, PA. 2014.

554. Ibid. P.2.

555. Op. Cit. Westfall. P. 813

556. Naze', Yaël, "Astronomical Arguments in Newton's Chronology," Dept. AGO, Universite' de Liege, 2012.

557. Op. Cit. Davis. Page 1.

558. Ibid. P. 3.

559. "The Chronology of Ancient Kingdoms Amended" London. 1728.

560. "Ibid. P. 8

561. Op. Cit. Christianson. P. 568.

562. Ibid.

563. Ibid.

564. Ibid.

565. Ibid. P. 569.

566. "Collections for the History of the Town and Soke of Grantham." Edmund Turnor, London. 1806, P. 165.

567. "Stukeley, William. "Memoirs of Sir Isaac Newton's Life" Ed. by A. Hastings White. London, 1936.

568. Op.Cit. "I.N. Correspondence" VII:289.

569. Op. Cit. Christianson, P. 570

570. Ibid.

571. Ibid.

572. Op. Cit. Westfall, P. 832.

573. Op. Cit Christianson, P. 572.

574. Ibid. Pp. 865-866.

575. Ibid. Pp. 858-861.

576. Op. Cit. Christianson, P. 572.

577. Ibid. P. 513.

578. Op. Cit. Westfall, P. 862.

579. Op. Cit. Keynes MS 130.11.

580. Op. Cit. Westfall, P. 863. This anecdote is attributed to Andrew Michael Ramsey, a Scotsman, the tutor of Bonnie Prince Charles, a future member of the Gentlemen's Club of Spalding (with John Theophilus Desaguliers) and The Royal Society of London.

581. Op. Cit. Keynes MS 130.6 Book 2.

582. Op. Cit. Christianson, P. 575.

583. Ibid.

584. Ibid.

585. Stukeley, William. "Memoirs of Sir Isaac Newton's Life" Ed. by A. Hastings White. London, 1936. PP. 82-83.

586. Op.Cit. Westfall. P. 869

587. Ibid.

588. Ibid. P 870.

589. Op. Cit. Keynes MS. 130 (6) Book 1.

590. "Journal Book of the Royal Society," March 23, 1727.

591. "The Political State of Great Britain," March 1727, P. 328.

592. Op. Cit. Westfall. P. 870.

593. Op. Cit. Christianson. P. 576.

594. Op.Cit. Westfall. P. 870.

595. Ibid. P. 871.

596. Ibid.

597. Bodelian Library, New College, MS. 361.4 f. 139.

598. Op. Cit. Christianson, P. 576.

599. Op. Cit. Westfall, P. 872.

600. Ibid. P. 872-873.

601. Yahuda Collection of Newton Manuscripts. MS 17.3, f. 11. Jewish Natl. and University Library, Jerusalem.

602. *Indiana Monitor and Freemasons Guide.* "Middle Chamber Lecture" *Indiana Grand Lodge of F&AM, 1946.*

603. Ibid. "Charge of the Entered Apprentice Degree."

BIBLIOGRAPHY

Alexander, H.G. "The Leibniz-Clarke Correspondence," Manchester U. Press, U.K. 1956.

Baily, Francis. "An Account of the Reverend John Flamsteed" London, 1835-37.

Bauer, Alain. "Isaac Newton's Freemasonry," Inner Traditions, Rochester, VT. 2007.

Boyer, Carl B. "Cartesian & Newtonian Algebra in the Mid-18th Century," Warsaw, 1968.

Brakke, David. "Canon Formation & Social Conflict in 4th Century England," *Harvard Theological Review*, Cambridge, MA, 1994.

Burnet, Gilbert. "History of His Own Times," Oxford, England. 1823.

Carpenter, Audrey T. "John Theophilus Desaguliers" Bloomsburg, London, 2011

Chaloner, William. "Guzman Redivivus" London, 1699.

Christianson, Gale. "In the Presence of the Creator," Free Press, New York, 1984.

Cohen, J. Bernard. "Isaac Newton's Papers & Letters …," Cambridge, MA, 1978

Conduitt, John. "Newton's Life at Cambridge." Keynes MS. Cambridge, MA, 2004.

Cooper, Charles Henry. "Annals of Cambridge," U. of Michigan Library, 1842.

"Correspondence of Isaac Newton," ed: Turnbull, Scott Hall & Tilling, Cambridge, UK, 1977.

"Correspondence of H. Oldenburg," ed: Rupert & Marie Hall, Madison, WI, 1965.

Cranston, Maurice. "John Locke: A Biography," London and New York, 1957.

Davis, Ernest. "How Did Newton Go So Far Off Course?" Soc. Industrial & Applied Mathematics, Philadelphia, PA, 2014.

Desaguliers, J. T. "Course of Experimental Philosophy." London, 1763.

"(The) Diary of Abraham de la Pryme," ed. Charles Jackson, Durham: Andrews & Co. 1870.

Gleick, James. "Isaac Newton," Pantheon Press, New York, 1995.

Gordon, Thomas. "A Cordial for Low Spirits" 3rd ed. London, 1763.

Hall, A. Rupert. "Desaguliers, J.T." ...*Dictionary of Scientific Biography*, Scribner & Sons, 2008.

Hazard, Paul. "The European Mind," World Publishing Co., Cleveland, OH, 1963.

Hervival, John. "The Background to Newton's *Principia*," Oxford, U.K., 1965.

Hoffman, Joseph H. "Leibniz in Paris," Cambridge University Press, Cambridge, U.K. 2008.

Holmyard, Eric J. "Alchemy," Dover Publications, U.K., 1990.

"Indiana Monitor," Indiana Grand Lodge of Freemasons, 1946.

"Joseph Halle Schaffner Collection of Scientific Manuscripts," U. of Chicago Library, 1977.

"Journal Book of the Royal Society," London, U.K.

Joutard, Philippe. "Les Camisards," Virtual Museum of French Protestantism, Paris, 1934.

Kerr, Philip. "Dark Matter," Crown Publishing, New York, N.Y. 2002.

"Keynes Collection of Newton Manuscripts," King's College, Cambridge, U.K.

King, Lord Peter. "The Life & Letters of John Locke," London, U.K. 1858.

Klopp, Onno. "Die Werke von Leibniz" (The Works of Leibniz), Hanover, Germany, 1866.

Leibniz, Wilhelm Gottfried. "Die Philosophischen Striften," U. of Michigan Library, 1875.

Locke, John. "Letter Concerning Toleration," London, 1689.

Manuel, Frank. "A Portrait of Isaac Newton," Cambridge, MA, 1968.

"Mint Papers in the Public Record Office." Parliament, London, U.K.

Newton, Isaac. "Mathematical Principles of Natural Philosophy," B. Motte, Oxford U. 1729.

Newton, Isaac. "Wastebook," 1665.

Naze, Yaël. "Astronomical Arguments in Newton's *Chronology*," U. de Liege, Belgium, 2012.

"Philosophical Transactions" of the Royal Society of London. London, 1665 to present.

"Portsmouth Papers," (Newton's papers donated to Cambridge U. Library, U.K. 1872.)

Rees, Julian. "John Theophilus Desaguliers," *Julian Rees Freemasonry* website, 2012.

Stukeley, William. "Memoirs of Sir Isaac Newton's Life," ed. A. H. White, London. 1936.

Swift, Jonathan. "Journal to Stella," ed. Harold Williams, Oxford U. Press. 1948.

Thomson, Garret. "On Locke," Wadsworth/Thomson, Belmont, CA. 2001.

Turnor, Edmund. "Collections for the History of the Town & Stoke of Grantham," London, 1806.

Westfall, Richard S. "Never At Rest," Cambridge U. Press, New York, N.Y. 1980.

Westfall, Richard S. "The Life of Isaac Newton," Cambridge U. Press, New York, N.Y. 1993.

Whiston, William. "Collections of Authentic Records...," London, 1727-28.

Whiteside, David T. "The Mathematical Papers of Isaac Newton," Cambridge, U.K. 1967.

World Book Encyclopedia.

"Yahuda Collection of Newton Manuscripts," Jewish Nat'l and Univ. Library, Jerusalem, 1967.

Made in the USA
Charleston, SC
02 June 2016